ULYSSES AND THE SIRENS

Studies in rationality and irrationality

ULYSSES AND THE SIRENS

Studies in rationality and irrationality

Revised edition

JON ELSTER

Associate Professor, Department of History
University of Oslo

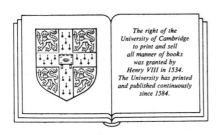

CAMBRIDGE UNIVERSITY PRESS

Cambridge

New York   New Rochelle   Melbourne   Sydney

EDITIONS DE LA MAISON DES SCIENCES DE L'HOMME

Paris

Published by the Press Syndicate of the University of Cambridge
The Pitt Building, Trumpington Street, Cambridge CB2 1RP
32 East 57th Street, New York, NY 10022, USA
10 Stamford Road, Oakleigh, Melbourne 3166, Australia
and Editions de la Maison des Sciences de l'Homme
54 Boulevard Raspail, 75270 Paris Cedex 06

First published 1979
Revised edition 1984
Reprinted 1986, 1988

Printed in Great Britain at the
University Press, Cambridge

Library of Congress catalogue card number 84-7654

British Library Cataloguing in Publication Data
Elster, Jon
Ulysses and the sirens. – Rev. ed.
1. Rationalism
I. Title
153.4'3   BF441

Revised edition   ISBN 0 521 26984 9 paperback
                   ISBN 2 7351 0081 2 paperback (France only)
First edition   ISBN 0 521 22388 1 hard covers
                   ISBN 2 901725 70 8 hard covers (France only)

CONTENTS

PREFACE TO THE REVISED EDITION

The only (but major) change in the present edition is that most of chapter II.5 on inconsistent time preferences has been completely rewritten. My friend Aanund Hylland of the Economics Department of the University of Oslo pointed out a gross mathematical error in the English edition, thus leaving what I thought to be a profound philosophical conclusion without a leg to stand on. Moreover, in a note dated 26 October 1982 he provided a detailed analysis of the correct mathematical structure of the problem. The results are given below. My conclusions have been reformulated accordingly. I should add that as usual his contribution goes much beyond the technical aspect of the problem; in fact the main conceptual arguments below are also due to his suggestions.

I would like to point out to the reader an article by Rebecca Dresser, 'Ulysses and the psychiatrists: A legal and policy analysis of the voluntary commitment contract', *Harvard Civil Rights-Civil Liberties Review* 16 (1982), pp. 777–854. The article cites my brief discussion of this issue (in II.2 below) and then goes on to provide a rich empirical material. Also, Thomas Schelling has discussed the problem of precommitment and strategic behaviour toward self in several recent articles, notably 'The intimate contest for self-command', *The Public Interest* 60 (1980), pp. 94–118.

J. E.

PREFACE AND ACKNOWLEDGEMENTS

Many philosophers and social scientists at some time in their lives have wanted to write fiction or poetry, only to find that they didn't have what it takes. Others have chosen philosophy or social science as a second choice when they decided that their first choice of doing mathematics really was not within their abilities. The present work is at the intersection of these two failures. But to fail is always to fail *at something*, and it leaves you with a knowledge of the kind of thing you unsuccessfully tried to do. In the essays collected here I have tried to exploit this knowledge for an analysis of rational and irrational behaviour.

The essays were written independently of each other, but have been rewritten to avoid redundancies and to incorporate further reflection. It may be useful to explain here how their topics relate to each other. Chapter I sets out the paradigm of individually rational behaviour, which is distinguished both from biological adaptation and from functional adaptation in societies. The main idea defended here is that the specifically *human* rationality is characterized by the capacity to relate to the future, in contra-distinction to the myopic gradient-climbing in natural selection. Chapter II then introduces the notion of imperfectly rational behaviour, the need for which arises because weakness of will may prevent us from *using* our capacity for perfectly rational behaviour. The notion of *binding oneself*, as did Ulysses before setting out towards the Sirens, is the crucial concept of the chapter, though the alternative strategy of 'private side bets' is also explored. Chapter III is essentially a list of problems in rational-actor theory, with a view to evaluating the power of this theory compared to norm-oriented or structuralist approaches. I con-clude that the rational-actor theory is logically prior to its competitors, though not necessarily more successful in each particular case. In chapter IV some of the problems discussed in chapter III are singled out for more intensive discussion. In particular I try to explain how contradictory beliefs and contradictory desires can be understood as *meaningful* even if *irrational*. There is, in other words, a descending sequence of perfect rationality, imperfect rationality, problematic rationality and irrationality which, in spite of the very diverse material included, lends a conceptual unity to the essays that justifies their being collected in book form.

Underlying all the essays is a particular view of the philosophy of science which I hope to be able to set out more fully elsewhere. A brief outline may prepare the reader for some of the ideas explored below.

(i) There are basically three modes of explanation in science: the causal, the functional and the intentional.

(ii) All sciences use causal explanation.

(iii) The physical sciences use only causal explanation, least-time principles and other variational formulations being merely analytical artifacts without explanatory power.

(iv) There is no place for intentional explanation in biology. This statement is defended in chapter I below.

(v) There is no place for functional explanation in the social sciences. This statement is defended (and qualified) in I.5 and II.8.

(vi) In biology a distinction can be made between sub-functional causality (mutations, senescence) and supra-functional causality (beneficial or harmful spill-over effects of individual adaptations). This distinction is briefly touched upon in chapter I.

(vii) In the social sciences a similar distinction can be made between sub-intentional causality and supra-intentional causality. The former refers to causal processes taking place within the individual, forming or perverting his intentions. This is the subject of much of chapters II and III. The latter refers to causal interaction between individuals. In my *Logic and Society*,[1] which is in a sense a twin volume to the present book, I discuss this subject at some length.

(viii) Animal and human behaviour should be studied with the notions of function and of intention as *regulative ideas*. Not all

[1] Elster (1978a).

animal behaviour is functional, and not all human behaviour is rational or intentional, but there is a well-grounded *presumption* that this will typically be the case.

Chapter I was originally presented at the Fourth International Congress of the International Organization for the Study of Human Development, Paris, 1977. The present version has benefited from the comments of Roger Masters, Arthur Stinchcombe and George Williams. A very much shorter version of chapter II was first presented at the ECPR Workshop on Political Theory, Louvain, 1976. Finn Tschudi then helped me by pointing out the closely related work of George Ainslie, from whom I later received comments and access to unpublished manuscripts that proved very important for the development of my ideas. I also would like to thank Francis Sejersted, Sissel Reichelt, Dagfinn Føllesdal, John Perry, Michael Bratman, Amélie Rorty, Peter Hammond, Arthur Stinchcombe and Robert Goodin for criticism and advice. Chapter III was presented at the Séminaire International sur l'Economie Sociologique, Paris, 1977. I would like to thank John Harsanyi for stimulating discussion during the gestation period of the paper, and Robert Goodin for constructive criticism. Chapter IV partly overlaps with chapter 4 of my *Logic and Society*, but there are large differences both in the material itself and in the way in which it is organized. Among those I am in debt to here are Amélie Rorty, Eugene Genovese and Paul Watzlawick, the first for important suggestions and the latter two for confirming that I had indeed understood them aright.

I

PERFECT RATIONALITY: BEYOND GRADIENT-CLIMBING

I.1 INTRODUCTION

The aim of this chapter is largely polemical and critical. I shall argue that in spite of certain superficial analogies between the social and the biological sciences, there are fundamental differences that make it unlikely that either can have much to learn from the other. The difference, essentially, lies in the distinction between the *intentional* explanations used in the social sciences and the *functionalist* explanations that are specific to biology. Donald Davidson[1] has argued that the attempts at psycho-physical reduction are bound to hurt themselves on the stumbling-block of intentionality, and from a very different point of view a similar thesis is presented here with respect to psycho-biological reduction or analogy. The argument cuts both ways, against the use of sociological methods in biology and against the transfer of biological paradigms to the social sciences. Most of the space is devoted to the first problem, because it is less extensively discussed in the literature. I argue that even if natural selection can to some extent simulate intentionality, there are crucial differences in the fine grain of animal and human adaptation. Two such differences are discussed in some detail. In I.2 and I.3 a case is made for the capacity for *global maximization* being a specifically

---

[1] Davidson (1973). The characteristic feature of Davidson's view is that he is simultaneously materialist, determinist *and* anti-reductionist. The following passage brings out the essence of his view: 'If a certain psychological concept applies to one event and not to another, there must be a difference describable in physical terms. But it does not follow that there is a single physically describable difference that distinguishes any two events that differ in a given psychological respect' (p. 717). That is, to conclude from determinism and materialism to reductionism is to commit the same fallacy as when from the fact that everything has a cause one concludes that there is something which is the cause of everything.

1

human trait not found in natural selection. In I.4 a similar argument is made concerning the unique human capacity for *strategic behaviour*. In I.5 I turn to the second problem, drawing attention to the better-known difficulties of functionalist analysis in sociology. Briefly stated, my contention is here that in societies there is no general mechanism – corresponding to natural selection – that could permit us to infer that the latent functions of a structure typically maintain the structure by feedback.

Discussions of these matters have shown me that my argument lends itself to three misunderstandings. First, I do not deny that interdisciplinary research, pooling the empirical and theoretical resources of biology and of sociology, can be fertile indeed. In human evolution, for example, the social structure is part of the environment that determines whether a given mutation will be beneficial or harmful. At another level the biological components of language, intelligence or mental illness are by now well documented, even if the relative importance of nature and nurture is always a matter of controversy. My argument is directed only at the transfer of whole explanatory paradigms; at the appeal to intentions in biology and to functions in sociology.

Secondly, I do not deny that cases can be found where biological adaptation leads to deviation from local maxima and to attainment of global maxima, nor that functional explanation can sometimes be useful in sociology. I am only arguing that there can be no *general* presumption that global maxima will be attained by natural selection, and that latent functions do not *typically* explain the persistence of the social structures exhibiting these functions. We may invoke here the Kantian notion of a *regulative idea*, as opposed to a dogmatic one.[2] A regulative idea distributes the burden of proof, in the sense of postulating which features can be assumed as a working hypothesis in the absence of specific evidence to the contrary and which features must be shown to be present in each particular case. The statement 'Everything has a

---

[2]   *Kritik der reinen Vernunft*, B 670ff (A 642ff); *Kritik der Urteilskraft*, §70ff. The simplest example is perhaps Kant's reinterpretation of the 'principle of continuity' from a dogmatic assertion to the effect that the set of organic forms can be ordered in a continuous (or dense?) series, to a regulative principle that exhorts us to seek, between any two forms, an intermediate one. The statement 'Everything has a cause' is in Kantian philosophy a constitutive principle to which there can be no exceptions, whereas the idea that 'everything has a function' is a regulative one that does admit of exceptions, as is explained in n. 83 below.

function' should not be taken as a dogmatic statement about organisms,[3] but as a statement to the effect that we may legitimately assume that a given feature has a function – i.e. could not undergo small variations without loss of reproductive capacity for the organism concerned – until the contrary has been demonstrated. The justification for this regulative idea is, of course, the general mechanism of gradient-climbing by natural selection, as explained in I.2. On the other hand there is nothing that could justify the regulative idea that every feature of the organism realizes a *global* maximum, so that all variations – small or large – would imply a loss of reproductive capacity. For intentional adaptation exactly the contrary is true. Here we do have a general mechanism for attaining global maxima, and what needs a separate explanation is rather the failure to achieve this.

Thirdly, I would not want to be read as an anti-reductionist, at least not of the extreme variety that postulates an unbridgeable gap between animal and human adaptation. I believe that the human capacity for global maximizing must ultimately be explained as a result of the locally maximizing gradient-climbing in natural selection. In this sense I am indeed a reductionist. Observe, however, that the object of the reduction is the *capacity* to behave in this manner, and not specific cases where this capacity is exercised. I believe, that is, that rational behaviour must be reduced in two steps: first by subsuming it under the general capacity for rational problem-solving and secondly by explaining that *general* capacity by the workings of natural selection. The argument is similar to the one proposed by Peter Richerson and Robert Boyd[4] concerning the biological foundations of the *capacity* for culture, which in their model is very different from the biological foundations for cultural *behaviour*. By contrast the argument is clearly incompatible with the views proposed by C. D. Darlington[5] or R. D. Masters,[6] who tend to see *specific*

---

[3]   For a clear statement of this dogmatic (or non-non-Darwinian) view we may take the following: 'A "functionless site" is simply one the function of which has not yet been determined' (Mayr 1970, p. 127). A statement along the lines sketched in the present essay is the following: 'The experimental study of adaptation has unravelled adaptive values in such unobtrusive and inconspicuous details of organismic organization that one should think of a character as having survival value until the contrary has been demonstrated' (Curio 1973, p. 1049).

[4]   Richerson and Boyd (forthcoming).   [5]   Darlington (1969).

[6]   Masters (1975, 1976).

behavioural patterns in biological perspectives. I return to the specific–general distinction in I.3.

As a last introductory remark I would like to put forward what I hope may turn out to be a self-destroying prophecy. I do not believe that my criticism, should someone happen to read it, will have any great impact. The attraction of biological analogies on social scientists, in particular, seems to be so great that even the best minds are led astray. In the cabinet of horrors of scientific thought there is room, alas, not only for a Worms or a Lilienfeld, but also for a Durkheim or a Merton.[7] At the present moment I think one can confidently predict that ethology and sociobiology between them will generate a continuous stream of pseudo-scientific papers for some years to come. I do not deny, of course, the occasional utility of biological analogies as a source for new hypotheses, any more than I would deny that some scientists may get their best ideas when reading the Bible or the *Dialectics of Nature*. I do deny, however, that biological analogies should have any privileged status. Ideas should be judged by their descendants, not by their ancestors. I hope that the social scientist who proposes to spend his time on finding *the* social analogue of, say, dominance or flight behaviour in animals would first reflect on the pseudo-debates of the nineteenth century about *the* correct social analogue of the cell: individual or family? There is no reason why any such analogue should exist, and that's all there is to the question.

I.2 THE LOCALLY MAXIMIZING MACHINE

In this section I sketch a highly simplified account of the theory of natural selection. By keeping strictly to first principles I hope to avoid being too patently wrong on specific biological matters outside my competence. As the conclusions themselves will be on the level of first principles, I believe that my simplifications can be justified.

I conceive, then, of the organisms in a population as a machine receiving inputs in the form of mutations. For simplicity we assume asexual reproduction, so that mutations are the only source of genetic novelty. Alternatively we may skirt recombination by

---

[7] For accounts of biological models in the social sciences see Stark (1962), Schlanger (1971), Banton (ed.) (1961).

arguing that in the long run only mutations can disturb the biological equilibrium (in a constant environment). The stream of inputs is random, in the sense that there is no correlation between the functional requirements of the organism and the probability of occurrence of a mutation satisfying these requirements. By mutagens such as X-rays it is possible to increase the probability of mutations generally; by chemical mutagens it is possible to increase the probability of structurally defined subgroups of mutations, such as the probability of cytosine mutating to thymine as a result of deamination by nitrous acid; but it is never possible – and this is the *central dogma* of molecular biology – to modify the probability of functionally defined subgroups of mutations. An analogy may help here. Comparing mutations to misprints, we may increase the probability of misprints by breaking the glasses of the typesetter, but there is no way of selectively increasing the probability of misprints occurring in the second edition of a book that will correct the factual errors of the first edition.

We assume – crucially – that all mutations are small, being typically amino acid substitutions resulting from the misprint of a single letter in the genetic code. There are no doubt mechanisms, such as gene duplication, that can produce macro-mutations, but in the first place the evolutionary importance of these is far from being clear and, in the second place, such mutations, while large compared to amino acid substitutions, are small compared to the discontinuities that are found in human adaptation.[8] No gene duplication could produce a change of the order of magnitude of the switch from the horse-drawn carriage to the 'horseless' carriage.[9] As the main contention of the present chapter is that there is a basic difference between the local optimization through

[8]   For the first point, see Frazzetta (1975), pp. 93ff; for the second, *ibid.* pp. 20, 152. For one possible evolutionary consequence (*not* function!) of gene duplication, see Rigby *et al.* (1974), who argue that the duplicated gene can mutate to a functionally inactive one (one step backwards) and then further mutate to a viable and possibly superior form (two steps forwards).

[9]   Frazzetta (1975), p. 152. Cp. also Schumpeter (1934), p. 54: 'Add successively as many mail coaches as you please, you will never get a railway thereby.' For an alternative view on technological development, stressing the small cumulative changes, see Rosenberg (1976), pp. 66, 166 and *passim*; David (1975); Nelson and Winter (1974, 1976); cp. also nn. 27 and 28 below. Even if we accept, however, that many evolutionary changes are larger than one-step mutations, and that many cases of technical change are incremental rather than discontinuous, I believe that there remains a genuine difference that suffices for my case. Another important difference (Frazzetta 1975, p. 20) is that in evolution there is nothing corresponding to 'useful failures' in engineering. Evolution never learns from past mistakes.

small improvements and the global maximization that permits steps of any size, the precise definition of 'small' is not really important.

In the phrase of Jacques Monod, natural selection operates by chance and necessity.[10] While mutations are random, the selection process is deterministic, in the sense that the machine at any given moment has well-defined criteria for accepting or rejecting any given mutation. (This means that I shall not deal with genetic drift and with the problem of non-Darwinian evolution.) The mutation is accepted if the first organism in which it occurs benefits in the form of higher reproductive capacity. Since the organism will leave more descendants than other organisms, the new allele will spread in the population until it is universally present. (This statement implies that I shall not deal with frequency-dependent selection and other sources – such as heterosis – of stable polymorphism. See, however, I.4 for a discussion of polymorphism as related to mixed strategies.) Among the results of an accepted mutation is that the criteria for accepting or rejecting new mutations will change. The organism is now in a different state from what it was before the mutation, and may be harmed or benefited from different inputs. To put the matter briefly: the machine says Yes or No to each input according to criteria that change each time it says Yes. If the machine ever arrives at a state in which it says No to each of the (finitely many) possible inputs, we say that it has reached a local maximum. The population climbs along a fitness-gradient until it reaches a point from which all further movement can be downward only; and there it comes to a halt. For a given initial state, several local maxima may be accessible, the choice between which depends upon the random order in which the mutations happen to occur.

A further analysis of this *locally maximizing machine* must take account of the possibility of environmental change. If the environment changes, the criteria for saying Yes or No to mutations will typically also change. A mutation is not beneficial or harmful in itself, only with respect to a given genetic background (itself the outcome of previous mutations) and a given environment. With a changing environment it may very well be the case that even instantaneous local maxima are never attained, if the organism cannot keep pace with its surroundings. The notion of an

[10]   Monod (1970); see also Schoffeniels (1973).

'environment' is, however, ambiguous. In the first place environmental changes may refer to changes in the geological or climatic conditions to the extent that they cause evolutionary change without being themselves affected by it. (The last proviso is required to exclude endogenous climatic changes, such as the change in the atmosphere generated by the evolution of plants.) In the second place some parts of the environment are themselves evolving organisms or the effects of such evolution. If a population is constantly subject to exogenous environmental change, a steady state can never be attained, but to the extent that the environment is itself made up of (or is the effect of) evolving organisms, it makes sense to ask whether a *general equilibrium* – where all organisms have attained local maxima relative to each other – can be realized.[11]

The conditions for the existence and attainability of a general biological equilibrium could presumably be very complex. Here I only stress the general idea that evolution may be seen under the increasingly complex assumptions of a parametric environment, a strategic (or, in view of I.4, quasi-strategic) environment and an exogenously changing environment. In the abstract model used here I deal with the first case only, though I believe that the conclusions are easily extended to the second case. With the third case, however, entirely different considerations become relevant. In particular the phenomenon of *preadaptation* – stemming from the fact that 'any structure has properties beyond those for which it was constructed'[12] – permits the attainment of global optima that in a constant environment would have remained inaccessible. This, however, is a chance phenomenon only, not a general mechanism comparable to natural selection.

Enough should have been said by now to explain why the realization of local maxima in the organic world is not a matter of course. There is no logical objection to the idea of a world where the rate of change of the environment relative to the mutation rate is so high that most organisms most of the time are badly adapted to each other and to their inorganic environment. In the world we know, however, the infinitely subtle adaptations found in the structure and behaviour of organisms are facts that for millennia have evoked the wonder and (with less justification) the admiration of naturalists. In many well-documented cases the natural solution

[11] Winter (1971), p. 258.   [12] Salthe (1972), p. 9.

to structural and functional problems is strikingly close to the solution that would have been chosen by the engineer or the economist working on the same problem. In some cases animals and men *are* facing the same problems, so that the actual solutions can be compared. As shown by d'Arcy Wentworth Thompson in his classic work *On Growth and Form* as well as by several recent authors,[13] these solutions are often strongly convergent. In recent ecological work[14] nature is seen as an economist rather than as an engineer. Optimal budgeting, linear programming, profit maximization and cost minimization are now as much part of evolutionary theory as of economics.

It is sometimes said that the theory of natural selection is a tautology; that the survival of the fittest means the survival of the survivors. If by fitness we mean genetic fitness, this is true enough. If, however, we understand fitness as ecological fitness, as measured for example by the life span of the organism, the survival of the fittest is turned into an empirical proposition to which there are many important counterexamples. To take but one example, natural selection works so as to produce the optimal sacrifice of parents for offspring. Too much sacrifice for a given offspring may reduce the chance of having more offspring later on, whereas too little sacrifice would damage the 'investment' already made in the offspring. If, on the other hand, the aim was to maximize ecological adaptation, zero sacrifice would clearly be the optimal strategy; indeed the best strategy would be to have no reproduction at all. The confusion between ecological and genetic fitness occurs in various forms in the literature. A rather crass example is found in a recent work on the philosophy of biology, where the author claims that 'the process of childbearing in humans' shows that 'what may be useful to the group (e.g. a species) may have no utility at all for the individual or may even have negative utility'.[15] A more subtle error (or potential for error) underlies the frequent use of the term 'parental investment' in recent evolutionary theory.[16] Whereas economic investment means

---

[13]   Leigh (1971), part I; Frazzetta (1975), ch. 5 and *passim*. On d'Arcy Thompson, see Gould (1976).

[14]   For surveys see Cody (1974) and Rapport and Turner (1977).

[15]   Simon (1971), p. 82.

[16]   Cp. especially Trivers (1972), p. 139, who defines parental investment as '*any investment by the parent in an individual offspring that increases the offspring's chance of surviving (and*

the sacrifice of something (i.e. consumption) now in order to get more *of the same thing* later, parental investment means the sacrifice of something (i.e. ecological fitness) in order to get *more of another thing* (i.e. genetic fitness).

I.3   THE GLOBALLY MAXIMIZING MACHINE

For the purposes of the present argument the crucial features of the locally maximizing machine refer to what it *cannot* do. In particular the machine is incapable of *waiting* and of using *indirect strategies*. These notions are defined as follows. The machine is capable of waiting if it can say No to a favourable mutation in order to be able to say Yes to an even more favourable one later on. Suppose that of a given protein, form B is superior to form A and form C is superior to B, and that because of the structure of the genetic code one-step mutations are possible from A to B and from A to C, but not from B to C. If the mutation to B should occur first, the organism is incapable of saying No. The machine is capable of indirect strategies if it can say Yes to an unfavourable mutation in order to be able later on to say Yes to a very favourable one. Suppose that A is superior to B and C to A, and that one-step mutations can occur from A to B and from B to C, but not from A to C. If B comes about, the organism will not be able to say Yes. As a gradient-climber the organism has its myopic eye fixed to the ground, and is incapable of taking account of what happens behind the next hill. As one author puts it, 'future events or possibilities simply cannot have any effect on the gene pools of organisms'.[17] It is no doubt true that 'even mutations to codons that are completely synonymous with each other may in many instances alter the future mutational possibilities of the genotype',[18] but these possibilities cannot set up a selectional pressure *now* that could give an edge to an apparently neutral mutation over the *status quo*.

By contrast, waiting and the use of indirect strategies are crucial

hence *reproductive success*) *at the cost of the parent's ability to invest in other offspring'*. Investment in the economic sense would rather be 'any investment by the parent in an individual offspring that increases the offspring's chance of having surviving offspring (and hence reproductive success) at the cost of the parent's chance of having surviving offspring'.

[17]   Salthe (1972), p. 133.   [18]   Stebbins and Lewontin (1972), p. 24.

features of human choice. I suggest that man may indeed be seen as a *globally maximizing machine*, a characterization that goes back to Leibniz, who saw man as being uniquely capable 'reculer pour mieux sauter'.[19] Some examples of global maximization from economic and political life are:

	Waiting	Indirect strategies
Politics	Anti-activism	Anti-reformism
Economics	Patent system	Investment

A few comments may be in order. Investment is perhaps the simplest example of global maximization that requires bypassing a local maximum: one step backwards in order to take two steps forwards. As observed above, parental investment in the animal realm is not really an example of investment in this sense. If, for example, one generation accepted a less-than-maximal number of offspring for the sake of a larger number of grandchildren, this would indeed be investment in the strict sense, but no such idea has ever been entertained in the biological literature. The patent system has the paradoxical feature that 'by slowing down the diffusion of technical progress it ensures that there will be more progress to diffuse'.[20] As Joseph Schumpeter stressed, the maximal exploitation of present possibilities may often be an obstacle to the maximal creation of new possibilities.[21] As suggested by Maurice Meisner, this proposition may also be applied to activism as an

[19] Leibniz (1875–90), III, pp. 346, 578; VII, p. 568. These references actually invoke indirect strategies as a part of the *divine* rationality in the construction of the best of all possible worlds. Similar propositions about *man* also abound, such as the following: 'Les appétitions sont comme la tendance de la pierre qui va le plus droit mais non pas toujours le meilleur chemin vers le centre de la terre, *ne pouvant pas prévoir* qu'elle rencontrera des rochers où elle se brisera, au lieu qu'elle se serait aprochée davantage de son but, si elle avait eu *l'esprit et le moyen de se détourner*...Le bonheur est donc pour ainsi dire un chemin par des plaisirs; et le plaisir n'est qu'un pas et un avancement vers le bonheur, le plus court qui se peut faire *selon les présentes impressions*, mais non pas toujours le meilleur. On peut manquer le vrai chemin, en voulant suivre le plus court, comme la pierre allant droit, peut rencontrer trop tôt des obstacles, qui l'empêchent d'avancer assez vers le centre de la terre. Ce qui fait connaître, que c'est la raison et la volonté qui nous mènent vers le bonheur, mais que le sentiment et l'appétit ne nous portent que vers le plaisir' (v, pp. 175, 182; italics added). Cp. Elster (1975a), ch. VI, for a further discussion.

[20] Robinson (1956), p. 87.   [21] Schumpeter (1954), p. 87.

obstacle to long-term action.[22] A revolutionary class must be capable of waiting, of marking time, of saying No to favourable opportunities. Conversely, political reformism may be seen as the refusal of indirect strategies. With the techniques of incremental planning or Karl Popper's 'piecemeal social engineering'[23] only local maxima will ever be reached, whereas a revolutionary class is capable of saying Yes to unfavourable possibilities. (Incidentally, the distinction between local and global maxima is also neglected in Popper's work on biology, where he wrongly asserts that 'What Darwin showed us was that the mechanism of natural selection...can simulate rational human action directed towards a purpose or aim.')[24] These observations, needless to say, are purely formal and do not imply any particular political view. I am only saying that the human *capacity* for revolutionary behaviour – for marking time and using indirect strategies – is a feature that distinguishes man from the activist-cum-reformist (i.e. opportunist) behaviour of natural selection. As is argued at some length in chapter II below, this capacity often will not be used even when it would be desirable to do so; conversely there are often very good reasons against experimenting with situations that are very distant from the present one.[25]

A further difference, of course, is that man can increase the probability of occurrence of functionally defined subgroups of 'mutations' (i.e. new ideas, inventions or institutions). As Michael Ruse puts it, 'one can talk of many, if not most, new cultural elements appearing by virtue of the fact that they are needed'.[26] We are not constrained to sit back and wait for the right mutation to occur; we can actively seek out the new kind of invention or institution that is needed. Now the relative importance of randomness and directedness in technological development is a matter of some controversy, and at least one recent author has argued that random inventions can generate a process that simulates consciously directed research. [27] His argument, however,

---

[22]   Meisner (1967), pp. 166ff.   [23]   Popper (1957), pp. 64ff.
[24]   Popper (1972), p. 267.
[25]   One of these reasons is linked to the problem of endogenously changing preferences, discussed in II.6 below. Another reason stems from risk aversion; a third from the 'irreversibility effect' discussed by Henry (1974).
[26]   Ruse (1974), p. 432.
[27]   David (1975), ch. 1. David sets out to explain the link between factor-scarcity and factor-saving biases in technical change. He rejects the 'intentional' explanations

is intended to explain technological change in the nineteenth century, and does not pretend to have universal validity. It does indeed seem obvious that the modern large corporation very actively searches out new techniques with highly specific properties, in contradistinction to the more myopic learning by doing that may have characterized the small firm of the last century. Also, even if the *direction* of technological change is more or less random, the *rate* at which it goes on may depend crucially upon the need for inventions, as in other recent work.[28]

As a more general observation it should also be seen that even if random search is observed to take place in human choices, this does not mean that the search ultimately is generated by a random process. On the contrary, a prior calculation may have found a random search to be the most rational procedure, perhaps because a consciously directed search would involve unacceptably high costs of acquiring and evaluating information.[29] In the special case of technical change, an enlightened manager may prefer to leave his scientists free to do what they want to do,

proposed by Hicks (1932), Fellner (1961) and Kennedy (1964), and then argues that 'The drift of technological developments generated over time within a fairly stable economic environment needs to be viewed, first and foremost, as a distinctively *historical* phenomenon, inasmuch as it may arise through the myopic selections *past* producers made from among the different species of techniques with which they originally had to work. The element of "guidance" present in the long-run process is attached in large measure to the circumstances surrounding those choices, and involves no forward-looking, induced innovational responses to current market signals or future portents' (pp. 61–2). On his view, technical progress (mainly through learning by doing) is locally neutral, but nevertheless ends up by creating a global bias towards economizing on the scarce factors.

[28]   See esp. Nelson and Winter (1976), who argue that technical progress occurs through satisficing rather than maximizing (cp. also II.4 and III.5 below). When gross profits drop below a certain critical level, innovative and imitative activity is turned on. The search is local and unbiased (i.e. random), but the result may exhibit specific patterns depending on the search context. (There is an inconsistency in the model when Nelson and Winter include learning by doing among the search mechanisms, for as stressed by David (1975), chs. 1–3, this kind of technical change occurs through the mere operation of the production process and does not require any particular inducement. Another inconsistency is that Nelson and Winter (1974) refer to their theory as a neo-Schumpeterian one, in spite of the strong emphasis laid on *local* search as opposed to discontinuous inventions.) In natural selection, of course, neither the rate of mutations nor the direction of mutations is a response to the functional needs of the organism; there is a more or less steady stream of randomly directed mutations, as in David's model. The analogy, however, is not complete, for in David's model the stream of inventions is not a random walk *tout court*, but a random walk with elastic barriers, which constrains the *actual* stream of inventions (and not only the *expected* direction of inventions) towards neutrality. There is, in other words, an *hysteresis effect* (Elster 1976a) to which there is no analogy in natural selection.

[29]   Cp. II.4 and III.5 below for some doubts about this argument.

because this policy will attract better scientists and ultimately be more profitable than a policy where less qualified scientists spend a larger proportion of their time pursuing specific objectives.[30]

These last remarks bring us on to a new level of problems, and require some distinctions that will turn out to be crucial in the sequel. In particular we should distinguish between the choice of an action and the choice of a way of choosing. Each of these two choices may be made either deliberately or by trial and error, which leaves us with four possible combinations. In the preceding paragraph I discussed the case of a deliberate choice of a random search process, but for the purposes of the present argument it is more important to understand the converse possibility: trial and error generating deliberate and intentional choice.

At this point the reader may justifiably feel somewhat confused, for exactly which are the phenomena that are being compared? If we are contrasting animal and human adaptation, the appropriate comparison presumably would be between animal and human behaviour, whereas we have been staging a confrontation between natural selection and human choice. Actually three different phenomena are involved: animal adaptation, human adaptation and the natural selection that has fashioned them both. In order to bring out the relation between these three domains, I shall use the instructive example of *pursuit games*. In the theory of differential games there is a standard example called 'the homicidal chauffeur game', where an automobile on an infinite unobstructed parking lot attempts to run down a pedestrian.[31] The pursuer has a higher speed, but poorer mobility because of the larger radius of curvature of the car. It is intuitively clear, and it can be proved rigorously, that if initially the pursuer is very close to the evader, the optimal strategy for the pursuer is to drive *away* from the evader and then, when far enough away, turn around for a direct pursuit. One step backwards is required for two steps forwards; a typical example of the indirect strategies that man is capable of using and actually does use in many real-life pursuits.

In the animal realm such pursuits are found at two levels. At the individual level we can see the fox pursuing the hare across the fields any autumn day; at the species level the Fox is hunting

---

[30]   See Cotgrove and Box (1970) for evidence on this point.
[31]   Cp. Isaacs (1965) and Hájek (1975).

the Hare across the generations, continually adapting to the counter-adaptations of the latter. I shall have a few words to say about the species pursuit, and then dwell at somewhat greater length on the individual pursuit. The upshot of I.2 was that in the species pursuit, indirect strategies and waiting are impossible (in the simple model), for an organism that took one step backwards would not leave any descendants to take the two steps forwards later on, whereas an organism that refused to take one step forwards is inconceivable. (In reality, of course, genetic drift[32] and preadaptation invalidate this proposition, but these are essentially chance phenomena.) The question then becomes whether the local maximization of natural selection is capable of producing a global maximizer; whether the gradient-climbing process at the species level is capable of evolving individuals that can raise their eyes from the ground and look beyond the nearest hill. In an abstract sense we know that the answer must be positive, since man himself is both a product of natural selection and a deployer of indirect strategies. It may be useful, nevertheless, to take a closer look at the problem as it arises in the predator–prey context.

M. Edmunds[33] and E. Curio[34] have studied in some detail the behaviour of prey and predators respectively. Prey, it seems, do not use indirect strategies, but are quite capable of waiting; predators are capable of both. For example, even if flight may reduce the present danger, it may increase the danger at later times by signalling the existence of the prey to the predator; for this reason the prey has 'learned' (through selection) not to panic.[35] A symmetrical example of waiting in predators is the 'speculative and unobtrusive trot [which] brings the lion closer to a prey than any speedy, and hence warning run'.[36] Also 'a variety of animals are able to make detours while stalking',[37] and to intercept the flight path of the prey.[38] The prey, in turn, has evolved a counterstrategy to interception. This is not the direct counter-strategy of a continuous change in direction so as always to move away from the pursuer. Rather the prey uses the so-called

[32] Wright (1970, pp. 12ff) explains how random drift may carry a population over a 'saddle' of local maxima. Conversely Wilson (1975, p. 24) observes that genetic drift may prevent the species from ever reaching a *local* maximum, 'if the species perches on a knife ridge leading up to the adaptive peak'.

[33] Edmunds (1974).   [34] Curio (1976).
[35] Edmunds (1974), p. 251.   [36] Curio (1976), p. 133.
[37] *Ibid.* p. 137.   [38] *Ibid.* pp. 148ff.

'protean display', a randomly changing direction that confuses the pursuer without depending upon the path of the latter.[39] According to Curio 'relatively few predators have overcome the protean defense',[40] but one of these must be the cheetah cited by Curio himself, which uses a less-than-maximal speed in pursuing its victim because the 'deceleration allows the cat to follow each twist in the unpredictable route of its quarry'.[41]

This could be depicted as in the following scenario. In a first evolutionary stage both predator and prey follow the simple strategy of direct pursuit and evasion. In a second stage the predator evolves the indirect strategy of path interception. In a third stage the prey evolves the protean counterstrategy, and in a last stage the predator responds with the waiting behaviour of sub-optimal pursuit speed. I do not know whether the actual evolutionary process was anything at all like this, but at any rate the component stages are all well documented. The main point of the next to last paragraph is brought home by the observation that in this sequence each step is indeed advantageous to the species that takes it.

This digression into prey–predator behaviour shows, firstly, that animals *are* capable of globally maximizing behaviour and, secondly, that such behaviour is found in highly specific and stereotyped situations.[42] For the present purpose the second idea is the crucial one. The characteristic feature of man is not a programmed ability to use indirect strategies or adopt waiting

---

[39] Edmunds (1974), pp. 145–6; Curio (1976), pp. 153–4.

[40] Curio (1976), p. 153.

[41] *Ibid.* p. 147; quotation slightly modified.

[42] Barash (1977, pp. 3ff) describes an experiment where a dog and a squirrel were placed in a situation where getting food required the use of an indirect strategy, which was achieved by the squirrel and not by the dog. He explains this by arguing that in the case of the squirrels 'the ability to conduct successful detours was favored by natural selection, such that each population of squirrels came to be composed of individuals who were good at going away from goals in order to reach them'. It must be admitted that the experimental set-up described by Barash is not a 'highly specific and stereotyped situation' in the life of squirrels. Nevertheless it seems to be sufficiently similar to the real-life situations where the ability of 'going away from goals in order to reach them' was developed, so as not to constitute a serious objection to the general thesis of this essay. There is a continuum of cases here, so that the more generalized the capacity for indirect strategies, the more novel the situations in which it can be exercised and the more justified the ascription of mental states and intentions. At one end of the continuum is the cell described by Rosen (n. 44 below), at the other end the 'monkey genius' described by Wilson (n. 43); the squirrels described by Barash are somewhere in between.

behaviour in specific situations, but rather a *generalized capacity for global maximization* that applies even to qualitatively new situations. Given such facts as pleiotropy, preadaptation and genetic drift it is not very surprising, perhaps, that one-step mutations can produce two-step strategies. Such strategies, however, must receive a separate explanation in each particular case, and there is no general mechanism that can create a presumption for their presence. By contrast globally maximizing behaviour in man is immediately explained by his ability to relate to the future and the merely possible. He can choose *the* globally best alternative because he is capable of surveying *all* alternatives, all possible futures. Here it is rather the absence of global maximization that is in need of separate explanation in each case. Such failures to achieve a global maximization are the topic of chapter II.

We may say that *in creating man natural selection has transcended itself.* This leap implies a transition from the non-intentional adaptation, be it local or accidentally global, to intentional and deliberate adaptation. The breakthrough may perhaps be observed *in statu nascendi* with 'Imo the monkey genius' who, when given a mixture of sand and wheat, invented the indirect strategy of first throwing the mixture on the water (one step backwards) and then retrieving the lighter wheat grains (two steps forwards). Edward O. Wilson, from whom this description is taken, qualifies this behaviour as 'a qualitatively new element: throwing the food temporarily away and waiting a short period before retrieving it'.[43] I suggest that this qualitatively new element is precisely the deployment of the generalized capacity for global maximization in what was surely a wholly novel situation. I further suggest that with this generalized capacity *mind* enters the evolutionary arena. In cases of situation-specific indirect strategies (or waiting) there is no need to appeal to intentional or mental structures. Someone might want to contest this for the predator–prey examples given above, but any rate there can be no trace of intentionality in the behaviour of 'a cell [which] can, as it were, "see" several moves ahead, and make an energetically unfavorable move if by so doing it arrives at a position from which it can make an exceedingly favorable one in a subsequent transition'.[44] By contrast the use of globally maximizing strategies in novel situations must imply an

[43] Wilson (1975), p. 171.   [44] Rosen (1972), pp. 55–6.

analysis of the context, a scanning of several possible moves and finally a deliberate choice between them. 'La sélection s'opère, non parmi les possibles, mais parmi les existants', wrote François Jacob[45] in a phrase that is at the origin of the present approach. Man, again by contrast, can choose between unactualized possibles.

I believe that these ideas can throw some light upon the question recently treated by Donald Griffin[46] and Daniel Dennett,[47] whether and in which sense animals can be said to have a mental life, intentions, self-awareness, 'mental images' of absent objects, etc. Griffin, at one point in his argument, writes that 'Since both conspecifics and human observers can predict the future behavior of an animal from its intention movements, it seems remarkably unparsimonious to assume that the animal executing the intention movement cannot anticipate the next step in its own behavior.'[48] This, I submit, is valid for men but not for animals. In the explanation of human behaviour the burden of proof is on the one who denies intentionality and anticipations; in ethology it is the other way around. Also Griffin has difficulties in making the notion of animal intentions an operational one: 'But suppose a dog *did* anticipate events likely to occur tomorrow? How could we recognize this fact from observing its behavior today?'[49] Here I submit that one could devise tests where the animal had a choice between locally maximizing and globally maximizing behaviour, and take the occurrence of the latter as evidence for a genuine mental representation of the future. Dennett, in his discussion of 'personhood', lists six criteria that must be fulfilled if some agent is to count as a person. Here I shall offer only some remarks on the relation between his third and fourth criteria. According to the third a necessary condition for someone being a person is that we treat him as an intentional agent. Dennett then goes on to observe that this also covers our attitude towards animals and even plants, and adds the (fourth) criterion of *reciprocity*. A person, that is, must be an agent 'to which we ascribe not only simple beliefs, desires and other Intentions, but beliefs, desires and other Intentions *about* beliefs, desires and other Intentions'.[50] In the

[45] Jacob (1970), p. 313.
[47] Dennett (1976); see also Dennett (1971).
[49] *Ibid.* p. 50.

[46] Griffin (1976).
[48] Griffin (1976), p. 44.
[50] Dennett (1976), p. 181.

terminology of I.4, a person must be capable of acting upon anticipations about anticipations. I submit, however, that a weaker criterion will do the same job, viz. the capacity for global maximization.

I.4 STRATEGIC BEHAVIOUR IN ANIMALS AND MEN

In I.2 a brief reference was made to a distinction between a parametric and a strategic environment. (See also III.2 for this distinction.) I will now argue that natural selection always acts as if the environment is parametric, even when it really is a strategic one, whereas man is capable of taking the strategic nature of the context into account. (In I.2 I dealt with the relation between a population and the other populations that make up its environment, whereas here I deal with the relation between an individual and the other individuals in the population to which it belongs. The logical point, however, is the same.) My main contention can also be stated by saying that man – in contrast to natural selection – is capable of realizing the solution to games where no actor has a dominant strategy.

The parametrically rational actor treats his environment as a constant, whereas the strategically rational actor takes account of the fact that the environment is made up of other actors, and that he is part of their environment, and that they know this, etc. In a community of parametrically rational actors each will believe that he is the only one whose behaviour is variable, and that all the others are parameters for his decision problem. Acting upon these inconsistent beliefs the actors will generate unintended and perverse consequences of the kind explored by social scientists from Marx to Keynes, or from Mandeville to Boudon.[51] Such behaviour is irrational from a collective point of view, even if individually each actor satisfies the criteria of rationality. A necessary (but insufficient) condition for collective rationality is the transition to strategic thinking. In the strategic or game-theoretic mode of interaction, each actor has to take account of the intentions of all other actors, including the fact that their intentions are based upon their expectations concerning his own.

[51] See Elster (1978a), ch. 5, for many examples; also Boudon (1977).

This was thought for a long time to involve an infinite regress,[52] but frequently this is not the case. Using the concept of an *equilibrium point* it is possible to cut short the infinite regress and arrive at a uniquely definable and predictable course of action that will be chosen by rational men. (But see III.2 for exceptions to this statement.) From the present point of view the crucial fact is that human actors not only make their choices on the basis of expectations about the future, as was pointed out at the end of I.3, but also *on the basis of their expectations about the expectations of others.* This is the true Leibnizian monad, each individual reflecting the totality from his point of view. The transparency and symmetry of this interaction ensures that the fate of the actors is in their own hands, whereas a community of parametrically rational actors will be in the grip of causal forces that elude them and that perpetually make their plans come to naught. At any rate strategic actors will escape what we may call supra-intentional causal forces. In chapters II and III I will return to the darker issue of sub-intentional (largely biological) causality.

I will now argue that there is no such strategic interaction in the animal realm, and that the neglect of this difference between the social and biological domains has led several recent authors down a blind alley. To set out the distinction in its simplest form, we shall look at two games that will be solved differently in a human society but identically in animal societies. The first is the Prisoner's Dilemma, which has been extensively studied by psychologists, economists and political scientists. [53] I shall spell out the structure of this game in a somewhat unusual form, where it appears as a game between 'me' and 'all others'. Let variables x and y range over the set of strategies {C, D}, where C stands for cooperation and D for defection, and let /x, y/ mean 'I choose x, all others choose y'. The Prisoner's Dilemma is then defined by the fact that for each actor (i.e. 'me') the relevant alternatives are ranked in the following order of preference:

---

[52]   Rémont de Montmort (1713) wrote about such mutual interdependence: 'Les questions sont très simples, mais je les crois insolubles. Si cela est, c'est un grand dommage car cette difficulté se rencontre en plusieurs choses de la vie civile. Quand deux personnes, par exemple, ayant affaire ensemble, chacun veut se régler sur la conduite de l'autre.' Cp. also III.2 below for games that genuinely are without a (non-cooperative) solution.

[53]   Rapoport and Chammah (1965), Olson (1965), M. Taylor (1976a) are surveys of psychological, political and philosophical aspects of this game.

(1) /D, C/
(2) /C, C/
(3) /D, D/
(4) /C, D/

It is immediately seen that whatever the others do, my best strategy is always D. As the others are in the same position, they will also choose D, the ensuing and fully predictable outcome being /D, D/, which is worse *for everyone* than /C, C/. This shows why strategic interaction is not a sufficient condition for collective rationality. (Here it is the *sub-optimality* of the outcome that destroys the collective rationality; a more complex problem is discussed in III.2.)

Among the innumerable examples of this structure from the social sciences we may single out the problem of work motivation. In an egalitarian society without solidarity between the workers, no one will put any effort into work even if it is better for everyone if everyone does so. For a biological example, we may turn to George Williams's explanation of the evolution of schooling in fishes.[54] Letting D stand for the tendency to seek towards the middle of the school and C for the absence of any such tendency, Williams argued that we have in fact a Prisoner's Dilemma where schooling evolved because it is individually favourable even if collectively it may lead to the extinction of the population. *Ceteris paribus* it is always better to be in the middle of the school than at the outskirts, because the fish in the middle are less exposed to predators. If, however, everyone seeks to be in the middle, the school as a whole becomes more compact and more exposed to predators. A simpler example is provided by aggression: in a population of peaceful organisms an aggressive mutant will get the upper hand, but its descendants may peck each other to death.

The second game, to be compared with the Prisoner's Dilemma, is less well known. It has been extensively studied by Amartya K. Sen under the heading of the 'Assurance Game',[55] and differs from the Prisoner's Dilemma in the ranking of the first two alternatives:

(1) /C, C/
(2) /D, C/
(3) /D, D/
(4) /C, D/

[54] G. C. Williams (1966), pp. 212ff.   [55] Sen (1967, 1973, 1974).

This game differs from the Prisoner's Dilemma in the crucial feature that *there is no dominant strategy*, i.e. no strategy that is the best whatever the others do. How should a rational actor behave in this game? With less than perfect information, he should use the maximin criterion and choose the strategy that guarantees him the highest minimum payoff. In the Assurance Game this is the strategy D, for the worst that can happen to him with this choice is alternative (3), whereas the worst that can happen should he choose C is alternative (4). If, on the other hand, we assume perfect information for all players, then they will all choose C in the confident expectation that everyone else will do the same, as no one has anything to gain from acting differently. In the Prisoner's Dilemma the requirement of full information is not necessary for the solution to emerge, but in the Assurance Game the slightest uncertainty or suspicion will make an actor choose D rather than C. Only in a fully transparent situation will the actors converge upon the collectively rational behaviour. Given perfect information, the difference between the two games may be expressed by saying that in the Prisoner's Dilemma the optimum /C, C/ is both individually inaccessible (no one will take the first step towards it) and individually unstable (everyone will take the first step away from it), whereas in the Assurance Game it is individually inaccessible and individually stable. (See III.2 for the game of 'Chicken', where the optimum is individually accessible and individually unstable.) Because human actors are able to act upon expectations about expectations, the stability of the optimum in the Assurance Game will make them converge towards it in spite of the individual inaccessibility.

For a sociological example of the Assurance Game, we may again look at the problem of work motivation, where Sen has argued that in a socialist society preferences should reflect the Assurance Game rather than the Prisoner's Dilemma. Hard work effort would not (or so I hope) be a dominant strategy under socialism. No one would prefer hard and in many cases monotonous work for its own sake, regardless of what the others are doing. Nevertheless *solidarity* with others could bring about the required effort. If I am certain that the others take their share of the work, I may actually prefer doing mine rather than being a free rider. Solidarity is *conditional altruism*, as distinct from the unconditional altruism of the categorical imperative and the unconditional egoism of capitalist society. (Cf. also III.7 for some further remarks on altruism.)

It is an empirical problem to determine whether the Assurance Game is often solved, in the sence of /C, C/ emerging as a result of individual calculations. Presumably the very stringent information requirements can only be fulfilled if the information is supplied from the outside (e.g. by the government acting as a coordinator) or if the community is sufficiently small and stable so that everyone can really come to know everyone else. In the present context, however, we are less concerned with the *probability* of the cooperative behaviour than with the very *possibility* of mutually dependent cooperative action. In human societies this possibility can be realized; in natural selection it cannot. I will now argue that a not uncommon fallacy of writers on natural selection is to think that *stability explains evolution*, so that the emergence of the solution in a game without dominant strategies can be explained by its immunity to free riders.[56] Individual accessibility is required for the solution to be realized in biological games, and individual stability can only assure its maintenance once evolved. I now proceed to some examples of this fallacy.

In the otherwise admirable book by E. O. Wilson on *Sociobiology* we find a first example of the fallacious reasoning from stability to emergence. In his chapter 'The prime movers of social evolution' (an expression that definitely suggests mechanisms for the *emergence* rather than just the maintenance of behaviour) we find the following explanation of schooling in fishes:

One potential variation on the selfish herd strategy is the utilization of a 'protector' that consumes part of the population but more than compensates by excluding other predators. The widespread coral fish *Pempheris oualensis* forms schools of a few hundred or thousand individuals that find shelter during the day in well-shaded holes, coral passages and caves facing the open sea. They share these hiding places with one or a few kinds of predatory fishes, mostly the cerranid *Cephalopholis argus*, which feed on them in limited amounts. Since the predators are territorial, the *Pempheris* gain to some extent by schooling and thus restricting their exposure during the daytime to only one or a few of their enemies. By jointly saturating the favored predators with more than they can

[56]   This conclusion was reached independently by Michael Taylor (1976b), who writes that 'The problem...is that, although it is reasonable to suppose that an equilibrium, once reached, will be maintained, there are not the reasons for supposing that it will be attained in the first place which there are in the case of a game played by rational human agents.'

consume, the individual members of the school are favored with an increased probability of survival.[57]

I read this text as *stating* that the sharing of hiding places with a predator is an individually stable adaptation, and as *implying* that no further explanation is required for the emergence of this behaviour. The adaptation is stable because any single fish that tried to make it on its own in the open sea would be more exposed to predation than it is in the caves. On the other hand this does not prove that the adaptation is individually accessible (e.g. a dominant strategy); indeed the 'safety in numbers' through joint saturation of the predators cannot have favoured the fish that first ventured into the caves. There must be some threshold beyond which there is safety in numbers (as is also recognized by Wilson in another connection)[58] and the evolution up to this threshold cannot be explained by invoking retroactive causality or anticipations. A similar ambiguity is found in Curio's discussion of 'swamping the appetite of predators' as a general counterstrategy of the prey.[59]

A second example concerns the use of *mixed strategies* in animal and human games. A mixed strategy is a probability distribution fixing for each pure strategy the probability that it will be chosen. A population of actors using mixed strategies should not be confused with a mixed population, nor with a population of actors each of whom spreads himself *physically* (and not only probabilistically) over several strategies.[60] The emergence of game theory as a discipline stems from von Neumann's 1928 proof that certain apparently insoluble games admit of a solution in mixed strategies. Now a genuine mixed strategy, involving non-zero probabilities for at least two pure strategies, can never be a dominant strategy. For social games this has the implication that realization of the solution requires perfect information, for animal games the

---

[57]   Wilson (1975), p. 38.   [58]   *Ibid.* p. 121.

[59]   Curio (1976), pp. 33–4.

[60]   Thus in the horse race the same macro-distribution of bets may be generated by three distinct mechanisms: each individual placing all his money on one horse according to a certain probability distribution (a mixed strategy proper); each individual distributing his money over many horses (a physical mix); and each individual placing all his money deterministically on one horse, different individuals choosing different horses. For the relation between the first and the second concept, see Dorfman *et al.* (1958), pp. 440–1, quoting from J. D. Williams (1954), p. 103. For the relation between the first and the third, see the discussion of Maynard Smith and Dawkins below.

implication that the solution can be realized only be accident. Let us explore these two propositions through some examples.

Among the rare attempts to explain real-life (and non-military) problems through the notion of mixed strategies the recent work of Raymond Boudon on education and relative deprivation may be cited.[61] In his work on the latter problem he tries to explain the classical and paradoxical finding from *The American Soldier* that the level of frustration in the army was highest where the objective possibilities of frustration were largest. Imagine, for simplicity, a cohort of 20 Military Policemen and another cohort of 20 airmen. The first belongs to a group characterized by small possibilities for promotion and low level of frustration, whereas in the second both promotion potential and frustration are high. Let us further assume that in order to have any chance at all in the 'promotion game' you must stake one franc's equivalent of extra effort. The promoted receive the equivalent of five francs in remuneration. Five of 20 airmen and 2 of 20 MPs will achieve this, all participants (i.e. all who have staked one franc) having the same chance of success. It is then easy to see that all 20 of the airmen will stake one franc, with 15 out of 20 being disappointed, whereas only 10 MPs will enter the game, of whom 8 are disappointed. The reason why only 10 MPs enter the game is that each of them finds it individually rational to use the mixed strategy of entering the game with probability 1/2. This ingenious and elegant demonstration suffers from the defect that the use of the mixed strategy is rational only if each individual is certain that the others will do the same, which requires quite an implausible amount of information about the other players. (See also III.2 for an additional difficulty.) Nevertheless this defect is an empirical one only, and there is nothing intrinsically impossible in the model. *If human beings were always as rational as they can sometimes be, this is how they would behave.*

No such general justification can be given for the emergence of the solution in animal games requiring mixed strategies. Actually, mixed strategies are even worse off in this respect than non-dominant pure strategies. The latter may emerge as solutions to a game where they *are* dominant strategies, and then be maintained even when the game is transformed (through environmental

[61] Boudon (1977), chs. IV–V.

change) into a game where they are individually stable without being individually accessible. This cannot happen with mixed strategies, because they cannot be dominant in any game whatsoever. (They might of course become fixed by genetic drift.) For an example where mixed strategies are used in evolutionary theory, we may look at 'the logic of animal conflict' as analysed by John Maynard Smith[62] (or rather at the simplified version of his analysis presented by Richard Dawkins).[63] We here assume that the population consists of two genotypes, hawks and doves, these being not the biological species, but two behavioural variants of the same species. When a dove meets a dove, each of them has a 50 per cent chance of winning 40 'evolutionary units' and 50 per cent of losing 10 units. When a hawk meets a hawk, each of them has a 50 per cent chance of winning 50 and a 50 per cent chance of losing 100. When a hawk meets a dove, the first wins 50 and the second loses 10 with certainty. It is then easy to show that the proportion of doves to hawks in the population will converge towards 5:7, i.e. stable polymorphism. So far, so good. The crucial and illegitimate step then comes when both Maynard Smith and Dawkins affirm that a similar situation can evolve without polymorphism, namely if each individual uses the dove strategy with probability 5:12 and the hawk strategy with probability 7:12. This would indeed be true in a population of human actors with perfect information, but is not for animal actors incapable of evolving a strategy that is optimal only against the same strategy chosen by everyone else. Conversely the polymorphism (i.e. the mixed population referred to above) could never emerge in a human population, because there can be no way of tacitly deciding which individuals shall adopt which strategy.

For a third example of the fallacy we may turn to a recent article by Gary Becker,[64] who argues that the notions of egoism and altruism are more subtle and intertwined than has usually been thought. Roughly the argument is that an egoist has a clear incentive to act as an altruist, because an increase in the income of the altruist will rebound on the egoist. A crucial assumption here is, of course, that the egoist is capable of correctly anticipating the altruist's action. Renouncing an increase in income that is brought

[62] Maynard Smith (1973, 1974).   [63] Dawkins (1976), ch. 5.
[64] Becker (1976), ch. 13.

about at the expense of an even larger reduction in income for the altruist could not possibly be a dominant strategy for the egoist. It is effective only against altruists and not against other egoists. Among the startling conclusions of Becker's analysis is that an altruist may actually be better off than an egoist, because the 'beneficial indirect effects on the behavior of others may dominate the direct "disadvantages" of being altruistic'.[65] Becker then applies the same scheme to the problem of genetic fitness, where he claims that the appeal to group selection or kin selection in order to explain altruistic behaviour is less indispensable than has been thought by most biologists. If altruist genes confer individual benefits on their bearers because others take account of them in order to maximize *their* benefits, then ordinary natural selection at the individual level is sufficient to explain the emergence of altruism.

In II.4 and III.7 I return to some aspects of the sociological half of this argument. Here I would like to question the biological half of it. Let us look at a population of egoists where a mutant altruist first appears. The egoists, of course, will treat him as if he were just another egoist, because they have no way of 'knowing' or 'anticipating' that the altruist will confer upon them some of the benefits they confer upon him. For this reason the altruist gene will have only losses and no gains, and will quickly disappear from the population. In other words, Becker seems to impute to lower organisms the capacity to act upon expectations that on my argument is specific to man. And even if the organisms had this capacity, I suggest (tentatively) that they would rather reason in the following manner: 'Why should we reciprocate towards the altruist, since this would make us worse off compared to him, even if in absolute terms we should all improve our lot?' What is maximized in natural selection is differential fitness, not absolute fitness. As Alexander Gerschenkron noted for another zero-sum game, 'mutually beneficial trade which enriches also the enemies is undesirable'.[66]

As a last remark I would like to observe that even in the animal realm game-theoretic solutions *may* emerge in the absence of dominant strategies, viz. in the case where the successive adaptations to the adaptations of others converge to the solution (as in

[65]   *Ibid.* p. 287.   [66]   Gerschenkron (1970), p. 65.

a damped cobweb cycle). An example of this case is provided by W. D. Hamilton in his game-theoretic analysis of 'extraordinary sex ratios'.[67] He studied the case of double parasitism (two parasitoids on one host); more precisely the situation where there are two types of females each of which is trying to maximize its genetic fitness through selection of a sex-ratio (ratio of males to total progeny) that is optimal relative to the ratio chosen by the other. Arguing first that fitness is proportional to the number of inseminations by sons plus the number of daughters, Hamilton shows that for a female using sex-ratio x on a host with another female using ratio x_0, the fitness will be proportional to

$$\frac{x}{x+x_0}((1-x)+(1-x_0))+(1-x)$$

For the female using x_0 the fitness will be proportional to the same expression, with x and x_0 changing places everywhere. If we now restrict the set of possible ratios to $\{0, 1/4, 1/2, 3/4, 1\}$ – a simplification that makes no difference to the analysis – the following payoff-matrix emerges:

		x_0				
		0	1/4	1/2	3/4	1
	0	?	1, 2.5	1, 2	1, 1.15	1, 1
	1/4	2.5, 1	1.5, 1.5	1.2, 1.3	1, 1	0.9, 0.6
x	1/2	2, 1	1.3, 1.2	1, 1	0.8, 0.7	0.7, 0.3
	3/4	1.5, 1	1, 1	0.7, 0.8	0.5, 0.5	0.4, 0.1
	1	1, 1	0.6, 0.9	0.3, 0.7	0.1, 0.4	0,0

Disregarding the undetermined (and biologically trivial) case of both females choosing to produce no males, we immediately see that the only equilibrium point (and thus the solution) of the matrix is when both players use 1/4. We also observe that the ratio 1/4 is *not* a dominant strategy, for if x chooses 1, x_0 will choose 0 rather than 1/4 and conversely. Nevertheless Hamilton is justified in saying that 'through trial and error, two naive players would quickly learn that constant playing of 1/4 was the optimum-yielding

[67]   Hamilton (1967).

strategy'.[68] If, namely, x_0 starts out with one of the set $\{0, 1/4, 1/2, 3/4\}$, then $1/4$ is x's best answer, and in the next round $1/4$ will also be the best counter from x_0. If x_0 begins with 1, x will counter with 0, to which x_0 will reply with $1/4$, which in turn will induce x to choose $1/4$. Thus whichever initial strategy is chosen by x_0, the sequence of replies and counterreplies will make the players converge upon the solution in a maximum of four steps. This shows that the presence of a dominant strategy is not a necessary condition for the game-theoretic solution to emerge, but nevertheless the point remains valid that in the absence of specific evidence to the contrary, there is no presumption that the solution will be realized in a game without dominant strategies. Hamilton offers such an argument; Wilson, Maynard Smith and Becker do not. Their procedure seems to rest upon unjustified assumptions concerning the burden of proof; they take for granted what must be demonstrated.

I.5   FUNCTIONALIST EXPLANATION IN SOCIOLOGY

In this part I turn to more familiar matters, which nevertheless seem worth while reconsidering. I here argue that functionalist explanation in sociology rests upon an ill-conceived analogy from biology, and that a closer analysis of purported functionalist explanations shows that in virtually all cases one or more of the defining features are lacking. Now there is no general agreement as to which features should enter into the definition of a functional explanation, and to the reader whose definition differs from mine the following may seem beside the point. Still I think that my use of the term is in fairly good agreement with the standard expositions by Robert Merton and Arthur Stinchcombe,[69] so that I am not setting up a straw man to knock down.

On my definition, then, *an institution or a behavioural pattern X is explained by its function Y for group Z if and only if:*

(1) Y is an *effect* of X;
(2) Y is *beneficial* for Z;
(3) Y is *unintended* by the actors producing X;
(4) Y (or at least the causal relationship between X and Y) is *unrecognized* by the actors in Z;
(5) Y maintains X by a causal *feedback* loop passing through Z.

[68] *Ibid.* p. 486.   [69] R. K. Merton (1957); Stinchcombe (1968).

In this paradigm the actors involved in X may be identical with the group Z, or the relation may be one of inclusion, overlap or disjointedness. Some comments on the criteria are in order. That functions are a subspecies of effects is, I think, fairly uncontroversial. To say that an institution 'has a function' must imply that it *does* something, i.e. generates some effect. The notion of a beneficial effect is rather more obscure. I shall take it to mean that Y is a local maximum of some state variable of which the actors in Z always want more rather than less. It would be unduly restrictive to require that Y be a global maximum, for then the biological paradigm would break down at the outset. Needless to say, the actors producing X may be engaged in an activity of global maximization (of some other variable). That Y be unintended and unrecognized is part and parcel of the Mertonian paradigm of latent functions, to which I am here restricting myself. On the other hand it is hard, but not impossible, to find the fifth criterion in Merton's account of functionalism.[70] In Stinchcombe's analysis, however, the existence of a causal feedback loop is made the central feature of functional explanation, and I believe this also reflects the view of most writers on functionalist theory.

I will now be arguing for a series of propositions. First, it is close to impossible to find any cases of functional analysis in sociology where the presence of all of features (1)–(5) is demonstrated. Secondly, there exists a naive brand of functional analysis (criticized by Merton) that from the presence of features (1), (3) and (4) concludes to the presence of feature (2) and often of feature (5). Thirdly, there exists a more sophisticated brand of functionalism (represented by Merton) that from the presence of features (1)–(4) fallaciously concludes to the presence of feature (5). Fourthly, there is a brand of (especially Marxist) functionalism that argues – fallaciously – that an institution can be maintained by its *long-term* effects if these satisfy criteria (2)–(4), even when the

---

[70]   In the explicit paradigm Merton (1957, pp. 50ff) lists eleven dimensions of his analysis; the feedback loop is not among them. In his more informal discussion, however, Merton several times implies that the ascription of (latent) functions to some pattern explains the existence and the persistence of the pattern. This, indeed, is the central idea of the pages (64ff) where he explains that the distinction between manifest and latent functions 'clarifies the analysis of seemingly irrational patterns'. The most explicit statement (with a rare occurrence of the term 'explain') is found in a reinterpretation of Veblen: 'Among these latent functions, which help explain the persistence and the social location of the pattern of conspicuous consumption, is its symbolization of "pecuniary strength and so of gaining or retaining a good name"' (p. 69).

short-term effects are harmful rather than beneficial. Fifthly – turning now to more positive statements – analyses satisfying criteria (1)–(3) and *either* criterion (4) *or* criterion (5) are of fundamental importance in the social sciences.

Starting with the last proposition, accounts satisfying requirements (1), (2), (3) and (5) may be called *filter-explanations,* whereas analyses satisfying criteria (1)–(4) may be dubbed *invisible-hand explanations.*[71] Militarily financed research may be analysed by a filter-explanation. If academic personnel apply for military funds in order to be able to conduct the research that they would have done in any case (i.e. with money from any other source), the Department of Defence may serve as a filter that selects some applications and rejects others.[72] The resulting composition of research will be beneficial to the military interests, while wholly unintended by the individual scientist, who can argue truthfully that no one has told him what to do.[73] This may also be called a case of *artificial selection,* where the feedback loop operates through the *recognized* effects of the structure whose persistence is to be explained. (See also III.4 for another example.)

For some cases of invisible-hand explanations we may also draw upon the sociology of science, viz. Merton's own work, on multiple discoveries and the 'Matthew effect' in science.[74] In the first example we have X equalling simultaneous discoveries, Y a functionally optimum amount of redundancy and Z the scientific community. In the second example we have X equalling disproportionate amount of recognition to senior scientists in case of co-authorship and simultaneous discoveries, Y more rapid dissemination of important results and Z the scientific community. In both cases Merton convincingly demonstrates the presence of features (1)–(4) of the functionalist paradigm. He also in both cases uses the term 'function', which *may* be interpreted as an implicit

[71] I borrow this terminology from Nozick (1974, pp. 18ff), though I use it to express a distinction that does not quite coincide with his.
[72] Glantz and Albers (1974).
[73] In an otherwise beautiful book of memoirs Ulam (1976, p. 232) seems to fall into this trap: 'These were the days of defense research contracts. Even mathematicians frequently were recipients. Johnny [von Neumann] and I commented on how in some of the proposals scientists sometimes described how useful their intended research was for the national interest, whereas in reality they were motivated by bonafide scientific curiosity and an urge to write a few papers.' The 'whereas' is misplaced, because (or to the extent that) the Department of Defence could screen out the proposals and retain those that were seen as having military potential.   [74] Merton (1973), ch. 20.

contention that criterion (5) is also satisfied. As already observed, Merton is rather ambiguous on this point; personally I tend to get the impression that Merton thinks of functional analysis as providing also an *explanation* of the phenomena to which these functions are imputed. As a last and rather more complex example of invisible-hand analysis we may take the case where X equals labour-saving inventions, Y reduction of the wage level and Z the community of capitalist entrepreneurs.[75] Here the actors involved in X are the same as group Z, which means that *intentional* analysis and *functional* analysis emerge as two alternative (and equally fallacious) approaches.[76]

I know of only one example where all of features (1)–(5) are actually present, viz. in the attempt of the Chicago school of economists to explain profit-maximizing as a result of the 'natural selection' of firms by the market.[77] The anomaly that led to this attempt was the following. On the one hand the observed external behaviour (choice of factor combinations and output level) seemed to indicate that firms in general adopt a profit-maximizing behaviour, by adjusting to market conditions. On the other hand the internal decision-making process of the firm did not seem to be guided by this objective; rather some rough-and-ready rules of thumb were found to be typical. To bridge this gap between the output of the black box and its internal workings, the economists in question postulated that some firms just happen to use profit-maximizing rules of thumb and others not; that the former survive whereas the latter go extinct; that the profit-maximizing routines tend to spread in the population of firms, either by imitation or by takeovers. If, then, we set X equal to a certain rule of thumb, Y to profit-maximizing and Z to the set of firms, we have a paradigm of functional analysis. The argument clearly is modelled on a biological analogy, and it works (to the extent that it works)[78] only because the notions of fitness, survival, reproduc-

---

[75] For more about this problem see Elster (1978a), ch. 5, and III.2 below; cp. also the references in n. 27 above.

[76] That is, when all behave in a way that is to their benefit as a group, it is tempting to conclude *either* that they act thus in order to get these benefits *or* that their behaviour has this function.   [77] Cp. II.4 and III.5 below.

[78] In addition to the problems discussed in III.5, we may add the local–global difficulty: unless we assume that all possible rules of thumb are represented in the population of firms, there is no presumption that a global maximum will be attained by this mechanism.

tion and inheritance can be transferred without too much modification.

In this case the feedback loop is explicitly demonstrated. In most cases, however, it is postulated rather than demonstrated. A large body of sociological literature seems to rest upon an implicit regulative idea that if you can demonstrate that a given pattern has unintended, unrecognized and beneficial effects, then you have also explained why it exists and persists. I believe that if you open at random any book on deviation, crime or conflict you will find statements that support this interpretation. One such statement, truthfully taken at random from my bookshelf, could be the following: 'Conflict within and between bureaucratic structures provides the means for avoiding the ossification and ritualism which threatens their form or organization.'[79] By using the word 'means' the author implicitly commits himself to an intentional or a functional explanation of conflict. His evidence, on the other hand, only supports the statement that conflict may have the *effect* of preventing ossification. No feedback loop is sketched (and of course no intentions are demonstrated); nevertheless the total neglect of the issue of the *causes* of conflicts can only be explained on the assumption that the author tacitly postulates a feedback relation whereby the effect maintains its cause. My way of making sense of this approach is to impute to these authors the regulative idea that criteria (1)–(4) permit us to infer the fulfilment of criterion (5), in the absence of evidence to the contrary.

Arthur Stinchcombe is among the relatively few writers who have recognized that 'the nature of reverse causal links from consequences back to structure [is] a sore point in functional theory'.[80] He also sketches six distinct mechanisms that could fill this gap. The first is natural selection in the literal (biological) sense. The second and (I think) the sixth invoke 'natural selection' of firms by the market. The third relies on conscious planning, and is really out of place in this context. The fifth seems to be quite similar to what was called above a filter-mechanism. The fourth is explained in the following cryptic terms: 'Without planning, people may find consequences of behavior satisfying. Thus church

---

[79] Coser (1971), p. 60. From the same volume of readings Himes (1971) is very much in the same vein.   [80] Stinchcombe (1968), p. 85.

services might be maintained without much planning to achieve theological ends, because people find the social interaction, or the respectability, satisfying.'[81] This Durkheimian example has been discussed in some detail by I. C. Jarvie, who concludes that the functionalist analysis has no explanatory power, because people's 'reasons for going to church may have very little to do with what they are doing in going to church'.[82] I tend to agree with this conclusion (which is backed by an argument that the interested reader should consult), which means that the only successful example of functional analysis in sociology is the one I have already singled out, viz. selection of firms by the market.

To understand the origin of functionalist sociology we may begin by observing that in biology both the following regulative ideas are valid:

– Every persisting structure has a function (i.e. has beneficial effects through which it is maintained).
– Every persisting structure with beneficial effects has a function (more specifically, is maintained through these effects).

Were these propositions to be read as general laws, the second would be redundant, but the logic of regulative ideas is different. A regulative idea admits of counterexamples, and is stronger the fewer the counterexamples. As the class of counterexamples to the second proposition is smaller than the class of counterexamples to the first,[83] the second is worth stating in its own right. The above discussion of Merton and Stinchcombe concludes that in the social sciences there can be no regulative idea analogous to the second of these propositions. There can be no general presumption – with the burden of proof on him who holds the opposite view – that

---

[81]   *Ibid.* p. 86.
[82]   Jarvie (1968), pp. 198–9.
[83]   Counterexamples to the first proposition are found at four distinct levels. At the most fundamental level, one should not think of mutations as 'having the function' of generating the evolutionary process. Natural selection is not a result of natural selection (G. C. Williams 1966, p. 128); mutations require causal, not functional explanations. At an intermediate level, the theory of non-Darwinian evolution argues that the number of functionless sites (or rather site-occupiers) in proteins is very large indeed. At the more molar level pleiotropy is a general mechanism for generating and maintaining neutral or even harmful features. The counterexamples of the fourth level are also counterexamples to the second proposition: these refer to beneficial effects that arise as the statistical summation of many individual adaptations. G. C. Williams (1966, p. 209) refers to the misconception 'that when one demonstrates that a certain biological process produces a benefit, one has demonstrated *the* function, or at least *a* function of the process'. Cp. also Elster (1978a), ch. 5.

the relevant subclass of beneficial effects maintain their causes. *A fortiori* this must hold for the sociological analogy of the first regulative idea, which is justly criticized by Merton.[84] I believe, therefore, that the time has come for sociology to shake off its biological inheritance altogether. Merton performed an important service in criticizing the regulative idea that 'Everything has a function', corresponding to the first of the two propositions above. He also performed brilliant analyses of the invisible-hand variety, but was led to overemphasize the effects and neglect the causes of behavioural patterns by some implicit assumption similar to the second proposition.

I end with some brief remarks on Marxism and functionalism. A strange and sad feature of contemporary Marxist sociology and political science is the espousal of the less valuable methods of bourgeois social science, and a total lack of interest in the tools that really are tailor-made for Marxist analysis. By the second statement I refer to the Marxist neglect of game theory, which in my view is indispensable for a theory of exploitation or of domination.[85] By the first statement I refer to the use of functional analysis, often of the vulgar kind denounced by Merton. In Marxist writings on education, bureaucracy and indeed on most topics there seems to be an implicit regulative idea that 'Every institution or behavioural pattern in capitalist society serves the interests of capitalism and is maintained because it serves these interests.' Marxists seem to have lost their sense of the ironies of history, whereby societies can generate patterns that lead to their own destruction. In order to substantiate this naive brand of functionalism Marxists have invented a special gimmick, which is to manipulate the time perspective. If, say, the actions of the State go counter to short-term capitalist interests, this has the function of safeguarding long-term capitalist interests; heads I win, tails you lose. (See II.8 below for examples of such reasoning in Marx.) Now this is not only an arbitrary procedure, because 'any argument can be turned to any effect by juggling with the time scale'.[86] It is also a theoretically inconsistent one, because functional analysis cannot invoke in-direct strategies, as was explained in I.3. To the extent that the state

[84] Merton (1957), pp. 30ff.
[85] For first steps in this direction see Shapley and Shubik (1967) and Lancaster (1973).
[86] Brooke (1972), p. 93.

is maintained through the effects of its actions on the capitalist class, the negative short-term effects should make it disappear (or change) before the long-term positive effects come to be felt. Only intentional actors are capable of taking one step backwards in order to take two steps forwards later on, so that the short-term/long-term distinction logically leads to a conspiratorial interpretation of history, given the absence of empirical evidence for such intentions.

There are, of course, also many cases where Marxists have committed the more sophisticated fallacy of assuming that effects that are beneficial (in the short term) to the capitalist class tend to maintain their own causes; or that, to put it differently, patterns can be *explained* by a demonstration that their effects are beneficial for that class. To take but one example, again at random, Michael Kalecki comes very close to arguing that the business cycle can be explained by its beneficial effects for the capitalist class.[87] Full employment for long periods of time is politically dangerous, whereas permanent unemployment is economically dangerous, whence the need for a business cycle. Actually Kalecki hesitates or oscillates between a conspiratorial and a functional approach, while the historical record at most justifies the causal statement that the business cycle may have had these beneficial effects.

[87]   Kalecki (1971). For a book that abounds with propositions of this kind, see Bowles and Gintis (1976).

II

IMPERFECT RATIONALITY: ULYSSES AND THE SIRENS

'...but you must bind me hard and fast, so that I cannot stir from the spot where you will stand me...and if I beg you to release me, you must tighten and add to my bonds'. (*The Odyssey*)

II.1 INTRODUCTION

Ulysses was not fully rational, for a rational creature would not have to resort to this device; nor was he simply the passive and irrational vehicle for his changing wants and desires, for he was capable of achieving by indirect means the same end as a rational person could have realised in a direct manner. His predicament – being weak and knowing it – points to the need for a theory of *imperfect rationality* that has been all but neglected by philosophers and social scientists. The path-breaking work of R. H. Strotz[1] and George Ainslie[2] has laid the empirical and conceptual foundations on which all later work will have to build. In this essay I attempt a first step towards a synthesis. I also endeavour to broaden the empirical and conceptual base itself, by adding some examples from fields not considered in their work. Strotz mainly deals with examples from the theory of consumer behaviour, whereas Ainslie relies mostly on findings from experimental psychology. Their work is summarized and discussed in II.5 and II.7 respectively; Ainslie's work is also discussed in II.2 and II.9. In II.6 the reader will find a discussion of endogenously changing preferences, a problem closely related to the questions of dynamic consistency raised by Strotz. In II.3 and II.4 the critiques of rationality offered by Pascal and Descartes are presented and contrasted. In II.8 the analysis is extended from individual

---

[1] Strotz (1955–6), criticized in Pollak (1968) and Shefrin and Thaler (1977).
[2] Ainslie (1975, 1977).

behaviour to group behaviour; societies as well as individuals have found it useful to bind themselves, e.g. through constitutions. The problem of binding oneself is also relevant for many questions in the philosophy of mind (who binds whom?) and in moral psychology (who has the right to bind whom?). These issues run through the whole essay.

The general thesis being defended is that binding oneself is a privileged way of resolving the problem of weakness of will; the main technique for achieving rationality by indirect means. There is, however, another route that can also be taken. This alternative approach consists, roughly, in a rearrangement of the inner space of the person, without any causal mechanisms being set up in the external world. Three varieties of this approach are explored here, and contrasted with the method chosen by Ulysses: Ainslie's notion of private side bets, Strotz's and Pollak's notion of consistent planning, and Charles Taylor's notion of responsibility for self. I believe that the Ulysses strategy is closely related to the Aristotelian approach to psychology, whereas the alternative notions have close links to existentialist philosophy. I would not deny that some degree of self-control can be achieved simply by pulling yourself up by the bootstraps, but as is argued below more durable results are achieved by acting on the environment.

II.2   Towards a definition

I start by giving some examples of persons binding themselves, or *precommitting* themselves, as I shall also say as a stylistic variation. In order to stop smoking it is standard practice to set up some causal machinery that will add force to your inner resolution: to tell your friends about your intention so as to invite their sarcastic comments if you are backsliding; to go for a walk in the mountains so as to make cigarettes physically unavailable; to cross the street when you see a tobacco shop further on so as not to be exposed to the sight of cigarettes; to take cold showers in order to strengthen your will-power; to undergo hypnosis in order to induce aversion to tobacco; to make yourself believe that more cigarettes mean certain death within five years.

Ceasing to smoke is a relatively simple problem, for several reasons. In the first place temporary success often implies permanent success, in the sense that abstention for a prolonged period reduces the urge to smoke. In the second place addiction to nicotine is a fairly isolated feature of the individual, with few spill-over effects to other character traits. *Obesity* – a central problem in the literature on behavioural self-control[3] – differs in both respects. Being fat is a character trait (not only a physical feature) that is involved in most other traits as well; the desire to change it is a desire to become a different kind of person. Also the temptation of backsliding is much more slowly reduced than in the case of nicotine. In a recent survey,[4] techniques for self-control of weight were divided into two main categories: self-managed antecedent stimulus control techniques and self-initiated reinforcement control. Within each of these, three further subcategories are distinguished, one of which refers to manipulation of the environment. According to another study[5] this does indeed seem to be the most efficient method.

Persons with periodically recurring mental illness may (but rarely do) bind themselves in advance, by issuing instructions that when the next episode occurs, the instructions that will then be issued (refusal to be hospitalized or extravagant orders of fast cars) are not to be obeyed. The Norwegian 'Law of psychic health protection'[6] has the unique feature that a person may voluntarily seek irreversible admission to a mental hospital. To be precise, the medical director may lay down the condition for admission that the patient shall not be permitted to leave within three weeks of the admission date, even should he desire to do so.

The spontaneity of jazz musicians is an oft-cited, and in some cases well-attested, phenomenon. Some take precautions against their tendency to spend immediately whatever money they get hold of; others do not. In the former category was Johnny Hodges, who throughout his career with the Ellington orchestra insisted on being paid on a daily basis.[7] In the latter category was Charlie Parker, 'A man living from moment to moment. A man living for the pleasure principle, music, food, sex, drugs, kicks, his per-

---

[3] See Foreyt (ed.) (1977).   [4] Jeffrey (1977).
[5] Stuart (1971).
[6] I owe my information about this institution, and its uniqueness, to Helge Waal and Einar Kringlen, who have also provided valuable suggestions in other respects. See also Adserballe (1977, pp. 485ff) for a partially similar practice in Denmark.
[7] Jewell (1977), pp. 140–1.

sonality arrested at an infantile level.'[8] This difference between the two alto saxophonists is easily heard in their playing.

Readers of *Lucien Leuwen* will recall the moment when Madame de Chasteller recognizes her love for Lucien and, fearing what it may lead her into doing, binds herself by choosing a companion who is certain not to permit her the smallest indiscretion. 'Cet être si méchant me répondra de moi-même.'[9] We may pause here to observe the subtleties that nearly always arise in these cases. Madame de Chasteller also adduces a further motive for choosing a companion, the desire to punish herself for past indiscretions. 'Et la sévérité de cette punition tranquillisa sa conscience: madame de Chasteller se pardonna presque l'entrevue si légèrement accordée à Leuwen.'[10] Self-punishment may indeed be a technique for self-control,[11] but in the present case this would be redundant, because the punishment also has the effect of making the behaviour in question physically impossible. If Madame de Chasteller had punished herself by some other means, such as self-flagellation, one could impute to her the prudential motive of inducing a process of operant learning, though it would be hard not to suspect some neurotic component as well. With the 'companion strategy', however, prudence has led to the simpler technique of reducing the number of feasible options, and then the motive for punishment can only be neurotic or moral.

Given these introductory examples – many more will be given – we can proceed to a tentative definition of what it is to bind oneself. The criteria advanced below may very well turn out to be neither necessary nor sufficient for a precise rendering of our intuitive notions of precommitment, but they will have to do as a first approximation. An obvious requirement is that

(i)   To bind oneself is to carry out a certain decision at time t_1 in order to increase the probability that one will carry out another decision at time t_2.[12]

The crucial point here is that the expected change in the probability of the later action must be the *motive* for the earlier

[8]   Russell (1973), p. 232; also abundant evidence in Reisner (1974).
[9]   Stendhal (1952), I, p. 969.   [10]   *Ibid.*
[11] See for example Mahoney (1972); also the editors' introduction to Mahoney and Thoresen (eds.) (1975).
[12] '...self-control is merely the emission of one set of responses designed to alter the probability of occurrence of another set of responses' (Stuart 1971, p. 180).

one; not an unintended effect, nor a predictable and not unwelcome effect. The need to exclude the latter case is seen by considering the following thought experiment. If Madame de Chasteller had chosen her companion in order to punish herself; if, furthermore, the binding effect of that choice was predictable and acceptable to her; and if, finally, she would not have chosen that disagreeable person had she not committed her earlier indiscretions, even supposing she could predict her later ones – then this first criterion would not be satisfied and we would not have a case of binding onself. If the psychological stance just described seems implausible, I can only answer that a similar attitude seems to underlie the refusal of many persons to engage in complicated and strategic behaviour directed against themselves. For some persons, that is, the desire to stop smoking may be weaker than their desire not to be (or become) the kind of person who could bring about a state of non-smoking through binding himself. Such a person might engage in some activity knowing that it will lead to a state of non-smoking, which he desires; but the condition for that activity might be the existence of some other end which is furthered by it and which in itself would be a sufficient motive for engaging in it.

We may observe here that this is *not* the problem that some (desired) results may be impossible to achieve except as a by-product of activities undertaken for other ends. The individual who sets out to obtain pleasure or to make himself into a cultured person will usually be thwarted, unless at some point the means become ends in themselves. (Cp. also III.9 for some further comments on 'willing what cannot be willed'.) Nor is it a question of cost–benefit analysis in the narrow sense that the necessary calculations and deliberations will consume more time and energy than will be saved if the strategy is successful. Rather the issue here is one of cost–benefit calculus in a much broader sense: even if the deliberations do succeed in modifying the behaviour or the character in the desired way, *the very activity of deliberating* can modify the character for the worse, and in ways judged even more important, through the stultifying effects on spontaneity. It is possible to become addicted to will-power, and it may be as rational to take steps against this addiction as against any other. As Thomas Nagel observes in a somewhat different context, 'spontaneity and immediacy are of value in themselves'[13] and thus require prudential protection. His argument is that too much spontaneity now may reduce the possibilities for spontaneous behaviour later on; my argument is rather that a strategy for reducing the undesirable consequences of spontaneity may also reduce the overall amount of spontaneity in my behaviour.

Condition (i) also permits more complex and hierarchical methods, involving three or more decisions. If, for example, the pattern of manic-depressive episodes were depression succeeded by exaltation (in fact the usual pattern is the opposite one), then the following case might be envisaged. At time t_1 the person, being in the 'normal' or 'ground' state, issues the instruction that the instructions he will issue at t_2, during the depressive phase, to the effect that the instructions he will issue at t_3, during the manic phase, are not to be obeyed, are not to be obeyed. This assumes that his considered opinion is that a person in the manic phase is not necessarily irresponsible, or that treating him as irresponsible will aggravate the long-term problem even if easing the short-term one. In somewhat fanciful terms we might speak here of an alliance between the early and the late self against the intermediate and more docile self. (Three-step techniques are also explored by Ainslie, but in his examples the point is rather that the early and the late stage may combine against the middle one so as to make precommitment superfluous.)[14] In this case the 'ground state' can be clearly distinguished from the pathological ones, so that external observers would know which instructions to follow, but this might not always be so. If a person on one day issues an instruction that future instructions of some specific kind are not to be obeyed, and then retracts the meta-instructions the following day, what would be the criteria for deciding whether the self making the retraction is a more authentic one than the one that

[13] Nagel (1970), p. 73.
[14] Ainslie (1975, p. 478) offers, among several others, the following example: 'Another example might be a person with antisocial impulses who has found that acts of delinquency put him into unrewarding situations and thus tries to avoid the temptation to perform them. However, if he is afraid that he may get out of control and get himself into bigger trouble, he may stop avoiding the temptation to act up in smaller ways, so that the authorities (police, ward attendants etc.) will exert more effort to guard him. The long-range desire to avoid a major rampage causes him to look for devices that will constrain his future behaviour; because such a device must be chosen early, when the effectiveness of the reward it leads to is low, one that also produces an immediate thrill may be choosable, while one that stands on its own may not be.'

issued the meta-instructions, or the very self whose lack of authenticity made those meta-instructions necessary? In II.9 I return to some aspects of this problem.

The next criterion is more of an *ad hoc* one, but seems required for the following reason. On the first criterion, taken by itself or in conjunction with criteria (iii), (iv) and (v) below, any act of investment – i.e. any sacrifice of present goods in order to make more goods available later on – would count as binding oneself. This, I think, is counterintuitive. It might be necessary to bind oneself in order to make that sacrifice (see the discussion of criterion (iv)), i.e. to take a decision at t_1 in order to increase the probability of the sacrifice at t_2, but the sacrifice at t_2 is not necessarily an act of binding oneself, even though it increases the probability of certain consumption decisions being carried out at t_3. In order to exclude this and similar cases[15] I shall impose the further requirement that

> (ii) If the act at the earlier time has the effect of inducing a change in the set of options that will be available at the later time, then this does not count as binding oneself if the new feasible set includes the old one.

In II.9 it is argued that inducing changes in the feasible set is one of the several strategies available for binding oneself; the second requirement states that expansions of the feasible set shall not count as instances of *this* strategy. Some options must be *excluded* if we are to speak of precommitment. Once again we should insist upon the distinction between motives and predictable desired effects. Many acts of investment are irreversible, and as such have the consequence of binding the investor to some particular allocation of consumption over time (II.5 below). This may even be part of the motive for the investment, but it need not be. To see that an investment is not necessarily irreversible it suffices to consider the standard 'Austrian' cases where wine is left to mature or forests to grow. Such acts of 'sacrifice' or 'waiting' do induce an expansion in the future set of options, but they do not imply any commitment beyond the present, because wine can be drunk and trees be cut before they come to fruition.

A further criterion is that

> (iii) The effect of carrying out the decision at t_1 must be to set up some causal process in the external world.

[15]   E.g. Kotarbinski's notion of *flexible planning*, as exposed in Johansen (1977), pp. 119ff.

This excludes, for example, decisions to decide. The point here is not that the carrying out of a decision to decide simply is to carry out the later decision itself. I feel that a decision to decide can be carried out by setting up some mental attitude that can be described as 'resolution', 'firmness of purpose', etc. Nor is the rationale behind criterion (iii) that decisions to decide are without efficacy, though I think that in general they have very little impact. 'I decide that I shall decide that p' has the same ritual and redundant sound as 'if someone were to buy several copies of the morning paper to assure himself that what it said was true'.[16] Sartre's brilliant analysis of the gambler, whose decision to abstain from playing loses all causal efficacy when once more he faces 'the green felt', leads up to the same conclusion.[17] The need for the third criterion is rather that our intuitive notion of what it is to bind oneself seems to require that we temporarily deposit our will in some external structure; that we set up a causal process in the external world that after some time returns to its source and modifies our behaviour. Once again we must recall the first criterion above. The point is not simply that 'a human being is controlled by the environment, and he also controls part of the environment that affects him and others'.[18] To modify the environment in a way that in an unanticipated manner has an impact upon the modifier, is not to bind oneself. We are talking here about controlling the controller *in order to* control oneself.

Criterion (iii) also excludes what Ainslie calls 'private side bets', a decision to group future rewards so that they stand or fall together.[19] This bookkeeping rearrangement may indeed be of some importance, as I have learned from personal experience. The

---

[16]   Wittgenstein (1953), §265.
[17]   Sartre (1943), pp. 69–70.   [18]   Jeffrey (1975), p. 194.
[19]   Ainslie (1975), pp. 478ff; Ainslie (1977), pp. 18ff. The technical basis of this notion is the following. We assume that present effectiveness of future reward is a decreasing function of the time from now till the reward is due. We assume, furthermore, that the curve relating time to effectiveness is more concave than an exponential curve (for the privileged nature of exponential curves see II.5 below). This means that the relative effectiveness of a large reward in the distant future and a smaller reward in the near future may change when the corresponding curves cross, which they can never do if exponential. There is a switch point, that is, when the person stops preferring the large reward and begins preferring the smaller one. Ainslie then imagines a case where the subject is offered a choice between two such rewards a number of times in succession: the private side bet then is a decision to choose between all pairs simultaneously rather than making a succession of choices. It can then be shown that this decision procedure delays the switch and increases the probability that the larger reward will be chosen. See also n. 42 below for the notion of a *public* side bet.

odds that you will perform some unpleasant task now rather than postpone it for the future are increased if you tell yourself that your reasons for postponing it will be equally strong when the future time arrives. A present failure will predict future failures, so that the consequences of the choice become more fateful than if you look at the immediate sequel only. Nevertheless I do not think this ingenious strategy should be referred to as precommitment. The fact that it is a response to the same problem – weakness of will – that motivates the technique of binding oneself should not lead us into saying that it is an instance of that technique. Private side bets, like the 'strategy of consistent planning' that will be considered in II.5, are an alternative to the method of precommitment.

A fourth and equally important requirement is that

(iv) The resistance against carrying out the decision at t_1 must be smaller than the resistance that would have opposed the carrying out of the decision at t_2 had the decision at t_1 not intervened.

To take cold showers in order to develop the strength of will that will enable me to stop smoking is not a very good strategy if stepping under the cold shower requires the very will-power it is supposed to develop. The problem underlying condition (iv) is the very difficulty to which the strategy of Ulysses is a solution: our general resistance to uphill walking, and our preference for downhill strolls. In I.3 I argued that the capacity for *waiting* and for using *indirect strategies* ('one step backwards, two steps forwards') is among the features that distinguish man from other animals, but this is not to say that the capacity is always fully utilized. Only man is in possession of the generalized capacity for seeking global maxima at the expense of local maxima, but it is equally true that only man is susceptible of *akrasia*, because that notion only makes sense on a background of successful long-term planning and successful resistance to temptation in many cases. *A fortiori* only man is capable of overcoming his weakness of will through the use of techniques such as precommitment, private side bets, etc.

This implies that precommitment in some cases can be seen as an indirect strategy that enables us to use indirect strategies. If I am unable to take a whole step backwards, then I might perhaps be able to take half a step backwards, knowing that after that first half step I shall be committed to the second half and enabled to take the two steps forwards later on. As observed above, investment is a case in point. If I have designed a new type of fishing net that will enable me to catch twice as much as the old one, and if I know that while I make the new net I shall get so hungry that I will prefer to go fishing with the old and as a consequence never get enough time for uninterrupted work on the new, then *destruction of the old net* could be a rational choice: an indirect strategy compelling me to use the indirect strategy of investing in a new net. This is *not* a case of burning one's bridges, for if one intends to move forwards these bridges serve no useful purpose anyway. Destroying useful means of production that could have eased the strain during the construction of the new is a more radical procedure. If necessity is the mother of invention, then you may spur yourself into activity by making yourself necessitous. It is sometimes suggested that the rapid economic growth in societies that have been ravaged by war, such as Japan and Germany after 1945, should be seen in this light. I am more than sceptical towards this notion. It may be true that the destruction of outdated machinery has the *effect* of enabling a nation to escape 'the penalties of taking the lead', but on all interpretations of history but the conspiratorial one this would never be a *motive* for undertaking a war, as it would have to be for the first criterion above to be satisfied. (In I.5 I dealt (by implication) with the even more obscure suggestion that such precommitment could be a *function* of war; I return to a similar problem in II.8.)

The general problem is the following: for a given task of uphill walking (i.e. a task which I resist with a given force) and for a given strength of will, does there always exist a strategy of precommitment that (1) is within my will-power and (2) is capable of getting me ultimately to the top of the hill? ('Ultimately', because we might envisage a sequential hierarchy of acts of binding oneself, each of which requires a relatively small effort.) It was argued by Descartes (II.4 below) that anyone can achieve anything if he goes about it in a sufficiently roundabout manner. In a special case and in a special sense (II.6 below) this holds demonstrably even for persons with zero will-power. If we accept, at least for the sake of argument, that we are all-powerful in this sense, how should we then explain the fact that we do not always use those options that are available to us? By hypothesis we cannot invoke weakness of will. We can, however, invoke cost–benefit considerations, in either the narrow or the broad sense distinguished above. For some individuals the very act of deliberating might require an effort that lies above the threshold of their will-power. (Cp. Maxwell's demon, who could surmount the second law of thermodynamics only on the assumption that calculation is costless and frictionless.) For other individuals the process of getting to the top (which they want) would also induce some character change (which they resist), in which case it could be rational to refuse the option that is assumed to exist.

The last condition I shall impose is

(v) The act of binding oneself must be an act of commission, not of omission.

The distinction between omission and commission is, of course, notoriously hard to draw with precision, but then I am not here aiming very hard at precision. Let us first observe that when someone does not decide to do x, this does not in itself count as an act of omission; we must add that he also decides not to do x. Secondly, let us consider an example[20] that shows that one can bind oneself by omission: a man standing on a street corner, desperate for a cigarette, watching the tobacconist lock his shop and cutting off his access to cigarettes by not entering. Such cases are excluded by criterion (v), but only as an unintended by-product of other cases which in my opinion definitely should be excluded. This shows that criterion (v) can and should be refined, but as already stated I do not here pretend to give necessary and sufficient conditions, only to sketch in rough outline the contours of the notion.

For a case that shows the need for something like criterion (v), consider the following problem in the philosophy of education. I suspect that a not uncommon vision of the development of the moral and intellectual faculties of the child is something like a four-stage sequence. In a first stage the power of parent and teacher is just a brute fact, accepted only because there is no other alternative. In a second stage the child is still powerless to reject authority, but rational enough to see that he would not have

[20] Suggested to me by Robert Goodin.

wanted to do so even had he been able to. In a third stage the child is physically and legally capable of rejecting authority, but refrains from doing so because he sees that it is in his own interest to remain bound. In a last stage liberation takes place at the common initiative of all parties. Now whatever the moral appeal of this fairy-tale, I would not like to count the third (and *a fortiori* not the second) stage as an example of binding oneself. The fact that someone prefers not to leave a given state is not evidence that he would freely have entered that state from all of the states that are open to him. There are transaction costs and uncertainties involved that destroy the apparent symmetry of entry and exit. As we shall discuss in II.6, preferences are always relative to a past history of choices, and if the child had known from experience the states to which he prefers the state of being bound, his preferences might have been very different. It does not seem adequate to me to say with Gerald Dworkin that 'an important moral limitation on the exercise of such parental power...is provided by the notion of the child eventually coming to see the correctness of his parent's intervention',[21] for virtually any educational scheme could be extended so as to produce its own justification *ex post facto*. Rather I would say that the mark of a successful education is that the child comes to see that no such justification is possible, but that the parents nevertheless had to make *some* (unjustified) choice.

II.3   PASCAL

One way of making yourself act in a certain manner is to induce a belief from which that action will follow compellingly. In this section I will explore the logic of such *decisions to believe*, with particular reference to Pascal's wager argument. This argument has two parts. The first goes roughly like this:[22] since there is a certain positive probability that God exists, and since he that believes in the existence of God receives an infinitely large gain if he proves right, whereas only a finite amount is at stake, the principle of expected utility maximization requires that one should

[21] Dworkin (1972), who uses the Ulysses episode as a paradigmatic case of justified paternalism.
[22] For a lucid exposition, see Hacking (1975), ch. 8.

believe. (This, of course, assumes that eternal bliss is not reduced to present value at some positive discount rate, as it is in a recent extravaganza.)[23] Now 'belief' is a very particular kind of action, in that it cannot be performed just on the will's saying so. Whence the necessity of the second step in the argument:

Vous voulez aller à la foi, et vous n'en savez pas le chemin; vous voulez vous guérir de l'infidélité, et vous en demandez le remède: apprenez de ceux qui ont été liés comme vous, et qui parient maintenant tout leur bien; ce sont gens qui savent ce chemin que vous voudriez suivre, et guéris d'un mal dont vous voulez guérir. Suivez la manière par où ils ont commencé: c'est en faisant tout comme s'ils croyaient, en prenant de l'eau bénite, en faisant dire des messes, etc. Naturellement même cela vous fera croire et vous abêtira. – 'Mais c'est ce que je crains.' – Et pourquoi? Qu'avez-vous à perdre?[24]

Initially there is no reason for believing, only a reason for making yourself believe. The causal efficacy of a belief for a given end can never provide grounds or reasons for *adopting* that belief, with the possible exception of self-fulfilling beliefs.[25] Nevertheless this efficacy might constitute a reason for *precommitting* oneself to the belief, in the sense of setting up a series of actions that will have the predictable result of my coming to believe. In Pascal's argument these actions can be described as 'going through the motions'; acting as if one believes in order to generate the real thing.

Pascal's self-directed argument may be contrasted with the other-directed argument that comes more naturally to the social scientist. Arthur Stinchcombe offers the following perceptive analysis:

[23]   Azzi and Ehrenberg (1975). For another argument that could be invoked to show that eternal bliss adds up to a finite total, see Elster (1975a), p. 148.

[24]   *Pensée* 233.

[25]   Cp. II.9 and in particular n. 123 below for a brief discussion of this problem. The point is that in some cases the belief may not only change the world in some (desired) manner, but change it in a manner that makes the belief come true. More formally, let us assume that the state of the world y is a function f of my beliefs about the world x (and of a number of other variables that are kept constant for the purposes of the analysis). Let us further assume that my utility u is a function g of y. Let us also assume that the conditions of Brouwer's fixed-point theorem are fulfilled (see Quirk and Saposnik (1968) for a non-technical explanation), so that there exists an $\underline{x}$ such that $\underline{x} = f(\underline{x})$. We then define $\bar{x}$ as the value of x that maximizes $u = g(f(x))$. Adopting a self-fulfilling belief for its causal efficacy would then require $\underline{x} = \bar{x}$, which could only happen by accident. A second possibility, which could also come about by accident only, is that there are several fixed points, of which one could choose the one maximizing $g(f(x))$. This possibility is raised again in II.9 below.

There are two possible causal links between control over activities in the present and the structure of activities and values in the future. (a) Activities established by current power-holders, embodying their values, may serve other functions than serving those values. Such additional functions will preserve the activities, even if commitment to the value is low. (b) People become committed to what they are doing, perhaps in order to reduce cognitive dissonance, so that one way to socialize people is to get them to act in terms of that value without belief and allow belief to follow.[26]

The second of these two causal links is also at the heart of Pascal's argument, with the – enormous – difference that in his case the individuals *themselves* are being asked to manipulate their own beliefs with action as an intermediate link. That rulers or ecclesiastics can exploit the pomp of religious ceremonies to bolster religious faith against the attack of reason is, of course, well known. Take a characteristic passage from Stendhal: 'Il y eut un *Te Deum*, des flots d'encens, des décharges infinies de mousqueterie et d'artillerie; les paysans étaient ivres de bonheur et de piété. Une telle journée défait l'ouvrage de cent numéros des journaux jacobins.'[27] It is vastly more paradoxical that reason should adopt these methods against itself. Valéry, in his wonderful essay on Stendhal, was on the wrong track when he argued that Stendhal would have found the (second part of the) wager argument odious.[28] It is true that Stendhal detested the passive and unthinking imitation that is the basis of religion and tradition, but the exhortation to *active* imitation addresses itself precisely to the intelligent libertine of Stendhal's persuasion.

Let us take a closer look at the paradoxes of the decision to believe. Bernard Williams has argued convincingly[29] that even if

[26]   Stinchcombe (1968), p. 116.   [27]   Stendhal (1952), I, pp. 317–18.

[28]   'A des hommes de cette espèce, traditions et religions sont antipathiques par essence et même odieuses. Ils y voient des puissances fondées sur l'*imitation*, et cette imitation renforcée au besoin, comme le marque et le conseille fort bien Pascal, par la *comédie*: "Suivez la manière par où ils ont commencé; c'est *en faisant tout comme s'ils croyaient*, en prenant de l'eau bénite" etc. (Imaginer ici le visage de Beyle lisant cette phrase, si jamais il l'a lue' (Valéry 1957, p. 578).

[29]   B. A. O. Williams (1973); also Pears (1974, pp. 105ff), who points to a problem that, when applied to Pascal, can be thus formulated: in the gradual process of a growing belief and a dwindling reason, might there not come a point where the first is not yet strong enough to support the religious behaviour and the second no longer strong enough to do so? A rather different case where it might seem rational or desirable to manipulate yourself into believing something for which you lack rational grounds of belief is the so-called Newcomb's Problem, for which the reader is referred to IV.3 below and to Elster (1978a), ch. 4.

it is possible to decide to believe p, one cannot both believe p and believe that the belief that p stems from a decision to believe p. If the decision to believe p is to be carried out successfully, it must also obliterate itself from the memory of the believer. The point is not that the belief that p is incompatible with the belief that the belief that p is the result of some causal process; presumably all beliefs are causally produced. Rather the idea is that in the case of a decision to believe, the belief stems from the wrong sort of causal process, i.e. from a process quite unrelated to any grounds or reasons for believing.[30] The implication of this argument is that the decision to believe can only be carried out successfully if accompanied by a decision to forget, viz. a decision to forget the decision to believe. This, however, is just as paradoxical as the decision to believe:

> The Heart cannot forget
> Unless it contemplate
> What it declines[31]

You can *make* someone forget something, but not by telling him to forget it, which quite probably will have the opposite result if he takes the injunction seriously.[32] *A fortiori* you cannot simply decide to forget something either; unless, once again, you bind yourself in some manner by setting up some roundabout machinery to induce forgetfulness. The most efficient procedure would be to start up a single causal process with the double effect of inducing belief *and* making you forget that it was ever started up. Asking to be hypnotized is one such mechanism; acting as if one believes is another, to the extent that 'cela vous fera croire *et* vous abêtira'. The loss of the critical faculty is not simply a *by-product* of the self-induced faith, but an essential *condition* for that faith to be held seriously, and if it had not followed from the

---

[30] Cp. Davidson (1970) for this notion.

[31] Dickinson (1970), no. 1560. B. A. O. Williams (1973, pp. 150–1) sees an asymmetry between deciding to forget and deciding to believe, but his argument seems to rest upon a confusion between a decision to forget something which I have known and the decision not to acquire some new knowledge which I feel I can manage without. There is no reason why I should even attempt *complete* knowledge, but there are good reasons for a *cumulative* acquisition of knowledge. It is true that there are many acquired pieces of knowledge that are so unimportant that they can safely be forgotten, but by assumption this is not true of a piece of information that is considered worthy of being deliberately forgotten. This is the point of Emily Dickinson's poem.

[32] Cp. III.9 and ch. IV below for more about these paradoxical injunctions of the double-bind variety.

faith-inducing process itself a separate process would have been needed to bring it about.

Now even if this may lead to the faith being held seriously, many have wondered whether such a faith should be taken seriously.[33] It would have to be a very tolerant or uncritical God that bestowed grace upon someone whose faith was acquired in this manner; it would be too much like praising someone for being right while knowing that he was right for the wrong reasons. Now after the event (i.e. after the onset of faith) we might say of someone that the religious practice of acting as if he believed only had the effect of triggering off a faith which in retrospect was latent all the time, and we might argue that the genesis of the faith and the fact that it was acquired for the wrong reasons should be irrelevant if in fact it is held for the right reasons.[34] This, however, is a tricky argument. I submit that no one could accept it on his own behalf before the event, i.e. at the time when the wager has to be accepted or rejected. For either this claim would only be a piece of self-deception which would not deceive God, or it would be an authentic one that could only be accepted by someone who had already acquired an authentic faith. It may be possible to pull oneself up by the bootstraps, but no one can rationally count on being able to do so.

Unless I am mistaken, there is also in Pascal a second line of argument that is somewhat difficult to square with the wager. In the wager argument it is assumed that reason in itself cannot offer any argument for the existence of God, only for the utility of believing in that existence. In other contexts, however, Pascal seems to think that reason is capable of *arriving* at that belief by ratiocination, but that it needs the assistance of the passions in order to *maintain* belief:

Car il ne faut pas se méconnaître: nous sommes automate autant qu'esprit; et de là vient que l'instrument par lequel la persuasion se fait n'est pas la seule démonstration. Combien y a-t-il peu de choses démontrées! Les preuves ne convainquent que l'esprit. La coutume fait nos preuves les plus fortes et les plus crues; elle incline l'automate, qui entraîne l'esprit sans qu'il y pense...Enfin il faut avoir recours à la coutume quand une fois l'esprit a vu où est la vérité, afin de nous abreuver et nous teindre de cette créance, qui nous échappe à toute heure; car d'en avoir toujours les preuves présentes, c'est trop d'affaire. Il faut acquérir une créance plus facile, qui est celle de l'habitude, qui, sans violence,

---

[33] James (1896).   [34] Cargile (1966).

sans art, sans argument, nous fait croire les choses, et incline toutes nos puissances à cette croyance, en sorte que notre âme y tombe naturellement. Quand on ne croit que par la force de la conviction, et que l'automate est incliné à croire le contraire, ce n'est pas assez. Il faut donc faire croire nos deux pièces: l'esprit, par les raisons, qu'il suffit d'avoir vues une fois en sa vie; et l'automate, par la coutume, et en ne lui permettant pas de s'incliner au contraire.[35]

This seems essentially to be the classic Aristotelian view of moral education: you become a good man by performing good actions. Initially the performing of these actions is an uphill climb which requires effort and meets with resistance, but the result is to set up a *hexis* such that the same actions flow as naturally from it as water seeking its downhill course.[36] The distinction between knowing something in the abstract and knowing it in the sense of having the proof before your mind is also used by Aristotle in his solution to the problem of *akrasia*. The *akrates* knows what he ought to do, but only in the sense in which a sleeping geometer can be said to 'know' a geometrical theorem. One cannot constantly *keep* before one's mind all that one knows, even if one is able to *bring* it to mind under the appropriate conditions, which may be lacking in the heat of action. Now this is a 'solution' to the problem of weakness of will only in the sense of explaining how that phenomenon is at all possible,[37] not a solution in the sense of a strategy for overcoming it. A solution in the latter sense is forthcoming if we bring the Aristotelian theory of moral education to bear upon the problem of *akrasia*; we then get the view exposed by Pascal in the text quoted above. On this view reason has a double task. In the first place, only reason can arrive at the intellectual insight that God exists. In the second place reason knows that intellectual insight is not enough, and therefore starts up a series of actions that will engender 'automatic' or 'customary' belief, permitting me to act rightly without having to mobilize at each instant the whole battery of arguments.

[35] *Pensée* 252.
[36] *Nicomachean Ethics* 1103. A similar distinction is found in Mencius, between 'acting through benevolence and rightness' and 'putting into action benevolence and rightness' (Nivison 1976). There are fascinating analogies and differences between Aristotle and Mencius (in Nivison's interpretation) that are worthy of more detailed and competent exploration than I could give them.
[37] For discussions of this problem, see the articles collected in Mortimore (ed.) (1971); also (and esp.) Davidson (1969), who concludes that weakness of will is a form of *surdity* where the causal processes of the mind operate behind the back, as it were, of the deliberating self. The reasons which *cause* me to do *x* may prevail over the reasons that are *reasons* for doing *y*, even when the latter are stronger (*qua* reasons) than the former.

It should be fairly clear that this line of reasoning is very different from the wager argument. Let us try to bring out the difference in a more explicit manner. Writing belief$_r$ for the rational belief arrived at (and maintained by) ratiocination, belief$_c$ for 'automatic' or customary belief and p for the proposition 'God exists', the wager argument goes like this:

(1) I do not believe$_r$ that p.
(2) I believe$_r$ that I should always believe$_c$ that p or believe$_r$ that p.
(3) I do not believe$_r$ that I shall come to believe$_r$ that p.
(4) I believe$_r$ that it is impossible both to believe$_c$ that p and to believe$_r$ that I believe$_c$ that p because of a decision to believe$_c$ that p.
(5) Therefore I decide to act so as to bring it about (i) that I believe$_c$ that p and (ii) that I do not believe$_r$ that I believe$_c$ that p because of a decision to believe$_c$ that p.

Here premiss (1) is the very starting point for the argument, which addresses itself to an unbeliever. Premiss (2) is the conclusion of what I have called the first part of the wager argument, i.e. the reasoning in terms of expected utility maximization. Premiss (3) follows, as argued above, from premiss (1). Premiss (4) follows by Williams's argument. Premisses (2) and (3) give part (i) of the conclusion (5); part (i) and premiss (4) then give part (ii). By contrast the Aristotelian argument goes like this:

(6) I believe$_r$ that p.
(7) I believe$_r$ that I should always believe$_c$ that p or believe$_r$ that p.
(8) I believe$_r$ that it is impossible always to believe$_r$ that p.
(9) Therefore I decide to act so as to bring it about that I always believe$_c$ that p.

From the crucial difference between premisses (1) and (6) stem several further differences between the two arguments. Premisses (2) and (7) are identical in wording, but the word 'should' does not reflect the same kind of rationality in the two cases. Premiss (6) is in itself a sufficient reason for (7), whereas (2) can only be sustained by invoking the causal efficacy of the belief. Premisses (3) and (4) correspond in some sense to premiss (8), but the logic is very different. That (3) follows from (1) is conceptually necessary, as is also premiss (4); by contrast (8) only expresses a psychological difficulty. Both arguments conclude that one should bind oneself to a belief$_c$, but the wager argument has the added implication that one should bind oneself to forget the argument itself.

There is a phrase in Pascal that could be used as a tag for both arguments: 'Il n'y a rien de si conforme à la raison que ce désaveu de la raison.'[38] It is clear by now that this disavowal can either be taken in the strong sense of an *abdication of reason* or in the weaker sense of the *insufficiency of reason* alone. In II.4 we shall see that Descartes's critique of reason probably is weaker than either of these. Here we should insist on the fact that even the abdication of reason is a less radical notion than the *dethronement of reason* that we associate with the names of Nietzsche and Freud. In the wager argument it is reason itself that decides to abdicate; a second-level rationality deciding that rationality should be abolished. The dethronement of reason is more radical, because it assumes that all forms of rationality really are nothing but dressings-up of vital drives; in fact it is misleading even to speak of dethronement, because reason never governed in the first place. The dethronement of reason only effectuates *de jure* what always had been the case *de facto*: the supremacy of the passions.

II.4 DESCARTES

To the phrase by Pascal quoted at the beginning of the last paragraph corresponds this statement by Descartes: 'la principale finesse est de ne vouloir point du tout user de finesse'.[39] In the following pages I propose an interpretation of this phrase and, more generally, of the Cartesian theory of rational choice. As already stated, the critique of reason (*finesse*) implied by that statement probably is a rather weak one; it can be briefly characterized as a *critique of instant rationality*. I will argue that even though this critique does not imply the insufficiency of reason, it is not implausible to see a psychological connection between the two. For this purpose I begin by showing that Descartes does in fact have a theory, set out in *Les passions de l'âme*, which is very similar to the Aristotelian argument adduced by Pascal. Even though Descartes himself never makes that theory bear upon the theory of instant rationality, the fact that he holds both of these views and that there is a plausible manner of connecting them would seem to justify the interpretation proposed towards the end of the discussion.

[38] *Pensée* 272.   [39] Descartes (1897–1910), IV, p. 357.

Towards the end of the first part of *Les passions de l'âme*
Descartes draws a distinction between two ways of fighting the
passions:

ceux en qui naturellement la volonté peut le plus aisément vaincre les passions
et arrêter les mouvements du corps qui les accompagnent ont sans doute les âmes
les plus fortes; mais il y en a qui ne peuvent éprouver leur force parce qu'ils ne
font jamais combattre leur volonté avec ses propres armes, mais seulement avec
celles que lui fournissent quelques passions pour résister à quelques autres. Ce
que je nomme ses propres armes sont des jugements fermes et déterminés
touchant la connaissance du bien et du mal, suivant lesquels elle a résolu de
conduire les actions de sa vie.[40]

The will may overcome the passions through sheer will-power, but
also by using the indirect strategy of pitting the passions against
each other. Albert Hirschman has recently explored the widespread use of this notion in the seventeenth century,[41] but he does
not, perhaps, distinguish with sufficient clarity between the
analytical, the manipulative and the strategic purposes to which
it may be harnessed. The analytical purpose would be to determine
to which extent the passions actually tend to neutralize each other
in men as they are. The manipulative and the strategic approaches
would set passion against passion in order to modify the behaviour
– the behaviour of others in the manipulative case and the
behaviour of self in the strategic case. This modification could
operate in either of two ways. In the first place person A might
try to influence person B (leaving open the possibility that A and
B may be the same person) by associating some additional reward
or punishment with some of the courses of action available to B.
For the case of A = B, this is the method of public side bets.[42] In
the second place, A might want to change the character (i.e. the
system of passions) of B, so that even with a constant reward
structure a different choice would be made. To pit passion against

[40] *Ibid.* xi, pp. 366–7.
[41] Hirschman (1977), esp. pp. 20ff.
[42] A public side bet is an irrevocable change in the payoff structure, in contradistinction
      to the private side bets that can be reversed at will. As explored at length by T. S.
      Schelling (1963), the public side bets may be used to *improve* my outcome from a game-like
      situation, by *reducing* the payoff that I get under certain combinations of strategies. It
      is, of course, crucial that the side bet be credible, so that my opponent really acts upon
      the assumption of a modified payoff structure. It is a surprising fact, worthy of
      explanation, that no society (to my knowledge) has developed institutions, private or
      public, specializing in accepting side bets for the purpose of accommodating people's
      wish to bind themselves. Such institutions could be used for strategic interaction with
      others, or simply for self-control.

passion may take the form of changing the situation so as to make
new passions bear upon it, or changing the passions so as to bear
upon the situation in a new manner. I believe that all the cases
adduced by Hirschman (in addition to the purely analytical ones),
come in the category of reward-manipulation. I also believe that
Descartes's main idea is that behaviour modification can take place
through self-directed (strategic) character modification. The
following passage should sustain this interpretation:

Et il est utile de savoir que, comme il a déjà été dit ci-dessus, encore que chaque
mouvement de la glande semble avoir été joint par la nature à chacune de nos
pensées dès le commencement de notre vie, on les peut toutefois joindre à
d'autres par l'habitude...Or ces choses sont utiles à savoir pour donner le
courage à un chacun d'étudier à regarder ses passions; car, puisqu'on peut, avec
un peu d'industrie, changer les mouvements du cerveau dans les animaux
dépourvus de raison, il est évident qu'on le peut encore mieux dans les hommes,
et que ceux même qui ont les plus faibles âmes pourraient acquérir un empire
très absolu sur toutes leurs passions, si on employait assez d'industrie à les
dresser et à les conduire.[43]

Anyone can do anything; the smallest amounts of will-power
suffice for the most extraordinary feats of self-control, given an
understanding of the physiological mechanisms by which habits
are formed and changed. *Hexis* in Aristotle, custom in Pascal and
habit in Descartes are all seen as the end result of non-habitual
actions. The result may be an unintended and unforeseen one, if
one is ignorant of the causal process by which it is produced, but
if one has insight into the workings of the mind (as according to
Aristotle one should have),[44] it can be exploited for the purpose
of self-control.

I believe I have shown that the theme of precommitment is
indeed present in the Cartesian psychology, but it is certainly less
important than another theme which I now proceed to discuss.
This theme – the critique of instant rationality – is first found in
a famous passage from the *Discours de la méthode*:

Ma seconde maxime était d'être le plus ferme et le plus résolu en mes actions
que je pourrais, et de ne suivre pas moins constamment les opinions les plus
douteuses, lorsque je m'y serais une fois déterminé, que si elles eussent été très
assurées. Imitant en ceci les voyageurs qui, se trouvant égarés en quelque forêt,
ne doivent pas errer en tournoyant tantôt d'un côté, tantôt d'un autre, ni encore
moins s'arrêter en une place, mais marcher toujours le plus droit qu'ils peuvent

---

[43] Descartes (1897–1910), xi, pp. 368–9.
[44] *Nicomachean Ethics* 1114; see II.6 for a discussion of this requirement.

vers un même côte, et ne le changer point pour de faibles raisons, encore que ce n'ait peut-être été au commencement que le hasard seul qui les ait déterminés à le choisir; car, par ce moyen, s'ils ne vont justement où ils désirent, ils arriveront au moins à la fin quelque part où vraisemblablement ils seront mieux que dans le milieu d'une forêt.[45]

I will follow a two-step procedure in interpreting this text. In the first step I sketch a number of possible readings, two of which are singled out as equally plausible (and as equally different from Pascal's critique of reason). In the second step I cite some further passages from Descartes that tend to attenuate the contrast between Descartes and Pascal, even though I believe that a genuine difference remains. Throughout the discussion I draw upon modern economics and game theory, which have made possible a more precise discussion of the problems that Descartes wrestled with. Some of the notions developed below are also discussed, from a somewhat different perspective, in III.5.

The *first interpretation* of the passage that comes to the mind of an economics-minded reader is, I believe, the following: a continuous evaluation and reevaluation requires so much time that it can be expected to more than outweigh the time gained by the improved direction that issues from the evaluation. The traveller will get more quickly out of the forest if he follows some – perhaps arbitrarily chosen – straight line than if he constantly halts in order to adjust his direction. This interpretation is very close to the attempts that have been made[46] to reduce Herbert Simon's theory[47] of 'satisficing' or 'limited rationality' to a species of maximizing or total rationality. This reduction stresses that the use of rules of thumb or stereotyped decision principles, such as 'always follow a straight line when lost in a forest', can be optimal if they permit us to economize on the cost of gathering and evaluating information. To seek the abstractly optimal solution to a technical problem, for example, might require so much time and money that the firm would go bankrupt before the solution emerged. The reason why French firms regularly lose contracts to American competitors has been sought along these lines; the excessive rationality of the French becomes an obstacle to economic rationality. I have argued elsewhere that Leibniz's rationalism, or

[45] Descartes (1897–1910), VI, p. 24.
[46] See for example Riker and Ordeshook (1973), ch. 2.   [47] Simon (1954).

rather his attempt to translate philosophical rationalism into economic rationality, also is profoundly irrational from the practical point of view.[48] To the extent that the first interpretation of Descartes is correct, one could say that it constitutes an anticipated answer to Leibniz.

I do indeed believe that this interpretation is one of the two that with roughly equal plausibility may be imputed to Descartes. Before I go on to the other interpretations, I would like to stress that the decision to follow a straight line is a genuine *decision*; an act of commission, not of omission. It is made before the event, and is not a mere rationalization made up (or imputed to the actor) after the event, and having the occurrence of the event as its sole or main evidence. This point is important in view of the numerous pseudo-explanations that have been offered in recent years to prove that all kinds of apparently irrational behaviour 'really' are governed by the principle of rational choice. I return to this general problem in III.10. Here I only mention the argument of Douglass North to the effect that an *ideology* is 'a way of economizing on the costs of information and therefore [is] in general a rational response'[49] because it saves us the trouble of evaluating each situation separately and on its merits. Now someone might conceivably adopt an ideology, such as a rigidly negative attitude towards a minority group, for such reasons, but if this kind of explanation is to have any force one would have to locate the decision in space and time. To say that the fact of *not jettisoning* an ideology that one has taken over from one's parents is evidence that one has *deliberately adopted* the ideology in order to economize on the costs of information would be a fallacy similar to the one discussed towards the end of II.2. (From the discussion in I.5 it also follows that one should be very much on guard against the notion that an ideology could be rational even if not deliberately adopted, in the sense of being a *functional* response to a given problem. The natural selection of ideologies seems an extremely far-fetched notion, for which I know of no empirical evidence.)

In the last two paragraphs we have distinguished between four approaches to rational choice: maximizing rationality (Leibniz); satisficing rationality (Simon); 'satisficing as maximizing' (first

---

[48] Elster (1975a), ch. 3.   [49] North (1971), p. 122.

interpretation of Descartes); 'maximizing as satisficing' (natural-selection theories of rational behaviour). In a powerful and strangely neglected article Sidney Winter has offered some important arguments that tend to demolish all three alternatives to Simon's approach; these arguments also suggest the *second interpretation* of Descartes. Winter observes that the attempt to reduce satisficing to maximizing gives rise to an infinite regress, because 'this choice of a profit-maximizing information structure itself requires information, and it is not apparent how the aspiring profit maximizer acquires this information, or what guarantees that he does not pay an excessive price for it'.[50] Take the case of a multinational firm that decides not to enter the forward exchange market because the information costs of the operation would exceed the benefits.[51] Then we shall have to ask how the firm decided how much information to acquire before taking the decision not to acquire the information needed in the forward exchange operation. Unless one could prove (and I do not see how one could prove) that the deviation from the 'real' optimum converges to zero or at any rate rapidly becomes smaller for each new level in the hierarchy of information structures, this argument not only has the implication that in every decision there must be a cut-off point where calculation stops and you simply have to make an unsupported choice, but also that *this point might just as well be as close to the action itself as possible*. Why, indeed, seek for precision in the second decimal if you are uncertain about the first?

This line of argument could support a decisionist interpretation of Descartes, which would imply a very radical critique of reason. The only task of reason would then be to prove the impossibility theorem just sketched, and from that point onwards intuition or satisficing would be on their own, unsupported by formal reasoning. I believe that this interpretation is the least plausible of the three readings I am offering of Descartes's moral philosophy, because it is hard to fit in with the texts (quoted below) dealing with the calculus of self-interest. Nevertheless there seems to be a strand in Descartes's writings, and indeed in his character, that reflects this preference for the unsupported decision that is rigidly adhered to once taken. Even in the absence of the

[50]   Winter (1964), p. 252; see also Winter (1975).
[51]   Robbins and Stobaugh (1974), p. 130.

impossibility theorem, this preference could be supported by an aristocratic distaste for calculations of any sort and by an equally aristocratic predilection for absolute firmness of character, however eccentric. It is hard to read the correspondence of Descartes without being struck by this 'grand seigneur' aspect of his character; never explain, never apologize.

I now proceed to the *third interpretation*. This is to argue that not only the *time* spent getting out of the forest is increased if the traveller constantly stops to reevaluate the situation, but that this instant rationality actually makes the *path* itself longer than it would have been along an arbitrarily (or at least along an optimally) chosen straight line. Economists have discussed a very similar problem in the context of finding the optimal use of forecasts in planning. Following Milton Friedman, Clem Tisdell has argued, in a language very close to the one we use here, that

even if the policy-maker has some (positive) ability to predict, it may nevertheless be optimal for him to follow an inflexible policy. Indeed, [this paper] shows that, *ignoring the increased decision costs* which 'fine-tuning' policies may involve and the unfavourable uncertainty effects which they may generate in a group, deficiencies in the ability to predict may, even if there is (considerable) ability to predict, make flexible or zig-zag policies undesirable... Patterns emerge which are helpful from a prescriptive point of view and which also explain the rationality of actual behaviour that might otherwise appear to be irrational, e.g. the decision-maker who has predictive ability but does not adjust to his short-term predictions may well be acting rationally.[52]

In the phrase that I have italicized Tisdell explicitly distinguishes his own approach (corresponding to the third interpretation of Descartes) from the cost-of-decision approach (corresponding to the first interpretation). He also mentions, as a third argument for being inflexible, the 'unfavourable uncertainty effects' that are further discussed in II.8. Under certain conditions (discussed towards the end of the present section) inflexibility requires precommitment. Here, however, I will rather stress that Tisdell's analysis (and behind him, Descartes) does not imply a very radical critique of reason.

---

[52]   Tisdell (1971), p. 35; my italics. Leif Johansen (1972) has shown that matters are not quite that simple. The choice is not between following an initial decision as if it were absolutely correct and acting upon successive forecasts as if each of them were absolutely reliable; rather the optimum is to steer a middle course and take some account of the changing forecasts, while not changing direction to the extent that one would have done if the current forecast was always thought to give the correct value.

This point can be brought out by looking at one of Tisdell's main examples, the inflation–unemployment trade-off (the Phillips curve). The problem is also discussed by William Nordhaus, in his important work on the political business cycle. I will argue that Nordhaus's approach is closer to the notion of binding oneself, which by contrast is not immediately relevant on the Descartes–Tisdell approach. Tisdell shows that under certain conditions the optimal policy may be to hold a constant level of unemployment rather than to adjust it to current forecasts. Nordhaus's problem is quite different: his policy-makers do not have to abstract from current forecasts, but from electoral considerations. The main thrust of his analysis seems to be that voters and planners always attach some weight to the welfare of later generations, whereas politicians, trying to maximize votes at the next election, are exclusively concerned with the present. This has two consequences: in the long run society will choose a policy with lower unemployment and more inflation than is optimal; in the short run each electoral period will begin in austerity and end in potlatch. Among the possible remedies to this bias in the democratic system Nordhaus discusses the strategy of Ulysses:

A third possibility is to entrust economic policy to persons that will not be tempted by the Sirens of partisan politics. This procedure is typical for monetary policy, which for historical reasons is lodged in the central banks (as in the independent Federal Reserve System in the US or the Bank of England). A similar possibility is to turn fiscal policy over to a Treasury dominated by civil servants. It may be objected, however, that delegating responsibility to an agency that is not politically responsive to legitimate needs is even more dangerous than a few cycles. This danger is frequently alleged regarding central banks which pay more attention to the 'soundness of the dollar' or the latest monetarist craze than to fundamental policy problems.[53]

I return to some of these problems in II.8. Here I shall only observe that the strategy envisaged corresponds to a paraphrase of Pascal's formula: 'Il n'y a rien de si conforme à la politique que ce désaveu de la politique.' To remove monetary policy from the political sphere would itself be a political act; the abdication of politicians and not their dethronement. In his work on the same problem Assar Lindbeck also suggests depoliticization of some policy agencies as a possible remedy.[54] Among the other possible strategies discussed by Lindbeck, I was especially struck by his

[53] Nordhaus (1975), p. 188.   [54] Lindbeck (1976), p. 18, n. 8.

suggestion that elections could be randomly spaced so that politicians would not have an incentive for turning policies into means for electoral purposes. Albert Hirschman remarks that 'unpredictability is power';[55] you can control your environment by making yourself appear unpredictable. Conversely you may control yourself by making the environment an unpredictable one. (*The Lottery* by Borges pursues this notion to its logical conclusion, and beyond.)

As already stated, I do not think it possible to say, on the basis of the texts, whether the first or the third interpretation of Descartes is the more plausible one. They have in common the critique of instant rationality which I take to be the central point he is trying to make. There is virtually no question of a *temptation* to be resisted; the obstacle to full rationality is ignorance rather than weakness of will. The ignorance of someone who has never learnt geometry is different from the ignorance of the sleeping geometer; once we have acquired the insight that it may be rational not to adhere to the instant rationality, there is nothing to prevent us from following that insight. Such is, at any rate, the preliminary conclusion that follows from a reading of the cited text from *Discours de la méthode* taken by itself. I now cite some further passages that suggest a slightly different conclusion.

In Descartes's writings there is an interesting and (as far as I know) quite neglected analogy between his cosmological views and his views on society. Common to both are the tenets of *atomism* and of *optimism*; erratically moving particles will by themselves create a perfectly ordered universe, and egoistically motivated individuals will act so as to further the common good. I shall cite two passages so similar in wording that it is hard not to think that they have their source in some common inspiration:

Car *Dieu a si merveilleusement établi ces Lois,* qu'encore que nous supposions qu'il ne crée rien de plus que ce que j'ai dit, et même qu'il ne mette en ceci aucun ordre ni proportion, mais qu'il en compose un Chaos, le plus confus et le plus embrouillé que les poètes puissent décrire: elles sont suffisantes pour faire que les parties de ce Chaos se démêlent d'elles-mêmes, et se disposent en si bon ordre qu'elles auront la forme d'un Monde très parfait.[56]

---

[55] Hirschman (1977), p. 50. A reader of Luke Rhinehart's novel *The Dice Man* will recognize the force – and the weakness – of Hirschman's dictum.

[56] Descartes (1897–1910), XI, p. 34. My italics.

J'avoue qu'il est très difficile de mesurer jusques où la raison nous ordonne que nous nous intéressions pour le public; mais aussi n'est-ce pas une chose en quoi il soit nécessaire d'être fort exact: il suffit de satisfaire à sa conscience, et on peut en cela donner beaucoup à son inclination. Car *Dieu a tellement établi l'ordre des choses*, et conjoint les hommes ensemble d'une si étroite société, qu'encore que chacun rapportât tout à soi-même, et n'eût aucune charité pour les autres, il ne laisserait pas de s'employer ordinairement pour eux en tout ce qui serait de son pouvoir, pourvu qu'il usât de prudence.[57]

The two phrases that I have italicized must proceed from the same mould of thought. The underlying logic as well as the actual choice of words are too similar for any other conclusion to be possible. Let us now see how Descartes elaborates upon the sociological theory implied by the second of the above passages:

La raison qui me fait croire que ceux qui ne font rien que pour leur utilité particulière, doivent aussi bien que les autres travailler pour autrui, et tâcher de faire plaisir à un chacun, autant qu'il est en leur pouvoir, s'ils veulent user de prudence, est qu'on voit ordinairement arriver que ceux qui sont estimés officieux et prompts à faire plaisir, reçoivent aussi quantité de bons offices des autres, même de ceux qu'ils n'ont jamais obligés, lesquels ils ne recevraient pas, si on les croyait d'autre humeur, et que les peines qu'ils ont à faire plaisir, ne sont point si grandes que les commodités que leur donne l'amitié de ceux qui les connaissent. Car on n'attend de nous que les offices que nous pouvons rendre commodément, et nous n'en attendons pas davantage des autres; mais il arrive souvent que ce qui leur coûte peu, nous profite beaucoup, et même nous peut importer de la vie. Il est vrai qu'on perd quelquefois sa peine en bien faisant, et au contraire qu'on gagne à mal faire; mais cela ne peut changer la règle de prudence, laquelle ne se rapporte qu'aux choses qui arrivent le plus souvent. Et pour moi, la maxime que j'ai le plus observée en toute la conduite de ma vie, a été de suivre seulement le grand chemin, et de croire que la principale finesse est de ne vouloir point du tout user de finesse.[58]

For simplicity we may assume that Descartes has in mind something like the Prisoner's Dilemma (defined in I.4). He then seems to argue that even if it is rational to choose the non-cooperative strategy in a single game of this type, it could be rational to cooperate in a sequence of games. This general idea can be made precise in many ways, some of which are further discussed in III.7. Here I shall only sketch two interpretations that are valid under very contrasting conditions. In the first place an egoist might reason in the following manner. 'If I appear outwardly as a helpful and altruistic person, other persons will come to like me and be concerned with my welfare, so that they will derive positive utility from my consumption. This means that

[57]   *Ibid.* IV, p. 316; my italics.   [58]   *Ibid.* IV, pp. 356–7.

they will tend to act altruistically towards me, and the net result will be that my welfare is greater than it would have been if I had acted strictly egoistically. For in general the benefits of a sacrifice to the person for whom it is made exceed the cost to the person by whom it is made, so that given equal sacrifices on all sides, the benefit of the sacrifices made for my sake will exceed the cost of the sacrifices that I make for the sake of others.' This argument, which is rather similar to the ideas recently proposed by Gary Becker (and further discussed in III.7), works quite well if we confine ourselves to a single individual acting in a world of other individuals whose reactions he should predict in the specified manner. If, however, the other actors are allowed to reason in the same manner, and to know that all reason in this manner, the argument collapses, because no one would have any feeling of friendship towards a person who acts altruistically only to obtain the benefits from the friendship.

In the second place we might appeal to the analysis of supergames proposed by Martin Shubik and Michael Taylor.[59] The basic idea here is that if (1) the number of games is infinite, or a random variable, or finite but unknown to the players and (2) there is a discounting of the future, then it may be individually rational to choose the cooperative strategy in the Prisoner's Dilemma. Both of these conditions are very plausible in real-life situations. We do not know *when* we shall die (so that the first condition is fulfilled), but we do know *that* we shall die (and so the second also is fulfilled). The snag, however, is that the cooperative behaviour is not a dominant strategy in the supergame, even though it is part of the solution. This means that an individual would not choose that strategy unless he were very certain that the others were going to do so as well. In other words, the second approach to the 'rationality of altruism' runs into the opposite problem to the first one: the second approach is successful only if public and known to everyone, the first only if hidden and unsuspected. This also implies that in a world with uncertainty and suspicion – such as the actual world – *neither* approach will be successful.

Let us, however, abstract from this problem and assume that Descartes is right in arguing that it is rational in the long run to

[59]   See in particular M. Taylor (1976a).

help others, even if irrational in the short run. Returning now to the comparison between Descartes and Pascal, we might ask how one should go about it if one has decided that 'le grand chemin' is the optimal course. Will the abstract calculations suggested above be sufficient to let help be forthcoming even when at the expense of the helper, or should he rather try to set up a character from which help will flow 'sans violence, sans art, sans argument'? Should reason be present at each choice, or only once and for all at the choice that sets up the *hexis* from which the latter choices will then follow 'automatically'? Pascal says that the latter procedure is the best, and I think he is right. The arguments sketched above do not have such an intuitive and compelling nature that it is possible to keep them before me each time I am tempted to seek my short-term gain. The same argument holds for the traveller seeking his way out of the forest. Even if he has decided not to change direction 'pour de faibles raisons', these reasons may seem more compelling when thirst and fatigue overwhelm him. The meta-rational actor, who is able to predict this possibility, would then put blinkers on so as to make himself physically unable to gather the information that lends some force to these reasons; a visual analogy to the strategy of putting wax in the ears, chosen by Ulysses for his men. An analogy to the strategy chosen by Ulysses for himself would be to preset a course and then in some way make oneself unable to change it. Actually neither of these strategies corresponds to the Cartesian analysis of *Les passions de l'âme*, which would rather recommend a planned change of character, so that even if one were able to gather the information and to act upon it, one would not wish to do so. (For a discussion of these three techniques for binding oneself, see II.9.)

II.5   INCONSISTENT TIME PREFERENCES

This problem was first raised by R. H. Strotz some twenty-five years ago, in a justly famous article. It is closely related to the problem of endogenous change of preferences, the topic of II.6. To see the importance of these problems, and the relation between them, consider first the usual notion of rationality. A rational actor on the standard definition is simply one who has consistent and complete preferences *at any given point of time*.

I believe that the notion of rational man should be extended so as to include temporal considerations. To be precise, some consistency requirements should be imposed both upon the actor's *choice of successions* and upon his *succession of choices*. Non-fulfilment of the first requirement is exemplified by inconsistent time preferences, of the second by endogenous change of preferences.

As stated, the two problems are closely related, and it is possible to treat them within a unified framework, as in a recent article by Peter Hammond.[60] Nevertheless I believe there are good reasons for following the tradition and treating the two separately. Both inconsistent time preferences and endogenously changing preferences imply that past decisions are not followed up, and both mechanisms assume that this can occur even in the absence of external influences such as persuasion, propaganda, argument or experience. In this sense both mechanisms are non-exogenous. Inconsistent time preferences, however, do not imply any character modification of the individual, as do the endogenous preferences changes. No doubt these changes, being endogenous, must be explained through some fixed transformation laws that characterize the individual and that might be seen as constant higher-order character features. The change of character is merely the unfolding of a potential. Choice according to inconsistent time preferences, on the other hand, is the progressive unfolding of an *actual* and unchanging attitude towards time.

It is widely, but far from universally, agreed that for an individual the very fact of having time preferences, over and above what is justified by the fact that we are mortal, is irrational and perhaps immoral as well.[61] (For *societies* planning for an infinite

---

[60]   Hammond (1976). He argues on p. 163 that precommitment 'is not really a way of resolving inconsistency', and that it 'means no more than determining what really *is* feasible at any stage'. He then retracts somewhat, and sufficiently for our purposes, by adding that 'such an exercise is often far from trivial; indeed, it is often like a kind of technical progress'. I have no quarrel with this characterization: consistent planning is sophistication within the limits of the feasible, precommitment is sophistication amounting to a modification of the limits.

[61]   This is strongly argued by John Rawls (1971, pp. 284ff) for the intergenerational case (but see n. 62 below) and by Thomas Nagel (1970) for the intragenerational case. Ingenious arguments for the contrary view have been proposed by Derek Parfit (1973) and by B. A. O. Williams (1976). For the sake of argument I here assume the Rawls–Nagel view, so that time preferences always constitute a *problem*. I should add, however, that there is much to be said for the Parfit–Williams view, but presumably most of my arguments would be accepted even by them for the cases (and surely there are such cases) where time preferences correspond to weakness of will and not (as in the cases

future it may be irrational *not* to have time preferences, because otherwise consumption will be postponed indefinitely for the sake of more investment.)[62] A common view of the matter is, perhaps, the following. *Qua* rational beings, and abstracting from the problem that we know that but not when we shall die, we want to allocate our welfare evenly over time. A year is a year is a year; there are no rational grounds for preferring the present over the future simply because it is present. (I assume here that time preferences always imply a preference for the present over the future, which disregards the very interesting case of the miser and the important 'mixed cases' where you are a miser in order to become a spendthrift.) On the other hand there is the fact of weakness of will. We simply are not always able to follow our rational inclinations, and the time preferences may be seen as the formal expression of this inability. Someone preferring the present over the future *must* allocate a larger amount of consumption to the present than to the future, regardless of the rational or sophisticated (see below) arguments for doing otherwise. This interpretation of time preferences as weakness of will is crucial to my argument, which does not apply to cases (if such exist) when the preferences stem from a considered judgment that some stretches of life are inherently more valuable than others.[63]

Having a preference for the present will typically lead me to *regret* my past decisions when a new present – the past future – comes along and reveals itself as an equally worthy candidate for

discussed by Williams) to the character traits that give substance to my life. It should also be added that the arguments against indiscriminate altruism (treating any stranger as altruistically as my wife) are stronger than the arguments against indiscriminate treatment of all temporal moments; the first seems less compatible with substance of character than the second.

[62] If a society tried to choose the savings rate that maximizes total undiscounted consumption over infinite time, it would find that there is no such savings rate: for any rate below 100 per cent there is a higher rate that gives larger total consumption, but the 100 per cent rate itself gives zero consumption. (This statement, of course, depends upon a number of assumptions, spelled out, for example, in Heal (1973).)

[63] Peter Hammond has suggested (in conversation) that one could decide to spend more now and less in old age, because in the latter period the lowered consumption would be compensated by the happy memories about the earlier period. Many objections could be raised to this idea; here I only mention two. First, could not lowered consumption *now* be compensated by pleasant anticipations about later affluence? Second, the temporal externalities of consumption could be negative rather than positive, so that in my old age I would look back with bitterness on my earlier enjoyment. To the optimism of Tennyson's 'better to have loved and lost / Than never to have loved at all', we may oppose the pessimism of Donne's 'better to be foul than to have been fair'. The problem cries out for a mathematical treatment.

my attention. Now if one regrets a past decision, the rational thing would seem to be to *reconsider* it. If, in the past, I have decided upon an allocation of goods over (what was then) the future, and if I now come to regret the decision, would not the rational response be to reconsider the decision for what remains of the future? The problem is that my only disagreement with my past decision may be with the allocation of goods between the past and the present, whereas my former and my present selves may agree over what is now the future. And, as a matter of fact, economists have not argued that reconsidering a past decision is a way of making it more rational. Rather they have argued that such reevaluation represents an additional element of irrationality, at least under the conditions that we shall now go on to spell out more fully.

We assume that an individual has one unit of a consumption good that is to be distributed over a number of years. In the examples below only three-year cases are considered. The 'years' should be understood as 'naturally lumpy' units of time – reflecting a non-arbitrary division of the temporal continuum. For reasons discussed below I believe it important to look at the present as something more than a point of zero distance from now. It is, phenomenologically, a period that includes the mathematical present and that is separated in a 'natural' manner from other periods. Such natural divisions include the days, which are separated from each other by periods of sleep 'when I do not exist'; the time from pay-day to pay-day ('I shall start saving next pay-day'); a calendar year ('I shall stop drinking on 1 January next year') and so on. In the first year, the utility of the future consumption stream is $U = u(x_1, x_2, x_3)$, with $x_1 + x_2 + x_3 = 1$. In fact, we shall restrict ourselves to utility functions of the form

$$u = v_1(x_1) + v_2(x_2) + v_3(x_3) \tag{1}$$

with (a) $v_1' > 0$ and $v_i'' < 0$ for all i and (b) $v_1'(x) > v_2'(x) > v_3'(x)$ for all x. Condition (a) ensures positive and decreasing marginal utility of consumption, condition (b) captures the idea of time preferences, more specifically the preference for the near future over the distant future. It is assumed that the utility function at the beginning of the second year is given by $u = v_1(x_2) + v_2(x_3)$ and at the beginning of the third year by $v_1(x_3)$. This makes clear the sense in which the utility function is *constant,* and hence allows a discussion of the consistency (and inconsistency) of time preferences that is independent of the problem of preferences that change over time.

An important special class of the utility functions (1) is given by the following

$$u = -\frac{1}{r}(b_1 x_1^{-r} + b_2 x_2^{-r} + b_3 x_3^{-r}), \text{ with } r > -1, r \neq 0$$

$$u = b_1 \ln x_1 + b_2 \ln x_2 + b_3 \ln x_3, \text{ corresponding to } r = 0,^{64} \quad (2)$$

with $b_1 > b_2 > b_3 > 0$. Time preferences are embodied in the parameters b_i. The motivation behind the parameter r is best illustrated by the case where there are no time preferences (i.e. $b_1 = b_2 = b_3$). Then the optimal sequence will be (1/3, 1/3, 1/3), regardless of r. Yet this is insufficient to determine the choice between, say, (1/4, 1/2, 1/4) and (2/5, 1/5, 2/5). Intuitively one would say that the chosen sequence should be the one that is 'closest' to the equal distribution, but this notion can be spelled out in many ways, corresponding to different values of r.

Given these preliminaries, we are in a position to define and discuss the notion of *consistent* time preferences. At the beginning of the first year the individual chooses an allocation that maximizes $v_1(x_1) + v_2(x_2) + v_3(x_3)$, subject to $x_1 + x_2 + x_3 = 1$. Assume that this leads to the values x_1', x_2', x_3'. At the beginning of the second year the individual plans an allocation that maximizes $v_1(x_2) + v_2(x_3)$, subject to $x_2 + x_3 = 1 - x_1'$. Assume that this gives the values x_2'' and x_3''. The consistency of time preferences is then defined as the requirement that $x_2' = x_2''$, i.e. that the amount planned in the first year for the second is the same as the amount chosen in the second year when it actually arrives. Taking the logarithmic case, an example of consistent time preferences is $u = 4 \ln x_1 + 2 \ln x_2 + \ln x_3$, which gives the allocation (4/7, 2/7, 1/7). This allocation may be called *irrational,* in the sense of exhibiting a preference for the

---

64   The numerical values of the utility function are not supposed to have any significance in themselves; they just represent the individual's ordinal ranking of sequences of consumption goods. The preferences represented by the general expression converge to those represented by the logarithmic one as r approaches 0. The numerical value of the utility function does not converge in the same way, but we could obtain such convergence by replacing u, in the case of $r \neq 0$, with an equivalent though mathematically less convenient function.

present, but nevertheless it is *consistent*. A person with such preferences might regret part of his earlier decision, but would stick to the part of the decision that has not yet been carried out.

An example of *in*consistent time preferences is given by $u = 3 \ln x_1 + 2 \ln x_2 + \ln x_3$. A person with these preferences would plan in year one the allocation (1/2, 1/3, 1/6), but when the second year arrives the allocation for the remaining two years will be reconsidered and becomes (3/10, 2/10). All in all, this means that the *inconsistent allocation* will be (5/10, 3/10, 2/10). Such a person is not only myopic, but myopic in an inherently contradictory manner that never permits him to stick to past decisions. We shall see later that this latter feature is not only an *aspect* of his myopia, but in fact a specific *type* of myopia that may be overcome while leaving the basic myopia of preferring the present over the future unchanged.

Strotz asked whether this person might not, in spite of his inconsistency and irrationality, be rational enough to understand his predicament and deal with it in a rational manner. This is less strange that it might sound. Consider a person who has inherited a fortune and decides to spend it in the following way. In the first year he will spend half his fortune on an enormous spree, and then he will divide the other half evenly over the rest of his life. When the second year arrives, however, he prefers – true to his inconsistent (but constant) preferences – to spend half of the remaining half on a somewhat smaller spree in the second year, and then divide what now remains evenly over the rest of his life, and so on.[65] (Observe that the point is *not* that he has become addicted to the *dolce vita*. This possibility is discussed in II.6.) It is not at all psychologically implausible that such a doubly irrational person – having time preferences, and inconsistent ones at that – might know or come to know his own character and take precautions against his later selves so that they not betray him. In this case the obvious way out is to buy an annuity that cannot be reconverted into cash.

Inconsistent time preferences may be more frequent and important than consistent (if irrational) ones. E. S. Phelps and R. A. Pollak

---

[65] Cp. St Augustine's prayer, 'Give me chastity and continence, only not yet' (*Confessions* VIII, vii). My attention was drawn to this passage by Davidson (1969).

have proposed a general mechanism to explain how time preferences become non-exponential and thus inconsistent.[66] (Their work deals with intergenerational planning, but carries over to the individual case. Indeed, the approach may be better suited to the latter.) They argue that time preferences may be decomposed into two distinct discounting functions: one which gives an absolute priority to the present over all later times, which are given equal and smaller weights, and one which decays exponentially. I believe this to be psychologically plausible, because in the notion of time preferences we bundle two problems that can and should be separated: the absolute priority of the present, and the gradual shading-off of the future. The absolute priority of the present is somewhat like my absolute priority over all other persons: I am I – while they are all 'out there'. The shading-off is a perspectival phenomenon that admits of degrees of 'out-thereness': the far future is like a distant relative, while the near future is more like a close one. (It is at this point that the notion of a 'thick' present is required, for in continuous time it would be hard to make sense of the absolute priority of the present.) Of these two discounting functions the first, by itself or in conjunction with the second, destroys the consistency of the time preferences.

In the remainder of this section I shall discuss how the person with inconsistent time preferences might try to cope with his problem. It is a problem for two reasons: qua time preferences they are irrational, and in addition they are inconsistent. One may assume that the individual has a meta-preference for rationality, i.e. he would want to have utility functions with $b_1 = b_2 = b_3$ (in case (2) above). Also and almost tautologically, one may assume that the individual has a preference that his first-period preferences be restricted. Can the individual behave strategically in ways that satisfy one or both of these meta-preferences? I shall first consider two ways of ensuring consistency, and then discuss how they relate to rationality.

In the example of inconsistent preferences cited above we may define the *Ulysses allocation* as (1/2, 1/3, 1/6). The individual, that is, is able to bind himself to the allocation he prefers initially, and so achieves consistency. While a naive person would choose in each period unaware of the fact that later he will come to change his

[66]   Phelps and Pollak (1968).

mind, a sophisticated person would foresee this event and – if consistency is an overriding concern – take steps to prevent it. Another sophisticated strategy is to use the *allocation of consistent planning* discussed by Strotz and further elaborated by R. A. Pollak.[67] We here assume that the sophisticated person, unable or unwilling to bind himself, reasons as follows. 'If in the first year I choose some amount x_1 (never mind how this choice is made), then I shall have $1 - x_1$ available for consumption in later periods. In the absence of precommitment, and given my character as I know it, I shall allocate this amount over the last two periods to maximize $v_1(x_2) + v_2(x_3)$. The values x_2' and x_3' that are solutions to this problem are functions of $x_1 : x_2' = f(x_1)$, $x_3' = g(x_1)$. Knowing this, I should choose x_1 so as to maximize $v_1(x_1) + v_2(f(x_1)) + v_3(g(x_1))$.'

The psychological coherence of this strategy might not seem obvious. It assumes that the person is capable in the first period of choosing differently from what he would naively do (assuming what remains to be proved, viz. that this amount will differ from the one that will be chosen both in the inconsistent allocation and in the Ulysses allocation), yet that in the second period he is incapable of deviating from his naive choice. Yet this formulation is misleading, for in the second period there are not the reasons for deviating from naiveté that exist in the first period, viz. the danger of inconsistency. True, the second-period choice will be irrational, but the first-period choice was not in any case motivated by the danger of irrationality. It was motivated by the first-period preferences, defined with respect to a different feasible set from the one that the naive agent believed to exist. Given my character, and more specifically my time preferences, all feasible sequences are of the form $(x_1, f(x_1), g(x_1))$. These very same time preferences then tell me which x_1 to choose. This sophisticated strategy overcomes what could be called *myopia with respect to the feasible set*, i.e. the myopia that consists in neglecting how one's present plans are constrained by future choices. It does not, however, overcome (or intend to overcome) the myopia embodied in the time preferences themselves.

What reasons could there be for using the strategy of consistent

---

[67]   Pollak (1968). His discussion uses continuous time, and my argument is just an elaboration of a three-period discrete-time case offered in a note on p. 203 of his paper.

planning rather than the Ulysses strategy? First, and most obviously, there might not exist any feasible technique for binding oneself. Secondly, however, even if the Ulysses allocation was feasible, one might prefer the consistent allocation out of respect for the freedom of choice of later selves. The first-period self might be unwilling to bind the later selves, yet, anticipating their autonomous choice, he might try to make the sequence as good as possible according to his own (and their) preferences. This, I believe, could at least make sense for social planning. On the other hand, of course, precommitment will often be more difficult for social than for individual planning, so that the two reasons for choosing the consistent allocation over the Ulysses allocation might coincide.

I now turn to the rationality of these strategies. I shall first discuss this simply as a matter of evaluation: how do the two strategies fare according to the meta-preferences for having $b_1 = b_2 = b_3$? I.e., how closely do they approximate the egalitarian allocation? Next, and more tentatively, I shall discuss whether these meta-preferences could ever make a difference for first-period choice. Could one ever *choose* on grounds of rationality between the inconsistent allocation, the Ulysses allocation and the consistent allocation?

To evaluate the strategies by the rationality criterion, we must know more about the allocations to which they give rise. Let the superscripts I, U and C denote, respectively, the inconsistent allocation, the Ulysses allocation and the consistent allocation. Some results, proved by Aanund Hylland, are given here.

(i) $x_1^I > x_2^I > x_3^I$; $x_1^U > x_2^U > x_3^U$; $x_1^C > x_2^C > x_3^C$. These results hold for all utility functions of the general form (1). The proof is non-trivial only for consistent planning.

(ii) If we compare the Ulysses allocation with the inconsistent allocation, either may be the more rational one. In the numerical example given above, the inconsistent allocation was more rational. An example where the opposite holds, is given by the function $u = 5 \ln x_1 + 2 \ln x_2 + \ln x_3$. This gives the inconsistent allocation (5/18, 15/56, 6/56) and the Ulysses allocation (5/8, 2/8, 1/8). Sufficient and necessary conditions for the Ulysses allocation to be more rational are easily formulated for utility functions of the form (2). The Ulysses allocation is the more rational one if and only if $b_1/b_2 > b_2/b_3$, that is, if time discounting is more pronounced between the present and the immediate future than between two consecutive periods in the future. This is the case in the model of Phelps and Pollak, discussed above. It also corresponds to the discount functions discovered by Ainslie. The inconsistent allocation is more rational if and only if the opposite inequality holds. This might not obtain very frequently, but the possibility should be noted. A person might feel, for instance, that as long as he ensures a decent consumption for the next year, he can enjoy a high consumption in the current year with good conscience, forgetting that in the next year he will not want to have the high consumption level that he had planned for himself, since the low level of consumption initially planned for the third year would spoil his pleasure. The borderline case is given by exponential time preferences. Then even the naive approach produces a consistent allocation equal to, and thus as rational as, that of Ulysses.

(iii) If we compare the consistent allocation with the inconsistent one, either may be the more rational. We consider the class of utility functions with the general form (2), and exclude the case of exponential time preferences, when the two allocations are equal. Otherwise, the consistent allocation is more rational than the inconsistent one if and only if $r > 0$.

(iv) Let us write $=_R$ and $>_R$ for 'is as rational as' and 'is more rational than' in pairwise comparisons between strategies I, U and C. When we compared U and I, or C and I, there was no need for being precise about the criterion for comparison; the statements of (ii) and (iii) above hold unambiguously as long as a more equal allocation is considered more rational. To compare U and C we need a more specific criterion. Starting with a utility function of the form (2), we remove the irrational time preferences by replacing each b_i by the same positive number. But there is no reason not to respect the other aspects of the individual's preferences, which are represented by r. One can then provide examples that demonstrate the following possibilities:

$$U >_R I >_R C$$
$$U >_R I =_R C$$
$$U >_R C >_R I$$
$$C >_R I >_R U$$
$$C =_R I >_R U$$

$$I >_R C >_R U$$
$$I =_R C =_R U$$

The following possibilities can never arise:

$$C >_R I =_R U$$
$$I =_R U >_R C$$

This also holds for the general form (1) and for every reasonable criterion of rationality. But it is probably true for the three-period case only. Four cases remain unanswered: when the Ulysses allocation is strictly between the two others and where it is as rational as the consistent allocation but differs from the inconsistent one.

The two main results that emerge are that the pairwise comparisons between the Ulysses allocation and the inconsistent allocation, and between the inconsistent allocation and the consistent one, can go either way. If either of the two sophisticated approaches has been chosen, and is more rational than the naive approach, the rational meta-preferences can only applaud. Is there, however, anything the rational meta-preferences can effect to prevent adoption of a sophisticated strategy if it is less rational than the naive, inconsistent one? Could one, that is, opt for inconsistency in order to achieve greater rationality? Consider first the Ulysses allocation. If I foresee that this will give a less rational allocation over time than if I follow my naive bent, I might abstain from taking the steps – e.g. buying an annuity – that would enable me to stick to my first-period preferences. One might object that such abstention would be contrary to the assumption, viz. that my meta-preferences have no efficacy and that my first-period preferences determine my first-period behaviour as part of an optimal three-period scheme. If that scheme includes my buying a three-period annuity in the first period, I will do so. If the meta-preferences have literally no efficacy, this is indeed true. They may, however, have *some* efficacy: not sufficient to deter me from consuming naively, but sufficient to prevent me from going through the relatively complex procedure of buying an annuity. I leave to the reader to consider for himself whether this is psychologically plausible, keeping in mind that the possibility only arises when the time discounting is less pronounced between the present and the immediate future than between two consecutive periods in the future.

Consider next the strategy of consistent planning. Could a person be deterred from adopting this strategy by its being less rational than naive behaviour? This seems more difficult to envisage. Once I know that I shall change my mind in the future if I act naively in the present, I cannot go on acting naively. As argued in II.3 above, I cannot decide to believe that a certain sequence is feasible simply on the grounds that acting on that belief will have useful results. Rationality may be well served by naiveté, but a person who knew this would be insufficiently naive to draw any advantage from his knowledge. If one has meta-preferences for rationality, the best option would seem to be to work strategically to change the first-order preferences. I now turn to this case.

II.6   ENDOGENOUS CHANGE OF PREFERENCES

A general theory of human action – further explored in chapter III – can be sketched as follows. To explain why a person in a given situation behaves in one way rather than in another, we can see his action as the result of two successive filtering processes. The first has the effect of limiting the set of abstractly possible actions to the *feasible* set, i.e. the set of actions that satisfy simultaneously a number of physical, technical, economic and politico-legal constraints. The second has the effect of singling out one member of the feasible set as the action which is to be carried out. From this we immediately see that the act of binding oneself can either be directed towards a change in the feasible set or towards a change in the mechanism that picks out the feasible alternative to be realized. In II.5 we assumed that the Ulysses strategy implied an induced change in the feasible set; here we explore the second possibility. We assume that at any given moment of time the singling out of one member of the feasible set is effectuated through rational choice. (See III.6 for other mechanisms for the second filter.) This implies that precommitment must occur through acting upon the preferences. This may either take the form of deliberately trying to bring about a change in the preference structure, or of deliberately resisting a change that would otherwise have been brought about by endogenous mechanisms. We shall mainly be concerned with the last possibility.

The problem is virtually unexplored in the literature. There is a small but rapidly growing body of literature on the notion of endogenously changing preferences, but very rarely is it assumed that an agent can take an active or strategic attitude towards his own preferences.[68] Rather he is seen as the passive vehicle of preferences that change according to some logic that he does not himself understand. Some authors mention in passing that the individual can take his precautions against such change if he comes to understand the mechanism by which it is brought about; resistance to habit-forming drugs is the standard example. The implications of this approach, are, however, rarely worked out, and the main emphasis usually is upon the analytical and manipulative aspects: how do preferences change (endogenously), and how can this be exploited by other people? I will also discuss these aspects, and then relate them to our main theme.

I begin with a discussion of C. C. von Weiszäcker's seminal paper on endogenous change of tastes.[69] For simplicity he assumes (1) that current preferences depend only upon consumption in the immediately preceding period and (2) that the income of the consumer is to be allocated over two goods only. Recent work has shown[70] that the second assumption is crucial for the results obtained by von Weiszäcker, and that they do not generalize to the n-commodity case. I disregard this problem here, as I think there are philosophically important questions to be discussed even in the special case. The first assumption is a bit surprising, as it excludes the notion of cumulative character formation which many writers have had in mind when discussing endogenous preference changes.[71] It is probable, however, that the introduction of the

[68]   The most recent and thorough discussions are found in the symposium on Formed Habits, *Journal of Economic Theory* 13 (1976). Earlier contributions include Haavelmo (1944, pp. 17ff), Georgescu-Roegen (1950), Gorman (1967), Peston (1967), Pollak (1970), von Weiszäcker (1971), Cyert and De Groot (1975). A sceptical note is sounded in Stigler and Becker (1977). The strategic approach is used by Shefrin and Thaler (1977) and by March (1977). The former restate Strotz's problem so as to make it one of planned change of preferences, but their underlying psychological postulates, with a distinction between 'planner' and 'doers', seem rather shaky. The approach chosen by March is very close to the one adopted here, with an emphasis upon inconsistent and endogenously changing preferences.

[69]   Von Weiszäcker (1971). The 'endogenizing of extra-economic variables' could be used as a general characterization of the most exciting work going on in contemporary economics. Von Weiszäcker is a past master of this art; see also von Weiszäcker (1973).

[70]   Pollak (1976).

whole consumption history as a variable would complicate the analysis so as to make it virtually unmanageable, and that at the present stage of research the strategy chosen by von Weiszäcker is a wise one.

Economists, when studying the consumer's choice, use more or less interchangeably three distinct notions: preferences, utility functions and demand functions. Given various conditions, which we assume fulfilled, any two of these concepts may be deduced or constructed from the third. Suppose that the consumer at time t has a preference structure P_t, represented by a utility function u_t, from which we can derive a demand function f_t which to each set of prices and income correlates a certain (two-component) commodity vector chosen by the consumer: $\mathbf{q}_t = f_t(p, m)$. We then assume that present demand is a function of demand and consumption in the immediately preceding period: $f_t = F(f_{t-1}, \mathbf{q}_{t-1})$, where F is some functional that represents the constant character traits underlying the changing preferences and governing their change. More specifically, we assume that F is such that there exists a g such that $\mathbf{q}_t = g(p, m, \mathbf{q}_{t-1})$. This latter form is the only one used by von Weiszäcker. Successive applications of the function g generate a sequence $\mathbf{q}_i$ of commodity bundles, which under certain conditions (whose economic interpretation is not clear) converges to a point $\mathbf{q} = h(p, m)$ that is independent of the initial bundle. The relation h may be formally interpreted as a demand function, as to each price–income set it correlates a certain commodity bundle. To this demand function there also corresponds (given some controversial assumptions) an 'as if' utility function U, in the sense that we can predict the bundle $\mathbf{q} = h(p, m)$ by assuming that the consumer is maximizing U, given p and m. Finally we may construct the 'long-term preference structure' P with the property that $\mathbf{x}P\mathbf{y}$ if and only if $U(\mathbf{x}) > U(\mathbf{y})$.

Let us return to the instantaneous preferences P_t. There is really no need to index these by time, because the only relevant difference between P_{t_1} and P_{t_2} is the consumption in the immediately preceding periods $t_1 - 1$ and $t_2 - 1$. If consumption in these periods was the same, then preferences in the following periods

---

[71] See especially Georgescu-Roegen (1950). The excessive generality of this paper may explain its sterility in begetting further research.

will also be the same. We may, therefore, more usefully index preferences by consumption in the preceding period, writing $\mathbf{x}P(\mathbf{y})\mathbf{z}$ for '$\mathbf{x}$ is preferred to $\mathbf{z}$, given that consumption in the immediately preceding period was $\mathbf{y}$'. Von Weiszäcker now proved the following theorem, valid under conditions that verbally may be expressed as inertia or conservatism of the consumer:

Given two commodity vectors $\mathbf{x}$ and $\mathbf{y}$, then $\mathbf{x}P\mathbf{y}$ if and only if there exists a sequence of vectors $\mathbf{r}_1 \ldots \mathbf{r}_n$ such that $\mathbf{r}_1\ P(\mathbf{y})\mathbf{y}$, $\mathbf{r}_2\ P(\mathbf{r}_1)\mathbf{r}_1$, $\mathbf{r}_3\ P(\mathbf{r}_2)\mathbf{r}_2 \ldots \mathbf{r}_n$ $P(\mathbf{r}_{n-1})\mathbf{r}_{n-1}$, $\mathbf{x}P(\mathbf{r}_n)\mathbf{r}_n$.

The theorem says, in other words, that $\mathbf{x}$ is better than $\mathbf{y}$ according to my long-run preferences if and only if there exists a path from $\mathbf{y}$ to $\mathbf{x}$ such that each step of the path is an improvement according to the instantaneous preferences at the beginning of the step. *If* the long-term preferences are interpreted as my 'real' or my 'rational' preferences, then the theorem implies that even if there is a conflict between my short-term preferences and the long-term ones, in the sense that $\mathbf{y}P(\mathbf{y})\mathbf{x}$, this conflict can always be overcome by the use of indirect strategies. It is a childhood fantasy come true: a walk in a landscape where from any given point you can always come to any higher point without ever having to go uphill, because the landscape contours change as a function of your path.

Von Weiszäcker also gives an ingenious (and controversial) example of this approach at work. In fig. 1 the amounts of goods q_1 and q_2 are measured along the axes. Line AA represents the budget line of an industrial worker. Line BB represents the budget line of a farmer. Initially the person in question is a farmer enjoying consumption bundle $\mathbf{y}$. I_1I_1 is the long-term indifference curve passing through $\mathbf{y}$ and I_2I_2 the short-term indifference curve corresponding to the preferences at $\mathbf{y}$. The point $\mathbf{z}$ is the long-term equilibrium point if the farmer were to move to the city. The point $\mathbf{x}$ represents a consumption bundle having the following properties:

(1) $\mathbf{z}P\mathbf{x}$
(2) $\mathbf{x}P\mathbf{y}$
(3) $\mathbf{y}P(\mathbf{y})\mathbf{x}$

If the farmer consumes $\mathbf{x}$ when living in the city, there will be a surplus available for taxation. Now city life (both in version **z** and *a fortiori* in version **x**) does not look very attractive from the point of view of the farmer, even though (in both versions) it is superior according to his long-term preferences. The theorem now tells us that there exists a sequence of points r_i that can bring him painlessly from **y** to **x**. (The reason why we consider the transition to **x** rather than to **z** will be clear in a moment.) The snag, however, is that as the curves are drawn, the initial part of the sequence must lie above both budget lines, because all r_i must lie above $I_1 I_1$. The latter statement is justified as follows. By definition each r_i satisfies the condition of the theorem that there exists a sequence of short-term improvements from **x** to r_i (viz. $r_1, r_2 \ldots r_{i-1}$), and according to the theorem this implies that $r_i P y$ for all r_i, which again means that all r_i must lie on indifference curves higher than $I_1 I_1$. Von Weiszäcker proposes the following

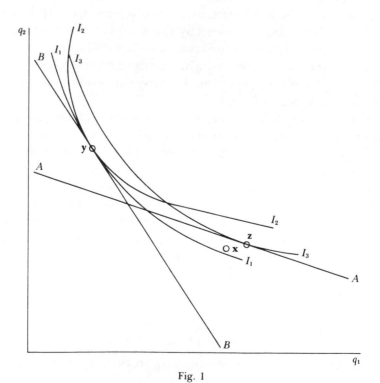

Fig. 1

solution to this problem. The government could subsidize the intermediate points r_i that lie above AA. When there arrives an r_i below AA, the government transfers the farmer to the city, gives him an income permitting him to buy x and retains the difference between z and x for itself in order to get back the money spent on subsidies. The farmer is better off (because xPy) and the government makes a profit because the subsidies are given only for a limited period of time, whereas the income from taxation can be perpetuated indefinitely, through taxation of the farmer's descendants.[72] Thus all is for the best in this Pareto-optimal world.

Or is it? We are discussing the case where an external agency could *manipulate* the individual with endogenously changing tastes, by putting him in a sequence of situations that will bring him smoothly and painlessly into a certain state that he could not have achieved by himself. If this is to be ethically acceptable, we must assume that the individual – if rational – would have done the same himself, given the same knowledge about the causal process underlying the preference change. We must assume, that is, that he would have applied for a loan to bring the intermediate points within his feasible set, planning to repay the loan when the final state is realized. I do not contest that this may happen in some cases. In particular I believe that the choice of a university education may be seen in this perspective. On the other hand I am unable to see that it would be irrational for an individual to refuse the offer of a subsidy, or to refrain from applying for a loan. And if it could be rational to refuse such offers, then I submit that it also is unethical to manipulate the individual through such offers.

This point merits some elaboration. Let us distinguish between coercion, seduction, persuasion and voluntary choice. The differences between these concepts are brought out by looking at the relation between preferences before the fact and preferences after the fact. Coercion and voluntary engagement are the two extreme ends of the spectrum. *Coercion* takes place when an individual prefers x over y, and continues to do so even when someone (physically) coerces him into doing y. *Voluntary choice* means that the individual initially prefers y over x, and does y for that reason.

---

[72] Actually von Weiszäcker (1971) only shows this to be true if the social rate of discount is sufficiently low.

(He may come to prefer *x* to *y* after the fact, but this is irrelevant in a discussion of the reasons for doing *y*.) *Seduction* occurs when an individual initially prefers *x* over *y*, but comes to prefer *y* over *x* once he has been coerced into doing *y*. Valmont's seduction of Cecile de Volanges is the classic depiction in literature of this process. Amartya Sen, when discussing that very problem raised by von Weiszäcker, seems to think that seduction is ethically justified:

> The labourer in question could actually prefer to be in one sector rather than in another, e.g., working in peasant agriculture rather than in wage employment in the town. It would be foolish to attribute all such preferences to 'irrationality' of some kind or other; there may be nothing remotely irrational in having a preference for being one's own master in one's farm even at a lower income, rather than working as a 'wage slave' in some factory, or indeed in some other farm. What is, however, more easy to argue is the case for avoiding the assumption of stationary tastes. Preferences about one's way of life and location are typically the result of one's past experience and an initial reluctance to move does not imply a perpetual dislike. The distinction has some bearing on the welfare aspects of employment policy, since the importance that one wishes to attach to the wage gap as a reflection of the labourer's preferences would tend to depend upon the extent to which tastes are expected to vary as a consequent of the movement itself.[73]

The same argument, when transferred to *Les liaisons dangéreuses*, presumably would not find many adherents. Now von Weiszäcker is making a stronger case for the justification of moving people from the countryside to the city, by relying on persuasion rather than on seduction. *Persuasion* means, then, that an individual is led by a sequence of short-term improvements into preferring *y* over *x*, even if initially he preferred *x* over *y*. My contention is that persuasion is more similar to seduction than to voluntary choice. This, at least, holds when the persuasion is not accompanied by a statement of intention informing the individual that he is about to be manipulated. Exploiting intrapsychic mechanisms that are unknown to the individual can never be justified. This, of course, does not imply that the individual should be protected from influences from the environment that tend to change his prefer-

[73]   Sen (1975), pp. 53–4.

ences; learning and experience, 'the angled road',[74] are essential to the development of the person. It does imply, however, that planning other people's experience is unethical. It also implies that we must refuse Robert Nozick's contention that inducements are never coercive;[75] they are if they are made for the purpose of leading the individual somewhere he might not want to go. There is no essential difference between coercion and seduction, nor between seduction and this form of persuasion.

Aristotle has an answer to this argument. 'Only an utterly senseless person can fail to know that our characters are the result of our conduct; but if a man knowingly acts in a way that will result in his becoming unjust, he must be said to be voluntarily unjust.'[76] In other words, the individual's failure to predict the impact of his present behaviour on his future preferences is a sign of his irrationality, and should not, by implication, form the basis for blaming the inducer. This observation seems correct in the standard case where the character (*hexis*) set up by a series of actions of a certain kind is just the disposition to perform that kind of action. Today, at least, we certainly should know that smoking will bring about addiction to smoking. The workings of the mind, however, are also subject to more complex laws. Repetition of some action may bring about a disposition *not* to perform that kind of action, as when people saturate themselves with sweets in order to bring about an aversion to sweets; and it may be difficult to know in advance which acts of repetition are habit-forming and which are habit-curing. The mechanism may be even more complex, as when a series of actions A interact with an existing disposition B so as to produce a tendency to perform actions C. (Does use of marijuana lead to heroin?) It is unreasonable to require that

---

[74]   Experience is the Angled Road
Preferred against the Mind
By – Paradox – the Mind itself –
Presuming it to lead

Quite Opposite – How Complicate
The Discipline of Man –
Compelling Him to Choose Himself
His Preappointed Pain –
(Dickinson 1970, no. 910)

[75]   Nozick (1969a).
[76]   *Nicomachean Ethics* 1114.

everyone should have full knowledge of these mechanisms, and equally unreasonable to ignore the fact that many groups have an incentive to acquire information about them and exploit them. In other words, no *individual* could acquire the knowledge about *all* these temptations that a specialized *group* could acquire about *one* of them. The injunction 'Know thyself' would in fact also be logically inconsistent, because the causal processes involved are themselves (higher-order) character traits that can be modified through conduct and so on.[77]

When discussing persuasion, we should distinguish between two issues. One is whether it is morally obligatory for the persuader to inform the object of the persuasion about his intentions; this question has been answered in the positive. A second is whether it could ever be rational for the individual to refuse the offer. If this question is answered in the negative, the first question loses much of its interest. I believe, however, that it should be answered in the positive. As is observed by Robert Pollak,[78] the scenario by which a 'myopic nonsmoker is led to become a heavy smoker...is entirely consistent with von Weizsäcker's assumptions', and yet it is difficult to conclude that the individual is better off in the end state than in the initial state. The step from 'long-term' or 'stable' preferences to 'real' or 'rational' preferences has not been justified by von Weizsäcker. Nothing is as stable and definitive as death.

The discussion of the paternalistic state may be seen in the light of these notions. To the extent that bans on cigarette advertisements stem from the actual or potential consumers themselves, who want to protect themselves against the Sirens of publicity, one should not talk about paternalism. The same holds for the proposal to introduce one television-free day a week in order to stimulate political or cultural activities; or the obligatory use of safety belts. It goes without saying, I believe, that the individuals are free to bind themselves (through laws) to bind themselves (with safety belts), or to protect their 'deeper' values against their more impulsive ones. The hard problems arise when these restrictions are imposed on the individuals, against their *ex ante facto* (and perhaps their *ex post facto*) preferences. I think it fairly clear that the government does not have the right to screen the public from

[77] Cp. also II.9 below.   [78] Pollak (1976).

television one day out of seven if the public does not want to be screened. It is much less obvious that the government should not have the right to make the use of safety belts obligatory, for here the state is asked to pay the bill if an accident happens.

The question, in a nutshell, is whether the welfare state implies or justifies the paternalistic state. Some people say Yes, and their aversion to paternalism then makes them reject the welfare state. Others also say Yes, and accept paternalism because they accept the welfare state. Personally I tend to say No, and to argue for a welfare state without paternalism. If people do not want to bind themselves, they should not be made to choose between being bound and getting no help if they hurt themselves as a result of not being bound. The spontaneous participation in risky activities, or even more importantly the spontaneous refusal to engage in body-building activities (what about obligatory physical exercise during the lunch hour to save the state hospital money?), should be respected. (Here, of course, it is crucial that there is some correlation between the extent to which individuals engage in risky activities and their contribution to social-welfare funds: otherwise their refusal to bind themselves would not be an expression of spontaneity, but an attempt to operate as free riders.) Ultimately the issue is one of a long and healthy life versus a rich life in accordance with one's preferences. If an assembly of informed individuals decide that they would rather have few resources for doing what they like than more resources for doing what is imposed on them, what authority could override their decision?

II.7 PRECOMMITMENT IN ANIMAL BEHAVIOUR

Among the many striking observations offered by Ainslie is the evidence that animals are able to use strategies of precommitment. Two of his examples are the following:

It is well known that pigeons will peck a key that has been associated with food, even when not pecking leads to much greater reward. Ainslie found that pigeons would regularly peck a red key for 2-sec access to food where not pecking led to 4-sec access to food beginning 3 sec later. If the key lit up green 12 sec before it was due to light up red, some of the subjects came to peck it on a majority of trials when its only effect was to prevent the key from lighting up red later in the trial... Subjects apparently learned to peck the key when it was green only if this forestalled the temporary effectiveness of the red key.[79]

The tendency of hungry pigeons to actively avoid certain opportunities to get food seems inconsistent with the orthodox concept of reward. If the fixed number of pecks on a key required for a single food reward is high but not so high that the pecking ceases (between 50 and 2000), pigeons will peck a second key whose only effect is to make the original key unavailable for a period of time (a time-out)...[The] subjects that sought time-outs from the opportunity to get food were those that presumably faced close choices between resting and working for poor reward. In such a situation their choice could be expected to vacillate between the alternatives. If we suppose that ambivalent behaviour is less rewarding than that of sticking to either alternative, the subjects might seek a device that bound their future behaviour to one or the other, or at least reduced the frequency of change.[80]

The first case is a straightforward example of weakness of will, overcome through the method of precommitment. The second case also has clear analogies in human behaviour; we may recall, for example, the Cartesian traveller in the forest. These findings apparently contradict a major implication of the present work, which is that men are neither angels (i.e. fully rational) nor animals (i.e. essentially myopic); they are imperfectly rational creatures able to deal strategically with their own myopia. Do the results reported by Ainslie imply that men should be debased to the level of animals, or animals elevated to the status of men? In order to present my argument for a negative answer to this question, I draw upon some distinctions developed in I.3 and further elaborated in III.7. In I.3 it was argued (1) that the capacity for global maximization is a unique and distinctive feature of man, and (2) that the examples of global maximization (e.g. the use of indirect strategies such as path interception in animal behaviour) found in the animal realm can evolve by accident only. Man has a *general* capacity for global maximization that he can deploy in qualitatively novel and unprecedented situations, whereas the scattered examples of such behaviour in animals are usually highly situation-specific.

In the present chapter I make a case for a more complex form of global maximization, involving the use of indirect strategies (i.e. precommitment) for the purpose of permitting indirect strategies (e.g. investment). The capacity for imperfectly rational behaviour

---

[79] Ainslie (1975), pp. 472–3.   [80] *Ibid.* p. 476.

in this sense is also a general one; the strategy of binding oneself applies to a large variety of situations and can exploit an extremely wide range of mechanisms. The fact that pigeons can be conditioned to bind themselves in situations that are both highly artificial and very specific should not be interpreted as evidence for a spontaneous use of precommitment in a very broad set of natural settings. And even if one could demonstrate that animals use precommitment behaviour in real-life situations, the explanation of this would have to be sought in evolutionary mechanisms such as preadaptation, pleiotropy or genetic drift. The appeal to a generalized capacity for binding oneself must be reserved for man. In particular, Ainslie's use of the term 'seek' in the last sentence of the second paragraph quoted above is misleading.

To repeat some of the ideas developed in chapter I, there is in human behaviour a *presumption of rationality* such that global maximization or strategies of precommitment – first-best or second-best rationality – are natural forms of behaviour that do not require any further explanation. Rather an explanation is called for when deviations from perfect and imperfect rationality are observed. In the animal realm the general mechanism of natural selection creates a *presumption of myopia*, and any given case of short-term sacrifice or precommitment behaviour would require a separate explanation. To the extent that animals could be shown to behave spontaneously in one of these future-oriented manners, we should ascribe to them mental experiences in the same sense in which human beings have mental experiences. The generalized capacity for (non-stereotyped) global maximization or precommitment behaviour presupposes an inner space where the possible states are represented. For future consequences to make a difference for present choice, they must somehow be present to consciousness *and be present as unrealized and merely possible*; this, I submit, is evidence of a mental life in a very strong sense. Such mental experiences may be found in the higher vertebrates, but Ainslie's pigeons lack the element of spontaneity that is required.

11.8 ABDICATION FROM POWER

The quandary of Ulysses also enters into any discussion of politics. Here I deal with two cases that seem especially important:

the problem of democracy and the problem of the capitalist state.

A direct democracy – either in the sense that all citizens vote on all issues instead of electing representatives, or in the sense that representatives can be recalled at any time – will tend towards zig-zag policies and constant reevaluation of past plans; it will be incontinent, vacillating and inefficient. Hegel is only one of the many political philosophers who have argued that this total freedom passes over into total unfreedom, both in the conceptual sense that liberty unlimited *is* slavery and in the causal sense that the anarchy of total liberty tends to prepare the ground for a dictator. I shall briefly indicate how classical and modern democracies have evolved different ways of coping with this problem.

In classical Athens all important decisions were taken in the assembly of citizens, meeting at least forty times a year. The assembly could reconsider its past decisions at any time, which would have left it an easy prey to demagogues or other manipulators had not certain institutional safeguards been established. M. I. Finley has drawn attention to two such institutions. The first is ostracism, which in practice was the right to banish well-known demagogues. Unlike Ulysses, the assembly could not always prevent itself from acting upon the song of the Sirens (but see the second institution below); it could, however, bar itself from hearing the song by expelling the singers. The second institution was called *graphe paranomon*, 'whereby a man could be indicted and tried for making an "illegal proposal in the Assembly" . . . *even if that proposal had been passed by the Assembly*'.[81] Finley observes that this arrangement differs from the corresponding safeguards in modern democracies: 'There lay the logic in the graphe paranomon, in the notion that by this procedure the demos was taking a second look at the proposal, rather than that one branch of government, the judiciary, was reviewing the actions of another branch, the legislature.'[82] He also suggests a contrast between the Greek approach to the stabilization of politics and the political scientists who have argued that some degree of *apathy* is a necessary prerequisite for the viability of democracy.[83] I shall now argue that both of these observations, while partly correct, are misleading in important respects.

[81]   Finley (1973), p. 26.   [82]   *Ibid.* p. 80.
[83]   *Ibid.* p. 67.

First, Finley seems to have underestimated the subtlety of the *graphe paranomon* (as described by himself). On his analysis the institution could be compared to the laws that have recently been passed in several countries, permitting consumers to annul instalment contracts within a certain period. (Strotz argues that buying on instalments is a device for precommitment,[84] but as in the manic-depressive case of II.2, it may be reasonable to precommit yourself against precommitments.) I believe, however, that a better comparison would be if the salesman not only ran the risk of having his contract annulled, but actually incurred a fine should it be annulled. Anyone wanting to exploit the impulsiveness of the people would then know that he ran the risk of being punished at the spur of a later impulse or when the impulse gave way to reason, and this must have acted as a deterrent against such exploitation. The *graphe paranomon* was a stabilizing device not only in permitting reason to regain the upper hand, but also in reducing the probability that it would lose out to passion in the first place.

Secondly, the Greek institutions and the phenomenon of apathy can hardly be set on a par as stabilizing mechanisms. It is absurd, I think, to suggest that a people could deliberately opt for apathy in order to protect itself against its tendency towards excessive meddling. Apathy may or may not have this *effect*; it may or – as is explained in I.5 – much more probably may not have this *function*; but it could never have been set up with this *intention*. A collective analogy to Pascal's self-induced loss of reason is impossible to conceive of. On the other hand the institutions of ostracism and *graphe paranomon* could very well have been set up in order to keep democracy within the limits required for efficiency and stability. And according to criterion (i) of II.2, this is required for these institutions to fall under the heading of precommitment. The mere argument that they have this stabilizing effect or (a more obscure suggestion) function would not be sufficient for this characterization.

In modern democracies a number of institutions can be interpreted as devices for precommitment. I observed in II.4 that the central bank can be seen as the repository of reason against the short-term claim of passion, an argument that has been

[84] Strotz (1955–6), p. 178.

developed in some detail by Francis Sejersted.[85] For classical liberalist policy, the exchange rate and the price level were seen as crucial parameters that under no circumstances should be transformed into political control variables. Mercantilism (and present-day neo-mercantilism) have rather stressed the need for current adjustments to the changing environment: would Ulysses let himself be bound to the mast if he knew that the shallow waters around the Sirens' island were too difficult for anyone but him to master? (The reader will recall that the problem was raised in the quotation from William Nordhaus in II.4.) Other institutions that have been accorded a similar autonomy for similar reasons include the Foreign Ministries of many countries and the BBC model of broadcasting, as distinct from the ORTF model. For these institutions it is possible to identify, with varying degrees of precision, the act of abdication whereby politicians have decided that certain values are too important, or certain tools too dangerous, to be subject to the current control of the politicians. The removal of monetary policy, foreign policy or broadcasting from the political sphere is itself a political act.

At another level the system of periodic elections can be interpreted in the same perspective, especially when the government does not have the power to dissolve parliament and order new elections. (The distrust of plebiscites is an expression of the same attitude.) In this interpretation periodic elections are the *electorate's* method of binding itself and of protecting itself against its own impulsiveness. We observed above, however, that for the *politicians* the system of periodic elections makes for a permanent temptation to lump the unpopular measures in the beginning of the electoral period and the popular ones towards the end, with sub-optimal consequences. We also noted Lindbeck's suggestion that the politicians in turn could bind themselves so as to avoid this temptation, by randomly spaced elections. This would provide a new answer to the problem of who shall guard the guardians, and indeed the randomly spaced elections could be the electorate's device for simultaneously binding itself and the politicians. Attractive as it is in some respects, the randomizing device would be too costly in other respects to deserve serious consideration.

[85] Sejersted (1973); also Elster (1975b).

(Similar objections apply to probabilistic methods of collective choice.)[86]

In II.4 we discussed two arguments for using rules rather than discretion in formulating economic policy: the cost-of-information argument and what one could call the cost-of-adjustment argument (offered by Friedman and Tisdell). Here we shall consider two additional arguments: one related to the sub-optimality created by strategic considerations and one related to the unfavourable effects of uncertainty on incentives. The sub-optimality argument has recently been discussed by Finn Kydland and Edward Prescott,[87] in a framework rather similar to the one used here. Their main idea is that optimal control theory, which at each point of time selects the best decision, given the current situation and given that decisions will be similarly selected in the future, is not the appropriate tool for economic planning:

The reasons for this nonintuitive result are as follows: optimal control theory is an appropriate planning device for situations in which current outcomes and the movement of the system's state depend only upon current and past policy decisions and upon the current state. But this is unlikely to be the case for dynamic economic systems. Current decisions of economic agents depend in part upon their expectations of future policy actions. Only if these expectations were invariant to the future policy selected would optimal control theory be appropriate[88]...Thus it seems likely that the current practice of selecting that policy which is best, given the current situation, is likely to converge to the consistent but *suboptimal* policy...The reason that such policies are suboptimal is not due to myopia. The effect of this decision upon the entire future is taken into consideration. Rather, the suboptimality arises because there is no mechanism to induce *future* policymakers to take into consideration the effect of their policy, via the expectation mechanism, upon *current* decisions of agents.[89]

The problem is related to difficulties treated elsewhere by Phelps and Pollak[90] and by Kelvin Lancaster,[91] but Kydland and Prescott give an added dimension to the problem by introducing the distinction between rules and discretionary decisions. They argue that in many cases the sub-optimality generated by the current discretionary decisions can be eliminated by the use of fixed rules

---

[86] Social choice by a randomizing mechanism, e.g. by letting the probability that some option will be chosen equal the proportion of voters who have it as their first choice, has the double advantage of guaranteeing minority rights and of being 'strategy-proof'. On the other hand the method could be exploited so as to make social choice too easily reversible.

[87] Kydland and Prescott (1977).

[88] *Ibid.* p. 474.

[89] *Ibid.* p. 481.

[90] Phelps and Pollak (1968).

[91] Lancaster (1973).

which preclude strategic considerations of the kind discussed. An interesting example, related to Lancaster's analysis of capitalism as a differential game between workers and capitalists, is the following:

A majority group, say, the workers, who control the policy might rationally choose to have a constitution which limits their power, say, to expropriate the wealth of the capitalist class. Those with lower discount rates will save more if they know that their wealth will not be expropriated in the future, thereby increasing the marginal product and therefore wage and lowering the price of capital.[92]

The argument may be read in a weak and in a strong sense. In a weak sense it only says that *given* the fact that decisions to invest are in the hands of the capitalist class, it is only sensible of the working class to guarantee the capital owners a reward on the investments. In a strong sense (implied by the reference to the difference in discount rates between workers and capitalists) it states that it is in the interest of the working class to leave the investment decisions to capital-owners, because otherwise the workers would prefer consumption now to consumption later and invest too little. The last argument is an old one, which has often been used as a justification for capitalism and income inequalities. The first is more original, because of the introduction of the strategic element and the meta-strategy (precommitment) proposed to overcome the strategic sub-optimality.

Turning now to the incentive problem created by uncertainties, this is closely related to the arguments for the 'rule of law' given by Max Weber and many others who have stressed the importance of a stable institutional framework for a growing economy. The problem is often stated as one of the need to be able to *predict* the decisions of the bureaucracy, but the Kydland–Prescott argument shows this to be a simplification. The ability to predict is a necessary, but not a sufficient, condition for dynamic optimality.

---

[92]   Kydland and Prescott (1977), p. 486. It is rather surprising that the authors do not in this connection (or, indeed, in their article) refer to the work of Lancaster (1973). If the phrase 'expropriate the wealth of the capitalist class' is to be read in the sense of an expropriation of *profits* (and not of the means of production and the power over investment decisions), then their problem is identical to the one raised by Lancaster, and his analysis presumably should have some relevance for theirs. In particular one should ask whether the symmetry of the differential game between workers and capitalists should not lead us to expect that the capitalist class also might find it useful to bind itself; one might expect that the effect of this double precommitment would be to achieve the optimum that is unattainable through current control of the variables.

In the absence of this condition, however, dire consequences indeed may ensue. Uncertainties about future decisions may stem from two distinct sources: the law may be *ambiguous* (as in ancient Chinese law)[93] or constantly (and unpredictably) *changing* (as in contemporary neo-mercantilism). Many authors from Leibniz onwards[94] have observed that the formal requirements of un-ambiguous and constant laws are in many respects more important than the need for just laws, because if you can predict the decisions of the court you can take precautionary measures that will protect you from unjust laws.

F. Sejersted[95] has argued that the rule of law in nineteenth-century Norway was a solution to the problems of the preceding despotism. This rule of law was later threatened by a further democratic development. Despotism and a highly developed democracy, not to mention a direct democracy, are based on the right to current intervention in all matters, whereas constitutional democracy is founded upon a set of stable institutions that cannot be undone at will once established. A crucial notion in this connection is the function of the *constituent assembly* that lays down the ground rules to be followed by all later generations. Only the constituent assembly really is a political actor, in the strong sense of *la politique politisante*; all later generations are restricted to *la politique politisée*, or the day-to-day enactment of the ground rules. The nation can bind 'itself' (a controversial notion) through the constituent assembly, by entrusting certain powers of decision to the judiciary branch, by requiring that the ground rules can only be changed by a two-thirds or a three-fourths majority, and so on.

The *paradox of democracy* can be thus expressed: each generation wants to be free to bind its successors, while not being bound by its predecessors. This contradiction has a structure similar to what has been called the central contradiction of capitalism: each capitalist wants low wages for his own workers (this makes for high profits) and high wages for all other workers (this makes for high

---

[93]   Needham (1956), pp. 521ff.
[94]   See Elster (1975a), p. 142, for Leibniz's views on this point. A strong advocate of this idea was Hume; cp. for example the exposition of his views in Miller (1976), pp. 162ff. Both Leibniz and Hume cite the classic account from Xenophon, where a tall boy with a short coat had forcibly exchanged coats with a small boy in a coat too long for him, and they both concluded that on a larger view of justice this is unacceptable because it undermines the institution of property.
[95]   Sejersted (1978); also (1973).

demand).[96] In both cases it is possible for any given generation (or any given capitalist) to eat its cake and have it, but all generations (or all capitalists) cannot simultaneously achieve this goal. The link to the problem of inconsistent time preferences (II.5 above) is obvious. The equivalent of the inconsistently irrational strategy can perhaps be found in recent Chinese politics, especially in the revolutionary phases where 'the plan loses significance in that it is constantly being revised'.[97] The Ulysses strategy is to precommit later generations by laying down a constitution including clauses that prevent its being easily changed. The constituent assembly has a unique and privileged character, not by right but by historical accident. In exceptional and unpredictable historical situations, representativity of persons and legitimacy of voting methods are decided on the spot; the drastic breach with the past leaves the assembly free to bind the future. The important condition, of course, is that the impact must come from without the political system; simple bootstrap operations are excluded.

It is interesting that several political thinkers have considered the possibility of a periodic constituent assembly, so that everyone once in his life would be allowed a say in the most basic problems of society rather than being under the tutelage of past generations.[98] This intention, while laudable, seems to harbour an irreducible contradiction. Let us assume, for example, that the constituent assembly has laid down (1) that there shall be constituent assemblies at thirty-year intervals and (2) that changes in the constitution between these assemblies must have a two-thirds majority. We then are led to ask which majority is needed in the later assemblies and who should decide it. If the original constituent assembly were to lay down the voting method for later assemblies, this would mean that it *was* privileged after all. If the later assemblies themselves are to decide the question, we immediately get into an infinite regress, for how shall the voting method be chosen? (In addition there is the issue whether a later assembly could suppress the system of periodic assemblies.) The reason why this infinite regress does not necessarily arise in the

---

[96]   Robinson (1956), p. 78; see Elster (1978a), ch. 5, for a further analysis of the logical structure of this contradiction.
[97]   Suttmeier (1974), p. 91.
[98]   Sejersted (1978) cites Thomas Jefferson and the Norwegian Henrik Stenbuch.

original assembly lies in the exceptional and charismatic character of the group, having its legitimacy in objective circumstances outside itself. These circumstances make for a unity and unanimity in the face of which procedural questions evaporate. (This, of course, is an idealized story, but not, I believe, an imaginary one.) The implication of this analysis is that later generations have no obligation to feel bound by their predecessors, but neither do they have any legitimate right to bind their successors. The constitution remains legitimate only because all alternatives lack legitimacy; it is a focal point in Schelling's sense or a 'bright line' in the sense of Ainslie (see II.9). If, say, in the constituent assembly 70 per cent voted for a required majority of two-thirds to change the constitution, whereas today 60 per cent are for a required simple majority only, this is not a legitimate basis for change.

We can take a closer look at this problem. At any given moment of time we may assume that there is a well-defined percentage $y = f(x)$ of the assembly that wants the majority required for a change in the constitution to be at least x per cent. Presumably y is a decreasing function of x; for simplicity we also assume continuity. (This can be interpreted in terms of individuals who have not quite made up their minds, being liable to vote for a proposed change according to some probability between 0 and 1.) If $f(50) > 50$ and $f(100) < 100$, there must be some fixed point $\bar{x}$ between 50 and 100 such that $\bar{x}$ per cent of the assembly wants the required majority to be at least $\bar{x}$ per cent. One could then argue that this $\bar{x}$ should be incorporated into the constitution itself, as the largest self-supporting percentage. One could argue, moreover, that $\bar{x}$ be currently modified in order to take account of changes in people's attitudes towards the relative importance of democracy and stability.

It would seem, however, that such attempts would be self-defeating. It would be pointless to bind future generations if they could unbind themselves in this manner. The only way out, perhaps, would be to incorporate a clause in the constitution that could not be modified by any generation, viz. that if in year t the percentage required for changes in the constitution is itself changed according to the above procedure, then this change should not come into effect before $t+30$. Only in this way could one be assured that the percentage $f(x)$ really reflected people's attitude towards democracy, rather than being a rationalization of some goal (i.e. some precise constitutional change) they want to achieve *now*. Assuming that the tendency over time is towards lower values of $\bar{x}$, this procedure could give acceptable results. If, however, the state of the opinion vacillates between fundamentalism and radicalism in the interpretation of constitutional law, the procedure would have the strange feature of placing a conservative generation in the situation where it has too much leeway for constitutional change; it would regret not being bound more tightly to the mast. Further reflection reveals further paradoxes. A liberal generation would want to enact illiberal measures in order to prevent the illiberal generation that is expected to follow it from enacting illiberal measures to bind the liberal generation that is expected to follow at one further remove, and so on. There is an inherent instability in all alternatives to the constitution handed down from the past, which retains its legitimacy *faute de mieux*.

The second set of problems to be discussed under the heading of political precommitment concerns the nature of the capitalist state according to Marxist theory. It is well known that during the heyday of classical capitalism the political power was not in the hands of the capitalist class. Should this be interpreted as the capitalists' abdication from power, and if so in which sense and for which purpose? In addition to Marx some further authors will be mentioned.

On the most general level (as found above all in the *German Ideology*) Marx's theory of the state can be stated in the following manner. Classical political theory from Hobbes onwards had assumed that the state was a means for realizing the cooperative solution to a Prisoner's Dilemma *played by all against all*.[99] Marx rejected this approach as being excessively general. Rather than looking at society as being made up of identical atoms having structurally identical (even if substantively opposed) interests, he argued that society should be broken down into two or more distinct classes, each of which has its internal Prisoner's Dilemma. He argued, moreover, that the capitalist state has the double task of facilitating the cooperative solution to the Prisoner's Dilemma played by the capitalists against each other and of preventing the cooperative solution (organization and solidarity) from emerging

---

[99]   For this perspective, see Baumol (1952), Olson (1965) and M. Taylor (1976a).

in the Prisoner's Dilemma played by the workers against each other.[100] (In addition there might be some tasks that are in the interest of both classes, such as the provision of public goods, but Marx argued that the development of capitalism would lead to these being increasingly assumed by private enterprise.)[101] The state's apparatus for repressing the workers is not relevant in this context. (It would be relevant only if established by the workers themselves, as suggested in the last quotation from Kydland and Prescott above.) We limit our attention, therefore, to the capitalist state as a tool for protecting the interest of the capitalist class as a whole against the interests of its individual members and for protecting the long-term interest of the class against its short-term interests. (I shall not deal here with the interesting problems that arise when individual short-term interests and collective long-term interests coincide, both being opposed to the collective short-term interest, as in the case of the 'imperialism of free trade'.)[102]

An example where the class interest entered into conflict with the individual interest is provided by the English Factory Acts, which, far from being a check on capitalist greed, were

the negative expression of the same greed. These acts curb the passion of capital for a limitless draining of labour-power, by forcibly limiting the working-day by state regulations, made by a state that is ruled by capitalist and landlord. Apart from the working-class movement that daily grew more threatening, the limiting of factory labour was dictated by the same necessity which spread guana over the English fields. The same blind eagerness for plunder that in one case exhausted the soil, had in the other torn up by the roots the living force of the nation.[103]

---

[100] In concrete terms, the task of the state is to facilitate cartels and employers' organizations and to prevent union formation. In appearance the English Combination Acts were directed against employers and workers alike, but in the first place there was a formal asymmetry in the fact that the statutes 'only allow of a civil action against the contract-breaking master, but on the contrary permit a criminal action against the contract-breaking workmen' (Marx 1867, p. 740), and in the second place the Acts were enforced to quite different extents against contract-breaking masters and workers.

[101] Marx (1857–8), pp. 429–30. Marx does not specify the mechanism that could bring this about, but at least two possibilities come to mind. Either some of the firms could achieve a size which would make it profitable for them to provide the goods singlehanded (Olson 1965, p. 29) or institutional devices (such as the patent system) could be invented to internalize the external economies. Marx certainly exaggerated this trend, but there is an important truth in the notion of capitalism constantly *reprivatizing* the activities that were undertaken by the state because the market system failed to provide them.

[102] Cp. Elster (1978a), ch. 5, for a discussion of this issue.

[103] Marx (1867), pp. 238–9.

Such cases are relatively simple to understand. As in forced cartellization[104] or in laws of expropriation,[105] the bourgeoisie may understand that it is in its own interest to be prevented from pursuing its own interest in an unrestrained manner, and bind itself accordingly. Other purported cases of capitalist abdication are more complex and ambiguous. In the case just cited, we were dealing with a state ruled by *capitalists* (though Marx adds 'and landlord') enforcing measures for the sake of the capitalist class as a whole. In other and more important texts Marx recognized that the state is *not* a capitalist state in the direct sense of being ruled by capitalists for their interest. On the contrary the political power was firmly in the hands of the aristocracy, as in England, or of a caesarist–bureaucratic regime, as in France. This separation of the economic and political power quite obviously creates a problem for a theory having as a basic statement that 'The executive of the modern state is but a committee for managing the common affairs of the bourgeoisie.'[106] It is to Marx's credit that he dropped this 'nothing but'-ism when he proceeded to detailed historical analysis. Nevertheless it remains to be shown that the modern state – besides being many other things – *also* is a committee for managing the common affairs of the bourgeoisie.

Marx adopted two different lines of argument in order to prove this for the English and the French cases respectively. In the articles for the *New York Daily Tribune*, the *Neue Oder Zeitung* and the Vienna *Presse* on English politics Marx stressed over and over again that the industrial capitalists deliberately abstained from taking political power because they feared that the concentration of economic and political power in one class would sharpen the class struggle and lead to a social revolution. The short-term

---

[104] See Mangset (1974) for an account of this phenomenon in Norway between the wars.

[105] Marx (1845–6), p. 340. Against Stirner, who saw the existence of these laws as a proof that the state was the real owner of 'private' property, Marx opposes a series of striking formulations. Stirner makes the *contradictions* of private property into the *negation* of private property. His argument amounts to saying that my watchdog is the real owner of my house. And finally, in a phrase where the double task of the state (protecting the capitalist class against the working class and against its own individual members) is clearly expressed: 'Weil die Bourgeois dem Staat nicht erlauben, sich in ihre Privatinteressen einzumischen, und ihm nur soviel Macht geben, als zu ihrer eignen Sicherheit und der Aufrechthaltung der Konkurrenz nötig ist, weil die Bourgeois überhaupt nur insofern als Staatsbürger auftreten, als ihre Privatverhältnisse dies gebieten, glaubt Jacques le bonhomme, dass sie vor dem Staate "Nichts sind"' (Marx 1845–6, p. 339).

[106] Marx and Engels (1848).

economic losses incurred by leaving power in the hands of the aristocracy were seen as smaller than the political gains (and the long-term economic gain) achieved by diverting attention and revolt away from the capitalist class and blurring the lines of class conflict. Marx quotes Juvenal in order to bring out the dilemma of the capitalist class, torn between its old enemy and its emerging one: *Et propter vitam vivendi perdere causas.*[107]

This explanation, however, hardly counts as an analysis of precommitment, because many of the criteria given in II.2 are unfulfilled. We can bring this out by staging a confrontation with some other views of English politics and with Marx's own account of French politics. In the *Economist* there appeared in 1862 an article with the striking title 'The advantage to a commercial country of a non-commercial Government',[108] where the author (Walter Bagehot himself?) argued forcefully that the commercial interests would abstain from taking political power if they knew their own good, because the aristocracy was far more capable than the 'rule of wealth'[109] of taking the disinterested long-term view. Similar views were voiced by Hyppolite Taine.[110] The same analysis was proposed by Schumpeter, who argued that the rule of the aristocracy was beneficial for the bourgeoisie because it 'needs a master'[111] to protect itself against itself. In these accounts it is at least arguable that criteria (i) and (ii) of II.2 are fulfilled. They all assume that the bourgeoisie deliberately restricted, or at least refrained from extending, its political power because it could not trust itself to maintain the stable environment required for long-term growth. Some options that might otherwise have been feasible were excluded by this strategy, and *this exclusion was the raison d'être for the strategy.* The last statement is not valid in Marx's case. For him the reduced freedom of action was a cost associated with the policy, not the very goal to be achieved. This means that criterion (i) was not fulfilled. The bourgeoisie abstains from power

---

[107] *Neue Oder Zeitung,* 12 June 1855. As far as I know, little attention has been paid to Marx's writings on English politics, even though they deal with the capitalist country *par excellence* and are much more consistent theoretically with his economic views than are the writings on French political history. Most (but not all) of these writings are collected in Marx and Engels (1971).

[108] I owe this reference, as well as other references in this paragraph, to Grindheim (1975).

[109] Bagehot (1966), p. 122.   [110] Quoted from Grindheim (1975).

[111] Schumpeter (1954), p. 139.

in order to manipulate the working class, not in order to control itself through a self-imposed master.

It seems quite clear that neither Marx's view of English politics nor the alternative theories mentioned satisfy criterion (v) of II.2. It would be absurd to say that the industrial capitalists abdicated from power; they had never had it. One cannot even argue with much plausibility that there was a deliberate decision not to take power, even though the fact that the Anti-Corn-Law League did not convert itself into a political party could be interpreted as a decision of this kind.[112] Rather, the best conceptualization would be to say that the aristocracy was free to maximize its own objectives with a reasonable profit to the capitalist class as a side constraint. This no doubt implies that the capitalist class would have taken power had its interests been seriously endangered, but this counterfactual formula does not provide the hard evidence needed for the satisfaction of criterion (v) above.

Now Marx never intended his account to be an analysis of precommitment, so he can hardly be criticized for the non-fulfilment of the criteria that enter into this notion. Rather his error was to single out the wrong actor, or to use the wrong concept of an actor. In the conventional sense of the term, only the aristocracy, with its internal fractions and conflicts, can be seen as a political actor in English politics at the time. The capitalists and the workers certainly had an influence on politics, but as constraints rather than as pursuers of goals. Marx certainly thought of the capitalist class as pursuing its economic goal through political means, and the non-participation in politics was then interpreted intentionally and instrumentally as the with-drawal from politics. Here Marx, far from neglecting the actor perspective in politics, tended to overemphasize the rational aspects of capitalist behaviour.[113] The same holds for the other authors cited above. Schumpeter may be right in saying that it was rational (i.e. advantageous) for the bourgeoisie to stay away from power, but we cannot conclude that this is why they stayed away from power.

---

[112] I owe this suggestion to Kåre Tønnesson. Marx makes the same point in his article on the Chartists, *New York Daily Tribune*, 25 Aug. 1852.

[113] Cp. in particular his conspiratorial interpretation of Palmerston's policies, in Marx (1971), pp. 278–9.

There is, of course, the question of the freedom of decision of the aristocracy within the constraints defined by the other classes. If a class is able to impose sufficiently strong constraints on the decision-makers, then that class may be the central political actor in a less conventional sense of the term. In this sense, for example, the Polish workers today can be seen as political actors, even if unorganized in the conventional sense;[114] similarly for many mobs and rioters throughout history.[115] We are so accustomed to the Hegelian–Marxist dichotomy between classes existing *in themselves* and classes existing *for themselves* that we forget the importance of the intermediate stage where classes exercise their influence through their existence *for others*.[116] If through this reflected existence they are able to achieve something approaching to what they could have obtained through organization, we may refer to them as 'quasi-actors'. Occasionally a group may be able to achieve more as quasi-actors than as actors, and might try to bind themselves by renouncing actorship. *Qua* responsible participants in the political give-and-take they might get less than through their nuisance value *qua* potential rioters. This notion is related to T. S. Schelling's observation that a stupid negotiator may obtain more concessions than a sophisticated one who is capable of seeing the justice of the adversary's claim.[117]

After this digression into the notion of a political actor, I turn to Marx's analysis of French politics, which *is* certainly intended as an analysis of precommitment. Marx's explanation of the *coup d'état* of Louis Bonaparte has much in common with Schumpeter's view of English politics, with the added feature that an act of abdication can be empirically proved to have taken place. The French bourgeoisie needed a master; it found him in Louis Bonaparte; it abdicated from power and transferred it to him:

Thus, by now stigmatizing as 'socialistic' what it had previously extolled as 'liberal', the bourgeoisie confesses that its own interests dictate that it should be

---

[114] 'The real threat to the government is neither the church nor the intellectuals, but the workers. Nobody knows what their reaction is likely to be in any situation. A prominent sociologist speaks of them as "the politically unorganized masses" and says their mere existence limits the government's freedom of movement' (*Sunday Times*, 25 Sept. 1977).

[115] Hobsbawm (1959), ch. VII.

[116] Cp. Evans-Pritchard (1940, p. 120): 'A man of one tribe sees the people of another tribe as an undifferentiated group to whom he has an undifferentiated pattern of behaviour, while he sees himself as a member of a segment of his own tribe.'

[117] Schelling (1963), pp. 22ff.

delivered from the danger of its *own rule*; that in order to restore tranquillity in the country its bourgeois Parliament must, first of all, be given its quietus; that in order to preserve its social power intact its political power must be broken; that the individual bourgeois can continue to exploit the other classes and to enjoy undisturbed property, family, religion, and order only on condition that his class be condemned along with the other classes to like political nullity; that in order to save its purse it must forfeit the crown, and the sword that is to safeguard it must at the same time be hung over its own head as a sword of Damocles.[118]

Surely it is only an accident that this magnificently rhetorical passage does not add the metaphor of Ulysses and the Sirens to the others. It *is* rhetoric, however, rather than analysis. Even if we concede Marx the point that the anti-capitalist nature of the Bonapartist regime was beneficial or even indispensable for the survival of capitalism as an economic system, it remains to be shown that this *explains* the emergence and maintenance of that regime. Abstractly speaking two such explanations are possible, of the functionalist and the intentional varieties. I refer to I.5 above for the suggestion that the anti-capitalist nature of the Bonapartist state can be explained through its function for the capitalist mode of the production. As for the intentional mode of analysis, it would require empirical evidence that the Bonapartist regime was deliberately set up by an act of abdication from power by the capitalist class. As far as I know no such evidence has been forthcoming. The reason why it might appear as if criterion (v) of II.2 is fulfilled in this case is the undeniable discontinuity of the *coup d'état*. The continued political supremacy of the English aristocracy could at most be seen as an act of omission of the English bourgeoisie, but the abrupt change of power from a liberal regime to a Bonapartist one satisfies at least one condition for this to be an act of commission by the French bourgeoisie. It is, however, at least as plausible to see the real actor in Louis Bonaparte himself. To say that the weakness of the bourgeoisie permitted his rise to power is not to say that the bourgeoisie permitted him to take power. To abdicate immediately before you are dethroned may improve appearances, but does not change the substance.

I conclude, then, that the analysis of democracy has offered some convincing examples of political precommitment; the analysis of

---

[118] Marx (1852), sect. IV.

the capitalist state has not. We should stress the crucial notion of the constituent assembly, not as a fictional device, as in contract theories of the state, but as a real historical assembly seeking to bind its successors. This is the closest analogy in society to the state of mind of Ulysses setting out on that dramatic part of his journey.

II.9   SOME CONCLUSIONS AND FURTHER QUESTIONS

Let us review the gamut of strategies of precommitment that have been discussed in the course of this chapter:

(1) Manipulation of the feasible set
    (a) Restricting the set of physically possible actions
    (b) Changing the reward structure by public side bets
(2) Manipulation of the character
    (a) Strengthening the will-power
    (b) Changing the preference structure
(3) Manipulation of information
    (a) Changing the belief system
    (b) Avoiding exposure to certain signals

To this we should add a strategy that fails to satisfy criterion (iii) of II.2, but that is also a response to the problem of weakness of will:

(4) Manipulation through a rearrangement of inner space
    (a) Using private side bets
    (b) Using consistent planning

Let us briefly comment upon these strategies and sub-strategies. Within the set of actions that change the feasible set I distinguish between, say, the strategy of going for a long walk in the mountains so as to make cigarettes physically unavailable and the strategy of telling your friends that you will stop smoking so as to change the reward system. The latter strategy also induces a change in the feasible set, because the option 'Continue to smoke without any sarcastic comments' now becomes unavailable. Within the character-modifying actions I distinguish between the general strategy of strengthening the will-power and the more specific strategy of modifying some particular desire: the first permits you to climb higher uphill slopes while the second lowers the height of the slope that is to be climbed. Within the set of actions that modify the information upon which further decisions are taken, I distinguish between the radical strategy of inducing new factual beliefs (including a strategy for inducing forgetfulness about the induction) and the moderate strategy of screening yourself from certain signals or cues in the environment. It is *not* a matter of avoiding exposure to information in the strict sense, which is as paradoxical as the induction of new beliefs;[119] only a question of avoiding exposure to conditions that might trigger off the efficacy of information already in your possession. You cannot deliberately avoid tobacco shops for the purpose of inducing forgetfulness about tobacco; on the contrary the need for constantly being on the lookout for such shops in order to cross the street before you come to them will more probably tend to strengthen your awareness of tobacco. Nevertheless exposure to tobacco in the concrete might be more tempting than the awareness of tobacco in the abstract, so that you could accept more of the latter as a cost of getting less of the former.

The most important of these strategies are probably methods (1b) and (2b). In most actual cases strategy (1a) is unfeasible or involves sacrifices too heavy, and would thus fail to satisfy criterion (iv) of II.2. The same, I think, holds for method (2a), which would often involve a form of overkill whose feasibility might do away with the problem itself. We should note, however, Ainslie's profound suggestion that strategies (4a) and (2a) may be closely related, i.e. that the technique of private side bets may involve a general strengthening of will-power. When the subject rearranges his inner space and reward system, so that a failure to follow up one decision (e.g. the decision to stop smoking) has negative implications for other decisions (e.g. the decision to diet), the interrelated system of goals and desires may come to exhibit the rigidity and inflexibility often associated with the notion of

[119] For the paradoxes of avoidance of information, see IV.4 below.

will-power.[120] As for strategy (3a), it would seem so costly as to be chosen only in a few extreme cases; strategy (3b) is frequently used, but is of doubtful efficacy.[121]

I submit that in most everyday cases the most efficient strategy involves a combination of methods (1b) and (2b). Realizing that through a series of actions I can achieve a *hexis* from which the desired actions will flow naturally ('sans violence, sans art, sans argument'), and that each of these actions is outside the immediate reach of my will-power, I may precommit myself to them by changing the reward system. This is how many people go about stopping smoking. To bring about the state of non-addiction simply by abstaining from smoking may be too hard; to set up a permanent system of public side bets is too complicated, and in any case unnecessary if a temporary system can bring about that state and thus make itself superfluous.

'After the age of forty, one is responsible for one's face.' This truth, equally hard to confront and to dispute, is but one aspect of the general fact of *responsibility for self*. One can never say 'This is simply how I am' as an excuse for conduct, for one could have made oneself into a different kind of person. In the philosophical literature this responsibility has been asserted from two distinct points of view. One, ultimately of Aristotelian origin, places the self squarely in the world of causal processes and argues that it can and should shape itself by exploiting these processes. This is the approach explored in the present chapter. Another, represented by Sartre and more recently by Charles Taylor, assumes that you can change yourself by redefining and redescribing the self. This would seem to be closer to the techniques of private side bets and of consistent planning. Like so many other writers, Taylor illustrates his approach with the problem of dieting:

Let us take the case of the man who is fighting obesity and who is talked into seeing it as a merely quantitative question of more satisfaction, rather than as a matter of dignity and degradation. As a result of this change, his inner struggle itself becomes transformed, it is now a quite different experience. The opposed motivations – the craving for cream cake and his dissatisfaction with himself at such indulgence – which are the 'objects' undergoing redescription here, are not

---

[120] Ainslie (1977) explores this at great length.
[121] Ainslie (1975), p. 478. A more positive evaluation is found in the editors' introduction to Mahoney and Thoresen (eds.) (1975), pp. 40ff. From their account, however, it is clear that 'stimulus control' shades over into other strategies, as when they refer to the rule 'always shop for groceries after a full meal'.

independent...When he comes to accept the new interpretation of his desire to control himself, this desire itself has altered. True, it may be said on one level to have the same goal, that he stop eating cream cake, but since it is no longer understood as a seeking for dignity and self-respect it has become quite a different kind of motivation...

Thus our descriptions of our motivations, and our attempts to formulate what we hold important, are not simply descriptions, in that their objects are not fully independent. And yet they are not simply arbitrary either, such that anything goes. There are more or less adequate, more or less truthful, more self-clairvoyant or self-deluding interpretations.[122]

Within constraints, saying makes it so: this is the important truth expressed here. In the social sciences this has been studied under the heading of self-fulfilling predictions, and Brouwer's fixed-point theorem has been invoked to show that in at least some important cases it is possible to describe the situation in a manner that takes account of the fact that the description modifies the state being described.[123] The central point of Taylor's passage, to which nothing corresponds in these studies, is that there may be several fixed points: several mutually incompatible ways of describing the situation each of which becomes true by virtue of being asserted. There are, of course, constraints that prevent any description from being a self-fulfilling one. These presumably correspond to higher-order character traits, and as such must be subject to the thesis that saying makes it so, within further constraints, and so on. Asserting 'This is how I am' is part description, part discovery, and part creation.

The Aristotelian and the Sartrian approaches supplement each other rather than contradict each other, at least if we are willing to attribute more importance to the constraints than Sartre himself does. The strategy of precommitment can be used to realize a state that is not attainable through simple redefinition. I, for one, believe that the constraints limiting the self-fulfilling descriptions are very strong, and become increasingly so when we go from the first-order description of the character traits to the higher-order descriptions of the first-order constraints. Anyone, however, admitting that there are *some* limits to the principle that

[122] C. Taylor (1976), p. 295; also C. Taylor (1971) makes the same point.
[123] Cp. n. 25 above. For a recent discussion, with full references to the economic and sociological literature, see Brams (1976), ch. 3. As far as I know there have been no attempts to link these issues to the analogous problems that arise in psychology, though the notion of *reflective equilibrium* elaborated by John Rawls (1971) could be interpreted in terms of fixed-point reasoning.

saying makes it so, must give *some* scope to the devices for binding oneself. The picture that can be seen both as a duck and as a rabbit, but not as both simultaneously, can serve as an analogy here.[124] The lines in the picture serve as a constraint for how the picture can be seen, but adding an extra line can change this constraint in what may be a drastic manner. Here the 'act' of switching from duck-vision to rabbit-vision corresponds to a redefinition of the situation, and the act of adding an extra line to the strategy of precommitment. Responsibility for self includes both types of action. (In IV.3 redefinition of self through a redefined other serves as one of the starting points for an analysis of love, and in IV.4 the same notions are brought to bear on the analysis of self-deception.)

In conclusion I would like to mention two disturbing problems to which I see no easy solutions. The first can be summed up in a phrase from William James, to the effect that 'the *highest* ethical life...consists at all times in the breaking of rules which have grown too narrow for the actual case'.[125] The lowest form of ethical life is presumably total and myopic impulsiveness. At a higher level is the life according to self-imposed rules or strategies of precommitment; and at the very highest level the deliberate breach of these rules when, all things considered, this seems justified. In order to see more clearly where the problem lies in this analysis, we may distinguish between five senses of 'action not governed by rules':

(1) Actions performed by a person lacking the concept of a rule
(2) Actions performed by a person who typically acts according to rules, but who either
  (a) fails to follow the rule in a particular case or
  (b) decides to break the rule in a particular case
(3) Actions performed by a person who has decided never to act according to rules and who either
  (a) has never followed the rules or
  (b) has followed the rules and decided to abandon them altogether

To see the relevance of these distinctions, consider the problem of free v. bound verse. Most poets writing bound verse would argue, I think, that this is a self-imposed and necessary limitation, and that the boundless freedom of free verse is destructive rather

---

[124] I owe this interpretation of Sartre to Dagfinn Føllesdal.
[125] Quoted after Ainslie (1977), p. 38, who also refers to the requirement of 'tolerance of ambiguity' as the mark of an adult person.

than creative. Only by restricting the infinitely large set of possible statements to the more manageable (but still very large) subset of statements satisfying the formal requirements of rhyme and meter can the poet create the setting where he can exercise his gift of choosing between such statements. The strict form of the sonnet permits the poet to 'put Chaos into fourteen lines and keep him there';[126] and a similar notion no doubt lies behind the feat recently performed by George Perec in writing a whole novel where the letter 'e' is nowhere used.

Against this classic line many other stances are possible. Some would argue that in order to write free verse one should have mastered the technique of bound verse (case 3b), and they would greet with scepticism the brand of poet who claimed the ability to dispense with this mastery (case 3a). Writers of both these persuasions would agree, however, that poetry is essentially different from mere talk (case 1), and that rules – if rules there be – should be mastered completely (unlike case (2a), corresponding to weakness of will). The most complex position would be that the highest poetical life is achieved by bound verse broken by the occasional regularity when it is required. It *is* important to bind oneself, to escape from the abyss of possibilities unlimited, but equally important to have a feeling for the occasions when perfection demands liberty of movement unfettered by rules, as in case (2b).[127] This last attitude would also seem to capture the idea expressed by William James, though case (3b) might also be a possible interpretation.

In the ethical, as distinct from the aesthetic case, the main problem is how to distinguish between cases (2a) and (2b); how to distinguish between breaking the rules for good reasons and breaking them for bad reasons. How can we know – and how can other people know – if a given piece of impulsive (not rule-governed) behaviour belongs to the highest or the lowest level of the mind? Exceptions recognized in advance as exceptions present no problems. What we want is a criterion for what *would have been* recognized in advance as a legitimate exception if the issue had been raised. Ainslie suggests[128] that in such cases we need *a bright*

---

[126] Edna St Vincent Millay (1975), Sonnet clxviii.

[127] 'Is there any keener joy·for a writer rigorously trained in artistic discipline, or for a borderline Protestant like Gide or Eliot, than becoming reverently conscious of strict rules which he may some day delight in breaking?' (Peyre 1967, p. 227).

[128] Ainslie (1977), p. 23 and *passim.*

line (or a focal point) in our inner space to tell us if a given exception is an *ad hoc* rationalization or a genuine one. Internalization of parental norms might be important here, in order to achieve this ideal of *control without rigidity.*

The problem can also be seen from the point of view of the person who has the task of binding us: under what conditions should he release us from the mast when we beg him to? Derek Parfit has constructed the following example:

> Let us take a nineteenth-century Russian who, in several years, should inherit vast estates. Because he has socialist ideals, he intends, now, to give the land to the peasants. But he knows that in time his ideals may fade. To guard against this possibility, he does two things. He first signs a legal document, which will automatically give away the land, and which can only be revoked with his wife's consent. He then says to his wife, 'If I ever change my mind, and ask you to revoke the document, promise me that you will not consent.' He might add, 'I regard my ideals as essential to me. If I lose these ideals, I want you to think that *I* cease to exist. I want you to regard your husband, then, not as me, the man who asks you for this promise, but only as his later self. Promise me that you would not do what he asks.'[129]

Parfit then goes on to argue that on one plausible way of thinking, 'she can never be released from her commitment. For the self to whom she is committed would, in trying to release her, cease to exist.'[130] This ingenious variation on the theme of *Catch 22* (of which more in III.9) does not, perhaps, carry total convincing power. It raises the same ethical questions as the obligation to keep deathbed promises, with some added complications of its own. These, however, are difficult matters, and not really germane to our problem. Instead of constructing a case of several successive selves, as in Parfit's example, we should imagine a situation where several selves coexist simultaneously and hierarchically, representing the lowest, the intermediate and the highest forms of ethical life as defined above. The question then is how other persons can pick out the authorized spokesman for the hierarchy; how they can decide whether the revocation of an order is issued by the lowest or the highest self. Other individuals have no direct access to *our* bright lines. Parfit seems to think that one should never give in, say, to a person begging me to give him the cigarettes he has begged me to withhold from him,[131] but this is to beg the very question raised by Ainslie and James, which is that sometimes I may have good reasons for asking to be released, in

---

[129] Parfit (1973), p. 145.   [130] *Ibid.* p. 146.   [131] *Ibid.* p. 145.

the sense of reasons that I would have accepted before I asked to be bound.

The second problem is even more murky. It concerns the spectre of infinite regress that must arise as soon as we introduce the notion of self-manipulation. We have discussed several cases of three-tiered selves, and in principle there seems to be no reason why this could not be extended to any number of levels. It is true that the number three crops up very often, and that plausible four-level cases are hard to construct. (Freud's trinity of id, ego and superego would correspond roughly to the lowest, highest and intermediate forms of ethical life respectively.)[132] Nevertheless the logical possibility of a hierarchy with indefinitely many levels is a disturbing one, and it is hard to know what to answer a person begging not to be released in the following terms: 'The rule-governed self that now speaks to you is one level above, and not one level below, that splendidly arrogant self who, invoking the Jamesian notion of the highest ethical life, begged you to release him. I grant you that this disrespect for rules is justified in the case of my neurotic and rigid superego, but not in the case of the moral rules that I adopt on the grounds of the categorical imperative and in the light of pure reason.' And – going from the point of view of the observer to that of the actor – can I *really* be sure that James's notion is not a temptation which I should resist? How can I know that my bright line is not constantly displacing itself 'behind my back' so as to justify, *ex post facto*, any exception to the rule?[133]

[132] Ainslie (1977), p. 38.

[133] For an example where many readers will recognize themselves, I quote from Arthur Stinchcombe (private correspondence): 'A problem along the same line I have thought about is the problem of judging research productivity of young scholars. Suppose that different people have an expected productivity of major innovations, so that a distinguished scientist might expect one major innovation every five years. But under those circumstances distinguished scientists might easily go ten years with routine work, while one with an expected major innovation every twenty years may be lucky enough to have his during his first five years. The question is whether you can so set up the system as to recognize or predict your mistakes. For instance, the Oxford common room may be a better predictive criterion than actual accomplishment. I recall that Whitehead recommended Russell for a fellowship over a higher-scoring candidate on a fellowship examination. The point here is that a norm to keep yourself universalistic may sometimes increase, rather than decrease your risks of error. I don't really believe it for this case, having made my mistakes often enough on both grounds. The argument reminds me of the one Claude Bernard argues so effectively against, of "clinical intuition". Maybe if you could fill universities with Whiteheads, and yet keep them from being corrupted by their powers and vanities; but in this world I doubt if that could come about, and binding oneself to performance universalism against your own clinical judgment of "deep science", is probably rational.'

I have no idea that would count as a solution to this problem, but I have a hunch about the lines along which a solution is most likely to emerge. We should invoke, I believe, an analogy from game theory, where the apparently infinite regress of 'I think that he thinks that I think...' does not prevent a game from having a unique and predictable solution, even in the absence of dominant strategies.[134] This approach is advocated, for example, by Harry Frankfurt in a well-known contribution to this debate.[135] I am not sure that I understand his arguments for, or indeed his version of, this solution, but I believe that this general kind of analysis offers some solid hope of escape. Perhaps one could appeal to fixed-point reasoning, in order to prove that for every person (or for some persons only?) there exists a level beyond which the preference structure repeats itself identically? I am fully aware that this suggestion is both extremely obscure and, to the extent that it is at all intelligible, pregnant with new problems, but I propose to leave the question at this point.

As a last word I would like to repeat a point made in the discussion of criterion (iv) in II.2. A full characteristic of what it means to be human should include at least three features. Man can be *rational*, in the sense of deliberately sacrificing present gratification for future gratification. Man often is not rational, and rather exhibits *weakness of will*. Even when not rational, man knows that he is irrational and can *bind himself* to protect himself against the irrationality. This second-best or imperfect rationality takes care both of reason and of passion. What is lost, perhaps, is the sense of adventure.

---

[134] There are, of course, games where the regress is a real one, so that there is no (non-cooperative) solution to the game; see III.2 below for a discussion of this issue.

[135] 'It is possible, however, to terminate such a series of acts without cutting it off arbitrarily. When a person identifies himself *decisively* with one of his first-order desires, this commitment "resounds" throughout the potentially endless array of higher orders" (Frankfurt 1971, p. 16). I believe that this 'resonance effect' should be taken as a *definition* of what it means to commit oneself decisively, and not as an effect of such commitment. In other words I cannot agree with Frankfurt when he goes on to say that 'It is relatively unimportant whether we explain this by saying that this commitment implicitly generates an endless series of confirming desires of higher orders, or by saying that the commitment is tantamount to a dissolution of the pointedness of all questions concerning higher orders of desire.'

III

PROBLEMATIC RATIONALITY: SOME
UNRESOLVED PROBLEMS IN THE THEORY OF
RATIONAL BEHAVIOUR

III.1 INTRODUCTION

The 'rational-choice' approach to human behaviour is without much doubt the best available model, but many problems concerning its scope and resolving power remain to be settled. In this chapter I present what amounts essentially to a list of such problems. It is not a survey of unresolved problems in the sense of Hilbert's 1900 address,[1] but a discussion of anomalies or 'critical points' in the sense of Oskar Morgenstern's 1972 article.[2] That is, I do not imply that these are well-defined questions to which there are at present no answers; rather that the issues

---

[1] At the Second International Congress of Mathematics in 1900 David Hilbert presented a list of twenty-three unsolved mathematical problems, of which some have since been solved, others have been shown to be unsolvable and still others remain unsolved. See also Reid (1970).

[2] Morgenstern (1972). These 'critical points' are the following. (1) Control of economic variables. By this Morgenstern refers to the problem of parametric v. strategic rationality, discussed in III.2. (2) Revealed preference theory. (3) Pareto optimum. Morgenstern does not believe that this notion permits us to avoid interpersonal comparisons of utilities; see also Morgenstern (1964). (4) Tâtonnement. Morgenstern joins the many authors who have criticized this fiction of general-equilibrium economics. (5) The Walras–Pareto Fixation. Here Morgenstern refers to the economist's obsession with free competition, which in Morgenstern's view is only a limiting case of no particular interest. (6) Allocation of resources. Here Morgenstern criticizes the economic profession for neglecting the impact of politics upon price formation and allocation. (7) Substitution. Here Morgenstern shows that in some cases the notion of a rate of substitution between goods in production is not defined. (8) Demand and supply. This section contains a critique of the notion of aggregate demand. (9) Indifference-curve analysis. Here Morgenstern shows that the notion of closed indifference curves harbours a contradiction. Other difficulties are also treated. (10) Theory of the firm. This is in part (as are also many of the other points) a restatement of (1) above. (11) Back to Cantillon. This is a plea for disaggregation (12) Personal and functional distribution. This is a criticism of marginal productivity theory, and a plea for the use of game-theoretical analysis. (13) Theory relevance. This section shows the inverse correlation between the empirical importance of economic phenomena and the intensity with which they are studied.

themselves are ill defined and the proposed solutions heavily dependent upon *ad hoc* assumptions. What is lost in conceptual clarity by these solutions often exceeds what is gained in technical tidiness.[3]

There is, perhaps, no alternative theory that can be singled out as *the* main competitor to the rational-choice model. A very general and abstract theory of action will permit us to distinguish between the main contenders. Any given piece of human behaviour may be seen as the end product of two successive filtering devices. The first is defined by the set of structural constraints which cuts down the set of abstractly possible courses of action and reduces it to the vastly smaller subset of feasible actions. The constraints are assumed to be given and not within the control of the agents; the reader is referred to the preceding chapter for the case of self-imposed constraints. The second filtering process is the mechanism that singles out which member of the feasible set shall be realized. Rational-choice theories assert that this mechanism is the deliberate and intentional choice for the purpose of maximizing some objective function, be it a real one (like profit) or a purely notional one (like the utility function representing preferences).

This two-step model immediately suggests two alternatives to the rational-choice approach. The first is the line of argument which I shall call Structuralist, denying the *importance* of rational choice, and indeed of the second filter in general, and asserting instead the all-importance of the structural constraints. In an extreme version this would mean that the constraints jointly have the effect of cutting down the feasible set to a single point; in a weaker and more plausible version that the constraints define a set which is so small that the formal freedom of choice within the set does not amount to much. Both Structuralism in Anglo-American social science[4] and Structuralism as a French methodological

---

[3]   'The only legitimate pejorative sense of "adhocness" reduces to a situation in which a theory's overall problem-solving effectiveness decreases, by virtue of its increasing conceptual difficulties' (Laudan 1977, p. 117; italics deleted).

[4]   As a representative example the following text may be cited: '...the structuralist would emphasize the bounding of political activity by social structure (including class) and values (including ideology). The behaviorist would emphasize political decision making within these bounds. The structuralist would study the fence around the cattle; the behaviorist would study the activity of the cattle within the bounds of the fence' (McFarland 1969, p. 135). There are some ambiguities here. I believe one should be

school[5] can with some effort be fitted into this definition. As a general theory of action it seems to me too obviously wrong to merit much discussion. At particular times and places the constellations of constraints may have been such as to exclude all but a very small subset of the possible actions, but for this to be generally true there would have to be some mechanism to bring it about, and in the Structuralist literature I have never come across any attempt to provide this. It is no doubt true that the ruling classes in most societies have tried to consolidate their rule by reducing the set of opportunities open to the oppressed classes, but this very statement implies that the ruling classes themselves were acting freely and rationally in their own interest.

Before going on to the second alternative, which is by far the most important, I would like to point to a more interesting version of the first alternative. Even if behaviour in any given case must be explained by the two-filter theory, one could argue that only the first filter is relevant for the analysis of *differences* in behaviour. One could argue, that is, that people's preferences and motivations are much the same at all times and places, so that differences in observed behaviour must be explained by differences in the opportunity set. Preferences, so to speak, cancel out, leaving the

rather hesitant in accepting the idea that *values* are constraints; they belong to the second filter rather than to the first. (An exception is lexicographically dominant values, discussed in III.3.) I also diverge from this view in that I conceive of Structuralism as theoretical rather than methodological. The Structuralist, on my definition, is not someone who *decides* to study the fence around the cattle rather than the movements within the fence, but someone who *asserts* that the cattle have very little freedom of movement within the fence.

5   As a representative text the following may be cited: 'La résistance que suscite la sociologie lorsqu'elle prétend déposséder l'expérience immédiate de son privilège gnoséologique s'inspire de la même philosophie humaniste de l'action humaine que certaine sociologie qui, en s'armant par example de concepts comme celui de "motivation" ou en s'attachant par prédilection aux questions de *decision-making*, réalise, à sa manière, le vœu naïf de tout sujet social: entendant rester maître et possesseur de lui-même et de sa propre vérité, ne voulant connaître d'autre déterminisme que celui de ses propres déterminations (même s'il leur concède l'inconscience), l'humaniste naïf qu'il y a en tout homme ressent comme une réduction "sociologiste" ou "matérialiste" toute tentative pour établir que le sens des actions les plus personnelles et les plus "transparentes" n'appartient pas au sujet qui les accomplit mais au système complet des relations dans lesquelles et par lesquelles elles s'accomplissent' (Bourdieu *et al.* 1968, p. 39). The rhetorical murkiness of this passage (representative in this respect as well) makes it difficult to say whether it states that the constraints are so strong as to make the choice unimportant; that the second filter operates through a mechanism other than that of rational choice; or that rational choice according to consistent preferences is uninteresting compared to the social process that generates and internalizes these preferences.

structural constraints with all explanatory power. For an illustration, take the variety of approaches to investment in precapitalist societies. Was the lack of investment due to a dearth of investment *objects*, as argued for example by Douglass North and Robert Thomas,[6] or to the absence of the *motivation* to invest, as argued by Eugene Genovese?[7] In general I believe that the economists, by some variety of Occam's razor, tend to assume that preferences are mostly similar across time and space,[8] whereas historians and sociologists are governed by their fear of committing anachronisms and imputing to premodern societies the preference patterns characteristic of their own. I do not believe this emphasis on constraints should be referred to as Structuralist, and it does not really represent an alternative to the rational-choice theory. Nevertheless it justifies an assertion to the effect that variance in behaviour is to be explained through the variance in opportunities, which is to some extent a downgrading of the rational-actor approach.

The second alternative, to which most of this chapter is devoted, questions the *reality* of rational choice and asserts that the mechanism singling out one member of the feasible set is a causal rather than an intentional one. This alternative comes in two versions. The most radical one asserts that in a number of cases the notion of rational behaviour is not even well defined; there simply is no uniquely prescribed action that a rational actor would choose. In III.2 and III.3 this case is argued for the important category of games without a non-cooperative solution; in III.5 for the situations where rationality leads to the infinite regress already discussed in II.4; and in III.9 for the contradictory mental attitudes that are more fully discussed in chapter IV. The less radical version accepts (or is non-committal about) the existence of a well-defined notion of rational behaviour, but argues that in some cases this ideal is not realized. In III.6 random behaviour and traditional behaviour are singled out as the two main sub-cases of this approach. In III.5 I also discuss a particular aspect of the

6   North and Thomas (1973), p. 62 and *passim*.
7   Genovese (1965), pp. 16–17.
8   See Harsanyi (1955) and Stigler and Becker (1977). There is a paradox here, that the staunchest defenders of the rational-actor approach should propose a theory having the undeniable effect of downgrading the importance of choice as compared to opportunities.

traditional-behaviour model, viz. the question of how the tradition is set up in the first place. The emergence of tradition through natural selection, or of a social analogy to that process, is the main mechanism that has been proposed. (Readers of chapter I will appreciate that even if this model were valid in some particular case, there would be no presumption that it could simulate rational choice.)

To these alternatives we may add a third, viz. the approach that denies the *stability* of rational choice, and that emphasizes the formation and the transformation of preferences. This issue was discussed at some length in II.6, and in III.8 I only return to the problem to make some additional points that are relevant for the present discussion. The comments upon subjective probability in III.4 also are relevant here, as I believe that the rational-choice theories based upon this notion (i.e. Bayesian decision theory) overestimate the stability of the probabilities that can be elicited by the standard methods.

I also discuss some of the traditional objections to rationality that are not often heard today, but that nevertheless retain some force. In III.3 the notion of lexicographic preferences – being the standard counterexample to the possibility of representing preferences by a utility function – is briefly discussed from the points of view of social anthropology and game theory. In III.7 the notion of altruism – being the standard counterexample to the self-interest interpretation of rationality – is equally sketchily approached from the points of view of biology, economics and sociology. Now we all know that rational-choice theory does not depend upon representability of preferences or upon egoistic motivations; nevertheless I believe that the formal solutions to these problems do not completely do away with the underlying substantial questions.

I conclude by arguing that even if rationality often is unimportant, or absent, or unstable, there is a hard core of important cases where the rational-choice model is indispensable. I argue, furthermore, that this model is logically prior to the alternatives, in the sense that the social scientist should always be guided by a postulate of rationality, even if he may end by finding it violated in many particular cases. This presumption is a 'principle of charity' similar to the one often used in textual interpretation. One should never take textual contradictions at their face value, but consider whether the context might not give a clue to consistency. Similarly one should always look very closely at apparently irrational behaviour to see whether there could not be some pattern there after all. Needless to say, charity should not be stretched too far, and there may come a point where the observer simply has to state that to the best of his understanding the behaviour has no rational motive.

III.2   GAMES WITHOUT SOLUTIONS

In this section I draw a distinction between parametric and strategic rationality.[9] Parametric rationality usually leads to a unique and well-defined prescription for behaviour, given the initial assumptions and expectations. The problem here is that these assumptions and expectations may themselves be irrational, because founded upon a naive belief about a constant (or parametric) environment. In strategic rationality this belief no longer operates, and instead comes the realistic insight into the strategic nature of the environment. Here, however, another problem arises: in strategic interaction there may be no uniquely defined mode of behaviour which is singled out as *the* rational choice.

There is something strange or even contradictory in the notion of parametric rationality. A parametrically rational agent believes himself to be free to adjust optimally (given his end) to a constant environment, and at the same time he can hardly fail to have some awareness of the fact that this environment is made up in part of other agents similar to himself. He could, of course, assume that the others are trying to adjust optimally to what looks to *them* like a constant environment, and then adjust optimally to their optimal adjustments. This, for example, is the strategy referred to as the Stackelberg solution in the duopoly problem.[10] It is clear, however, that this only makes the same paradox appear at a higher level. The contradiction can only be eliminated by transition to the strategic or game-theoretic mode of thinking. The strategically

---

[9]   In the history of science these approaches can be associated with the names of Max Weber and John von Neumann respectively.
[10]   See Coddington (1968), pp. 58ff; also Elster (1978a), ch. 5.

rational actor sees himself as a player in a game, which in the ideal case is defined by perfect information in the sense that all players have full knowledge about each other's preferences and knowledge. No one can then assume himself to be a step ahead of the others, and everyone has to take account of the fact that everyone takes account of everyone else before making his decision. This sounds like an infinite regress, but as was observed at the end of chapter II it is possible, through the notion of an *equilibrium point*, to short-circuit the regress and arrive at a uniquely defined solution for the game. An equilibrium point is a set of individual strategies each of which is optimal against the others. In other words, $(s_1 \ldots s_n)$ is an equilibrium point if for all i s_i is player i's best answer to $(s_1 \ldots s_{i-1}, s_{i+1} \ldots s_n)$. (I shall return shortly to a crucial ambiguity in the word 'best' here.)

The notion of parametric rationality, whatever its shortcomings, has at least the advantage that it is usually well defined. There are, certainly, maximization problems without solution, as when the objective function is discontinuous or the feasible set not compact. An important case is the non-existence of optimal plans in certain problems of planning for an infinite horizon.[11] In most applications, however, the assumption of a constant environment generates a unique action which is *the* rational thing to do, or at least a set of actions which are equally and maximally good. These actions may turn out to be self-defeating, if based upon assumptions about other agents that are incompatible with these agents' assumptions about themselves, but at any rate they are well defined. Strategic rationality in this respect is much more problematic, given the pervasive importance of games without a non-cooperative solution. In this section I discuss two categories of such games: variable-sum games without equilibrium points and variable-sum with several equilibrium points, none of which can be singled out as the solution. In III.3 a third category is mentioned, the constant-sum games without a von Neumann–Morgenstern solution.

A simple game without an equilibrium point is the following: 'Each player writes down a number. The player who has written the largest number receives from each of the other players a sum of money equal to the difference between the largest number and

[11]   Heal (1973), ch. 13, has a good discussion; cp. also ch. II, n. 62 above.

the number written down by that player.' It is intuitively clear, and can be proved easily,[12] that in this *fuite en avant* there can be no equilibrium point. The economics of hyperinflation may perhaps be understood as a game of this general form. In this case there is no equilibrium point because the strategy set is not compact, and the phenomenon probably is no more important than the cases where parametric rationality also fails to define a uniquely characterized behaviour.

Much more important are the no-solution games where there are *several* equilibrium points. John Harsanyi has recently offered a powerful analysis of this problem,[13] claiming that a solution can in fact be defined for all non-cooperative games. It is not possible to enter here into the details of his argument, but some critical observations may be offered. First, and most obviously, his solution concept does not satisfy the ordinary requirements of rational behaviour for at least some types of games. In fact, for a game such as the following Harsanyi argues that the players should use their maximin strategies, even if these are not optimal against each other:

	B_1	B_2
A_1	30, 20	20, 0
A_2	40, 0	10, 30

Commenting upon this argument, Harsanyi admits that 'it may be argued that this suggestion does not deserve to be called a "solution", because it lacks many of the desirable properties of true solutions. It may be called a "quasi-solution". One may even argue that it is just another way of saying that such games have *no* true solutions'.[14] This is indeed my opinion. The maximin strategy in such cases should not be called a rational strategy, for that would mean that if the other players are rational, then it is irrational for you to be rational. Use of the maximin strategy (or of *any* strategy) amounts to throwing up your hands and seeking a way out of the infinite regress simply because you have to *act*. The action, however, is a result of causal pressures building up and of mental fatigue, not of rational deliberation.

Secondly, and more controversially, it is not certain that Harsanyi's solution concept is satisfactory in the cases where it does

[12]   Owen (1968), p. 73.   [13]   Harsanyi (1977), chs. 7 and 14.   [14]   *Ibid.* p. 138.

pick out one equilibrium point as the solution. One of the important features of Harsanyi's book is the emphasis laid on the conceptual problems inherent in solutions involving mixed strategies. It is well known that in an equilibrium point of mixed strategies, mixed strategy s_i can never be unambiguously *the* best for player i against $(s_1 \ldots s_{i-1}, s_{i+1} \ldots s_n)$, for he will do equally well using any of the pure strategies entering in s_i, or indeed any probability mix of these pure strategies. This makes for a lack of stability of such equilibrium points that is somewhat disturbing, especially because a cautious player would rather use his maximin strategy if it ensures him the same payoff against the equilibrium strategies of the other players. Harsanyi solves this problem by singling out one strategy as privileged, viz. the *centroid* mixed strategy in which all the pure strategies have the same probability of being chosen. This implies that mixed strategies can enter into the solution to a game only if they are equiprobabilistic in this sense. This procedure is interpreted causally rather than intentionally; i.e. Harsanyi assumes that these probabilities will not be generated deliberately by a mechanical device such as flipping a coin, 'but rather by what amounts to an unconscious chance mechanism inside player i's central nervous system'.[15] In III.6 I return briefly to some of the conceptual implications of this approach. Here I shall only state that it is not at all obvious that it conforms to our intuitive notions about rationality. To bring out this point, consider the following game:

	B_1	B_2
A_1	2, 2	1, 2
A_2	2, 1	1, 1

As Harsanyi observes,[16] this is in a sense a variant of the Prisoner's Dilemma. For each player it is absolutely indifferent whether he chooses his first or his second strategy; he receives the same payoff in both cases, regardless of what the other does. He could also choose any mixed strategy with the same expected outcome. Nevertheless it is clearly to the advantage of the two players to arrive at (A_1, B_1) rather than (A_2, B_2). According to Harsanyi the centroid mixed strategy is the solution to this game, with an expected payoff of 3/2 to each player. I submit that this result is counterintuitive. The notion of a solution, surely, must be

---

[15]   *Ibid.* p. 114.   [16]   *Ibid.* pp. 278ff.

constructed so as to capture our intuitive notions about rationality; if intuition tells us that rational players would choose (A_1, B_1) and Harsanyi's theory tells us otherwise, so much worse for the theory. I do not want to be dogmatic about intuition here. In many cases our intuitions are rather shaky,[17] and then they have to conform to the theory rather than the other way around. Still there are some intuitions that are hard to give up, and I believe this to be one of them. That experimental studies[18] show the second strategies to be chosen by at least one player in about 20 per cent of the cases probably is not evidence against the reliability of this intuition. As observed by Rapoport, the defection can also be explained by assuming that for some players the difference between their own payoffs and those of the opponents also enters into the calculation, which means of course that the payoff matrix does not really reflect the utility payoffs of the players. In an experimental situation payoffs must be given in money or in similar material terms, and then there is always the possibility that interaction effects make the real payoff structure diverge from the material one. *If* the real payoff structure is as indicated in the game, I believe that choice of (A_1, B_1) is unambiguously the rational outcome, which can then serve as a constraint for all possible solution concepts.

The preceding considerations imply that in some cases at least a game-like situation offers no uniquely defined rational behaviour. Well-known cases from the game-theoretical literature are 'Chicken'[19] and 'Battle of the Sexes',[20] where a bargaining

[17]   Consider for example the following game (*ibid.* p. 287):

Player II

		B_1	B_2	B_3
Player I	A_1	6, 4	0, 0	0, 0
	A_2	0, 0	4, 6	0, 0
	A_3	0, 0	0, 0	2, 3

Here Harsanyi's theory prescribes that (A_3, B_3) be the solution. This seems well in line with some of our intuitions about the game, even if perhaps it conflicts with other intuitions. The role of conceptual analysis is to settle such borderline cases, while conforming (in the simplest possible manner) with our unshakeable intuitions. It may happen, as argued by John Rawls (1971), that before we arrive at a 'reflective equilibrium' some of our intuitions, even the ones that appeared absolutely firm, will have to be modified. I do not exclude the possibility that on further reflection Harsanyi's theory comes to look so attractive that I shall have to modify my intuition about what a rational player would do in the variant of the Prisoner's Dilemma given in the text, but at present I see no reason for doing so.

[18]   Rapoport *et al.* (1976), pp. 226–7.

[19]   Rapoport (1966), pp. 137ff; also extensively discussed in Rapoport *et al.* (1976).

[20]   Luce and Raiffa (1957), pp. 90ff, 115ff.

stalemate prevents a non-cooperative solution from emerging. An example, based on a generalized Chicken situation, may be useful at this point. In economic theory there is a well-known problem concerning the link between labour-scarcity and factor-bias in technical progress. From Marx to Hicks[21] it was taken more or less for granted that entrepreneurs have an incentive to economize on the scarce factors, not only through substitution, but also through biasing their innovations. In a justly famous contribution W. E. G. Salter[22] then showed that after substitution has taken place, all factors are equally scarce at the margin, so that entrepreneurs have no special incentive to bias their search one way rather than another. Two lines of argument were used to answer this contention. One is linked to the names of Kennedy, von Weiszäcker and Samuelson,[23] stating in essence that there are constraints on the set of possible innovations that make the bias a rational one. The other was proposed by William Fellner,[24] who argued that it was rational for entrepreneurs to bias their innovations if they expected the wage rise to continue into the future. The latter argument has been criticized by Paul David,[25] on the grounds that it neglects the importance of free riders in technical change. I will show that David's argument, when further elaborated, shows that the game played by the entrepreneurs is a game without a solution.

The reasoning behind the Marx–Hicks theory must have been roughly the following. It is beneficial for all capitalists if they all introduce labour-saving innovations, for then the aggregate demand for labour will fall, and wages accordingly. Therefore, an increase in wages may be expected to bring about labour-saving innovations so as to reduce the wages to their former level. This reasoning would have been valid if the capitalists acted as one actor, but it breaks down when applied to decentralized decisions. If all other capitalists are going to bias their innovations, the individual capitalist can act as a free rider; if they are not, his action can have only an infinitesimal impact on the wage level, assuming perfect competition. Now if the wage level is expected to rise in the future, it is rational for the individual entrepreneur to bias his search, as

[21] Esp. Hicks (1932), p. 129.
[22] Salter (1960), pp. 43–4.
[23] Notably Kennedy (1964).
[24] Fellner (1961).
[25] David (1975), pp. 36 n. 2, 54.

argued by Fellner, because this will enable him to preempt future wage rises to some extent. The question, however, is why the entrepreneur should have these expectations. The only rational basis for such expectations must be that the other entrepreneurs are not going to bias their search, but rather will go on acting as before; i.e. an assumption about a parametric environment. This assumption, however, can hardly be called rational. In any case, the entrepreneur will quickly unlearn this assumption when it turns out that wages go down rather than up, because all entrepreneurs – and not only himself – have introduced labour-saving innovations. The next step may either be that no one introduces this bias because everyone expects the others to do so, or that they all finally realize that the situation is a strategic one. In the latter case we have a generalized case of Chicken: if everyone else introduces labour-saving innovations, then it is rational for the individual not to do so, but if no one else does so, then it is in his interest to do so.

In this situation, as explained above, there is no behaviour that is *the* rational one, at least not if we are talking about strategic rather than parametric rationality. As long as the entrepreneurs believe that they are, each and individually, acting in an environment of other entrepreneurs who must go on acting as they did last year, then the notion of individually rational behaviour – given this belief – makes sense. The belief itself, however, is not a very sensible one. And as soon as the belief is supplanted by the more rational insight into the strategic and symmetric nature of the situation, the notion of rational choice simply evaporates and guessing has to take over.

I submit, then, that such games without solution constitute a deep anomaly in the theory of rational behaviour. If all games had a non-cooperative solution, then the strategically rational actor would be the perfect incarnation of the Leibnizian monad. He would be 'windowless', in the sense of not being able to communicate with others, and nevertheless his point of view on the universe would reflect and internalize all other points of view in a harmonious whole. The fact that such tacit coordination or preestablished harmony is not always possible, and that some choices *cannot* be made by the rational self, has implications for philosophy, psychology and the social sciences in general.

III.3   LEXICOGRAPHIC PREFERENCES

This preference structure is the standard counterexample that shows that not all transitive and complete preference orderings can be represented by a real-valued utility function. A vector $(a_1 \ldots a_n)$ is lexicographically preferred to another $(b_1 \ldots b_n)$ if and only if for some i, $a_i > b_i$ and for all $j < i$, $a_j = b_j$. An implication of this definition is that for all $j > i$, the relation between a_j and b_j is quite irrelevant to the evaluation of the vectors. In particular b_j can be vastly larger than a_j for all $j > i$, and nevertheless the vector **a** will be lexicographically preferred to **b** if a_i is slightly larger than b_i and $a_j = b_j$ for $i < j$. Or, in other words, for each i, the ith component of the vector is incomparably more important than the $i+1$'th one, so that there can be no trade-offs between the two. It is well known that this preference structure cannot be represented by an ordinal utility function,[26] nor by a von Neumann–Morgenstern one.[27] The last fact also has implications for game theory. The minimax theorem stating that all finite zero-sum games have a solution in mixed strategies crucially assumes that preferences are represented by utility functions that are unique up to a positive linear transformation. One might conjecture, therefore, that if the players have non-representable preferences, the zero-sum game may be without a solution. Peter Fishburn[28] has shown that this is indeed the case. To be precise, he has demonstrated that in zero-sum games with lexicographic preferences there are (1) cases where player I has a maximin strategy and player II a minimax strategy, but these are not optimal against each other and (2) cases where neither player has a maximin or minimax strategy. The last case is illustrated by the following game, where payoffs to player I are represented by three-dimensional lexicographic preferences:

[26]   See e.g. Luce and Suppes (1965), pp. 261ff.
[27]   Riker and Ordeshook (1973), pp. 37ff. We may note here that if the number of alternatives is a finite one, the preferences can always be represented by an ordinal utility function, whereas lexicographic preferences cannot be represented cardinally even in this case. For this reason the impossibility of cardinal representation is perhaps the more interesting of these theorems. We can also observe that lexicographic orderings are perhaps more frequent in political life than in economic life; see again Riker and Ordeshook (1973) and esp. M. Taylor (1973).
[28]   Fishburn (1973).

		Player II		
		s_1	s_2	s_3
Player I	t_1	1, 0, 0	0, 0, 0	0, 1, 1
	t_2	0, 0, 0	0, 1, 1	0, 1, 0

Assuming that I chooses t_1 and t_2 with probabilities a and $(1-a)$, and that II chooses s_1, s_2, s_3 with probabilities p, q, r, then the expected three-dimensional payoff to I is $(ap,\ r+\ (1-a)q,\ ar+(1-a)q)$. If $a=0$, then the worst that can happen to I is $(0, 0, 0)$, namely if II sets $p=1$, $r=q=0$. If $a>0$, then the worst possible outcome for I is $(0,\ 1-a,\ 1-a)$, for $p=r=0$, $q=1$. But this means that I cannot choose a so as to maximize this minimum outcome. For any positive a there is a smaller guaranteeing him a better minimum, but going to the limit and equating a to 0 does not give the best minimum.

What is the substantial importance of these formal results? It is easy, and to some extent justified, to dismiss them out of hand as irrelevant for the theory of rational behaviour. To my knowledge no one has yet offered an interesting example of a real-life zero-sum game with lexicographic preferences, and in any case they do not seem to offer any paradoxes that are not also found in parametrically rational agents with discontinuous objective functions or non-compact feasible sets. As for the non-representability of the preferences, this does not show that lexicographically governed behaviour cannot be made amenable to rational-choice analysis, only that this analysis cannot use the handy tool of the utility function. Nevertheless some substantial issues can be discerned behind the clouds of confusion that seem to arise in the discussion of these matters.

The first concerns the interpretation of lexicographically prior values as constraints on the decision-making rather than criteria for decision-making. We can say, of course, that at subsistence level calories are lexicographically more important than taste,[29] but a more natural interpretation may often be to say that the calorie

[29] Georgescu-Roegen (1954).

constraint should be added to the budget constraint for the definition of the feasible set. This lends some strength to the argument that rational choice may be *unimportant* and that the structural constraints defining the feasible set are more crucial. The Marxist aversion to theories of the consumer's choice can in part be explained by the fact that Marx wrote at a time when the budget constraint and the calorie constraint jointly had the effect of narrowing down the feasible set to a very small subset indeed, even though regional variations in consumption during the Industrial Revolution showed that it was possible to live at subsistence level in several different ways. [30] (The aversion in part can also be explained by the Marxist assumption that consumer preferences under capitalism are highly manipulable and thus *unstable*.)

The second issue is more important. It concerns the relation between 'rational behaviour' and 'economic behaviour'. Two opposed views may be quoted on this topic:

I have come to believe that the economic approach is a comprehensive one that is applicable to all human behavior, be it behavior involving money prices or imputed shadow prices, repeated or infrequent decisions, large or minor decisions, emotional or mechanical ends, rich or poor persons, men or women, adults or children, brilliant or stupid persons, patients or therapists, businessmen or politicians, teachers or students.[31]

A basic assumption... is that some kind of 'trade-off' will always be possible. Formally we can express this by assuming the so-called *Axiom of Archimedes*. This means in our example that if we have

$$(x_1, y_1) \text{ preferred to } (x_2, y_2)$$

we can always reverse the preference by increasing y_2; i.e. there exists a $y > y_2$ such that

$$(x_2, y) \text{ preferred to } (x_1, y_1).$$

This means that a loss of some units of one commodity can always be compensated by a gain of some units of another commodity or, to put it another way, *everything has its price*. It may be tempting to define economics as the science of things which have a price, in a very general sense. Questions of life and death and ethical principles like an absolute aversion to gambling would then be considered as belonging to the more general social sciences.[32]

I submit that the second view is the more reasonable one, precisely because of the fact of non-Archimedean preferences (of

[30]   A. J. Taylor (1960); for the implications of this fact for the labour theory of value, see Morishima and Seton (1961) and Elster (1978c).
[31]   Becker (1976), p. 8.   [32]   Borch (1968), p. 22.

which the lexicographic preference is a special case). When the Archimedean criterion is not satisfied, we are dealing with goods or activities which are in a sense non-comparable and do not lend themselves to the economic approach. This, of course, does not mean that they are unamenable to rational analysis. The failure of the economic approach to explain some forms of behaviour does not imply that we must invoke structural constraints, tradition, natural selection or chance; there can be rational non-economic behaviour. I believe that some controversial issues in social anthropology can be usefully restated in this framework. The debate of 'substantive' versus 'formal' definitions of economics[33] can be interpreted as a discussion of non-Archimedean versus Archimedean preferences. Where preferences have the Archimedean property, we can talk as if people maximize utility along a single dimension; otherwise the hierarchy of values must be explicitly recognized. The discussion of 'economic spheres'[34] is also related to this problem. When exchange is organized in hierarchically arranged spheres with different media of exchange, we are dealing with a non-Archimedean system. For a similar example from our own societies, medals are supposed to be 'without a price'.

The question can be raised whether these hierarchies exist in reality or in ideology only. Fredrik Barth argues that the economic spheres are not so watertight as they may appear to be,[35] and in our own societies it is well known that at least some honorific distinctions are for sale unofficially. (An important exception are military honours. 'Je ne vois que la condamnation à mort qui distingue un homme, pensa Mathilde. C'est la seule chose qui ne s'achète pas.')[36] The entrepreneurial function, stressed by Barth, of facilitating movement between spheres that in the official ideology are totally separate, is probably found everywhere. Nevertheless ideologies are also part of reality, and the stealthy transfer of goods across the barriers between spheres is a very different process from the automatic flow of commodities in modern economies.

[33] See the articles collected in LeClair and Schneider (eds.) (1968).
[34] See e.g. Bohannan (1955).
[35] Barth (1967).
[36] Stendhal (1952), I, p. 489.

III.4   SUBJECTIVE PROBABILITY

The two pillars of modern decision theory are cardinal utility and subjective probability. It is certainly a formal triumph of philosophy and economics to have related these subjective notions to operational and observable criteria. By giving the subject a series of choices between risky options, it is possible to define concepts that express the cardinal utilities associated by him with certain events as well as the subjective probability with which he believes they will occur.[37] The question, of course, is whether this operation really measures what it purports to measure; whether there are distortions inherent in the procedure that prevent the techniques from being valid. I shall not here discuss the problem of cardinal utility, except to mention the standard objection that it is inappropriate that the individual's attitude towards risk should be relevant for measuring the utility he attaches to *certain* outcomes.[38] Instead I shall argue that the notion of subjective probability is less useful for a theory of rational decision-making than is argued in the Bayesian literature, and that it is often more rational to admit ignorance than to strive for a numerical quasi-precision in the measurement of belief. By setting the standards of rationality too high, irrationality may ensue.

The Bayesian approach – using subjective probabilities – to human behaviour and choice is increasingly adopted by economists and philosophers alike.[39] One of its main implications is to eliminate the maximin criterion in decisions under uncertainty (i.e. total ignorance). In the first place, we are usually told, there is no such thing as total ignorance; and in the second place the only use for the maximin criterion is in the solution to zero-sum games where the environment (i.e. the other player) can be predicted with total certainty. Instead of the maximin criterion it is then recommended that we use the expected-utility criterion, or maximize the expected utility on the basis of some probability distribution defined over the set of alternatives. Of course no one has ever denied that this is a good criterion in many cases. The novelty of the Bayesian approach is to argue that it *should* always

---

[37] Luce and Suppes (1965) give a full survey of the field.
[38] Arrow (1963), p. 10, and Sen (1970), p. 97; but see also Morgenstern (1976).
[39] Thus Harsanyi (1975), arguing against John Rawls; also Harsanyi (1977), Raiffa (1968), Keeney and Raiffa (1976).

be used because it *is* always possible to define a set of subjective probabilities that can serve as a guide for action. In this section I would like to question this step from 'is' to 'ought'.

Given an event E and an agent X it *is* always possible to design a series of questions that will elicit from X a number that can be interpreted as his subjective probability assignment to E. We start out, for example, by giving him the choice between the following options:

> O_E: If E happens, you get a reward R. If E does not happen, you get nothing
> O_1: If a red ball is drawn at random from an urn containing p_1 per cent red balls and $100 - p_1$ per cent black balls you get the reward R. If a black ball is drawn, you get nothing

Assume that X prefers O_E to O_1. Assuming that he maximizes expected utility, we must conclude that he assigns to E a subjective probability larger than p_1. We can then repeat the same experiment with O_2 instead of O_1, where O_2 differs from O_1 only in that p_1 is replaced by the probability $p_1 + e$. If the agent still prefers O_E to O_2, we place before him the choice between O_E and O_3, where the probability is $p_1 + 2e$, and so on. Sooner or later we will come to a lottery O_n which X prefers to O_E, so that his subjective probability is smaller than $p_1 + (n-1)e$. We then give him the choice between O_E and O_{n+1}, where now we use the probability $p_1 + (n - 3/2)e$. We can continue in this manner as long as desired, and define the subjective probability with any degree of precision.

This is only one and the least sophisticated of the many methods that can be used to elicit subjective probabilities or degrees of belief. Nevertheless it brings out quite well *the possibility of hysteresis*[40] which is the central point that will be raised here. How can we be sure that the final probability $\bar{p}$ is independent of the path that has led up to it; independent, that is, of the particular values of p_1 and e that were chosen? We want $\bar{p}$ to reflect nothing but (and all of) the relevant information which the individual has in his possession concerning E; in other words we want $\bar{p}$ to be a *state variable*[41] describing a certain feature of the individual at a certain moment of time. If, however, the method for measuring the value of this variable has an impact upon the value we

---

[40]   Elster (1976a).
[41]   See Fararo (1973), pp. 200ff, 487ff. The definition of a state given by system theorists (e.g. Padulo and Arbib 1974, p. 21) is too general for the present purposes; see Elster (1976a) for further discussion.

measure, then the interpretation of $\bar{p}$ must obviously be very different. In this case $\bar{p}$ also depends upon causal processes that are irrelevant from the point of view of information or of subjective belief. There is good experimental evidence that such distortions due to *anchoring* arise in many cases.[42] (In addition there are the distortions due to various forms of wishful thinking[43] as well as the subtle phenomena of self-deception, discussed in IV.4.) These results do not, of course, hinge upon a comparison between the elicited subjective probabilities and the real subjective probabilities, for the latter concept is not an operational one. Rather they turn upon comparisons between different methods for eliciting the subjective probabilities, methods which should be equivalent but nevertheless produce different evaluations.

The point is not that we should discard belief statements that are the outcome of a causal process; all belief statements are causally produced. Rather the point is that we should exclude the belief statements that are generated by *belief-irrelevant* causal processes, i.e. causal processes where the causes include not only *reasons*, but also irrelevant causal factors such as mental fatigue (which is greater the lower is p_1 and the smaller is e), a preference for symmetry (why not 50 per cent?) or an aversion to symmetry (surely 50 per cent is too simplistic). In II.3 I discussed in some detail a case of such belief-irrelevant causal processes leading up to belief formation, namely Pascal's wager. One of the points made there was that we should not hold to or act upon a belief if we suspect it to be the result of such belief-irrelevant processes. If I have a periodic tendency to hallucinate *and I know this*, then I should take care not to act as if my beliefs were true. (Or if the hallucinations go together with a lack of judgment in this respect, I should take care beforehand to be prevented from acting upon them.) I submit that much the same holds for the subjective probabilities elicited by procedures such as the one specified above. I further submit that no method for improving upon this procedure could avoid this difficulty. Sophistication is generally of little avail here, as indicated above: if we point out to a subject his irrational or irrelevant preference for symmetry, he may replace it by an equally distorting aversion to symmetry.

[42]   Tversky and Kahneman (1974), pp. 1128ff.
[43]   See in particular Janis and Mann (1977).

Among the decision theorists who have espoused partially similar views one should especially cite William Fellner.[44] He argues that if the subjective probabilities are interpersonally controversial or intrapersonally unstable it may be rational to slant them in one direction or the other in order to avoid or reduce the regret and self-recrimination that can follow from acting upon such probabilities. The questions then arise, how much slanting and for what reasons? If the reasons are as adduced above, that 'the degree of calibration depends on the procedure of elicitation',[45] then there is no argument for stopping short of complete conservatism and use of the maximin criterion. This, however, is not what Fellner has in mind. If the reasons are that we are faced with an irreversible decision, Claude Henry has shown that it may be rational not to act upon the current estimate of the subjective probabilities, even assuming that they are not distorted by hysteresis.[46] Nothing that specific, however, is found in Fellner's argument. His reason simply seems to be the avoidance of the subjective discomfort that may be felt when we are proved wrong in the *ex post facto* sense. It is of course well known that bureaucrats and other decision-makers may be biased in their decision by this mechanism, because the blame attaching to a wrong guess is so much larger than the praise given for a right one. I strongly doubt, however, whether this is a practice that should be encouraged.

From these generally sceptical remarks several conclusions can be drawn. One possibility is to advocate the use of maximin reasoning in such cases. If I do not trust my subjective probabilities and if I have no theoretical foundation for a procedure that could correct my elicited probabilities so as to bring them closer to my 'real subjective probabilities', nor for a procedure that could define an interval within which these real probabilities are to be found, then surely I am in a state of total and genuine ignorance and should adopt the maximin criterion or one of the other criteria consistent with the Arrow–Hurwicz characterization of total ignorance.[47] The currently debated issues of nuclear power

[44]   Fellner (1965).
[45]   Tversky and Kahneman (1974), p. 1130.   [46]   Henry (1974).
[47]   Arrow and Hurwicz (1972); also Luce and Raiffa (1957), pp. 296ff. The characterization implies that only the best possible and the worst possible consequences are relevant for the choice between the alternatives.

and recombinant DNA seem to fall in this category. Even assuming that the risks of reactor failure can be numerically estimated,[48] there are political[49] and geological[50] factors involved where genuine uncertainty seems to prevail. In this case the maximin criterion would seem to be the most relevant one, as all the alternatives (hydraulic power, fossil power etc.) have approximately the same 'best consequences' as nuclear power. In the DNA discussion [51] it has been argued that one alternative ('forbid recombination') has much better 'worst consequences' and much worse 'best consequences' than the other ('permit recombination'), so that a weighted combination of maximin and maximax reasoning[52] would be appropriate. In this case, however, *there is no rational way of choosing the weights*; another instance where rationality is not defined.

Another possibility would be to use the method of *Gestalt hunches*. That is, instead of proceeding analytically and decomposing the decision-problem into its elementary sub-problems to each of which we assign subjective probabilities of the above-mentioned kind, we should operate directly at the level of the global problem and use our judgment to arrive at a practical conclusion. Take the case of the Vietnam war.[53] If it is true that the disastrous sequence of decisions made by the military and the political authorities relied heavily upon Bayesian decision theory and the assignment of subjective probabilities to elementary sub-problems ('My best guess is that the VC will attack within a week with 70 per cent probability' etc.), this could be taken as a natural experiment disconfirming the Bayesian method and

[48]   This may be granting too much. In particular the problem of human error involves not only common-mode failures, but also after-effects that may be hard to estimate. (See Feller 1968, pp. 118ff, for the distinction betwen these two problems.)

[49]   In Stanford Research Institute (1967) we find, for example, quantified probabilities for attempts to sabotage nuclear power plants which can hardly be taken seriously. In any case the plutonium handed down to later generations will continue to be material for nuclear weapons, and who can say with any confidence whatsoever what the chances are that a national government in a given country will be tempted to use this option a hundred or five hundred years from now?

[50]   For the geological uncertainties involved in the nuclear waste disposal problem, see de Marsily *et al.* (1977).

[51]   See Cohen (1977) for a survey. His conclusions do not support the statements in the text, which are made only to highlight the conceptual aspect of the problem.

[52]   See Luce and Raiffa (1957), pp. 282ff, 296ff.

[53]   The following remarks should be compared with Ellsberg (1971) and Janis (1972).

providing an argument for the superiority of the global *political* approach to such problems.

I have no firm evidence as to the truth of the antecedent of the preceding conditional statement. And even if it proved to be true, it could be argued that this only shows that the decision theorists were bad theorists and not that they used a bad theory. And even if it was conceded that the theory is bad, for the reasons given above, it could be said that the global approach of the politicians would also require subjective probabilities, guesses or hunches. My answer to this would be that people survive in politics because they are able to evaluate subjective probabilities with the minimum of distortion from belief-irrelevant causal processes. (The same holds for successful businessmen – not to be confused with successful firms.) To the extent that there is no comparable selection process screening out the unsuccessful and biased decision-makers in the army or in the government, one should take extreme care in interpreting the subjective probabilities stemming from such individuals. Now it is of course an empirical fact that people who survive in politics rarely have the formal training of the decision theorist, and their subjective probabilities often will not satisfy the standard consistency requirements. If the input to the political selection process had been composed only of decision theorists, then the output of decisions might have improved; but if the decisions were to be taken by (or on the basis of evaluations given by) decision theorists who have not been subjected to this screening process, then the quality of the output would surely deteriorate compared to the output produced by ordinary people selected for that crucial and elusive quality: judgment.

III.5   MAXIMIZING, SATISFICING AND NATURAL SELECTION

The last remarks of the preceding section immediately lead us to the cluster of problems cited in the heading of the present section, which are usually associated with such names as Herbert Simon, Milton Friedman, Gary Becker and Sidney Winter. I shall repeat and expand upon some of the points made in II.4, in order to show that the existence of well-defined rational behaviour may be questioned on grounds related to the cost of information. In order to present the argument in the proper setting, I shall first sketch some of the developments in the theory of rational behaviour that led up to it. In logical and partly in chronological succession I believe that we may distinguish between five distinct positions within this development.

The first position is the classical maximization approach, assuming total certainty or objective probabilities, no information and transaction costs, instant and faultless calculation, and so on. The importance of this paradigm as an idealized standard should always be kept in mind. It includes perfect rationality, in the sense of chapter I above, as well as imperfect rationality, in the sense of chapter II. The approach is subject to the difficulties raised in III.2, viz. that the optimum may in some cases not be defined, though not for the reasons discussed in the present section.

The second position is the theory of satisficing or of limited rationality, associated with the name of Herbert Simon and a number of later theorists.[54] The arguments for this view are partly empirical and partly logical. Empirically it is rarely the case that businessmen deliberately search for the global optimum in their feasible set. Rather they tend to set themselves some goal such as a minimum rate of profit, and then adopt the first course of action that happens to come into their minds (perhaps as a result of some standardized search process) and that satisfies this minimum requirement. Logically it can be argued that the abstractions implied by the classical maximization model are too heroic, and that the model could never be realized even in principle. The search for the optimum uses time that could have been spent more profitably.

The third position takes its cue from the last remark of the preceding paragraph. This is a modified maximization approach[55] that takes some account of the objections of the satisficers, by arguing that satisficing, properly understood, is just a species of maximizing with such elements as the cost of information included. The abstractly optimal position, e.g. the solution to a technical problem that might be optimal from an engineering viewpoint, may be economically irrational because it is too costly and time-consuming.

---

[54] Simon (1954, 1976), March (1977).
[55] Riker and Ordeshook (1973) exemplify this position.

The fourth position is in a sense the third stood on its head, not satisficing-as-maximizing, but maximizing-as-satisficing. The Chicago school of economists,[56] and Joseph Schumpeter before them,[57] have argued that 'rational' or maximizing behaviour really is the result of stereotyped or satisficing action, in the sense that the maximizers are just the satisficers who are selected by the market, or more generally by the struggle for survival, because they happen to have stumbled across the optimal rules of thumb. The Chicago economists, from Armen Alchian onwards, have presented several slightly different versions of this argument, one which explicitly denies that firms have maximizing intentions and one which states that we might just as well assume that firms have such intentions because in any case they act as if they did.

The fifth position is represented by a fundamental and somewhat nihilistic paper by Sidney Winter, initiating a long series of exciting pieces of work, much of it done jointly with Richard Nelson.[58] The main effect of his paper is to destroy the third position and implicitly to restore the second, but it also has important implications for the fourth. Winter's simple point, already stated in II.4, is that the attempt to redefine satisficing as a species of maximizing leads to an infinite regress, because the 'choice of a profit-maximizing information structure itself requires information, and it is not apparent how the aspiring profit maximizer acquires this information, or what guarantees that he does not pay an excessive price for it'. At some point this infinite regress must be cut short by intuition, unsupported by formal reasoning, and why not then make the cut-off point as close to the action itself as possible?

Winter also has cogent objections to the natural-selection theories of rational behaviour. From the fact that in an initial situation a rule of thumb employed by a given firm is the most profitable one, we can never conclude that it will remain so when that firm expands relative to other firms and thus changes the initial situation. Also he shows that under plausible conditions maximizers and non-maximizers may coexist in market equilibrium, and that maximizers may become extinct. Both of these

---

[56] In particular Alchian (1950), Friedman (1953), Becker (1976).
[57] Schumpeter (1934), p. 80.
[58] Winter (1964, 1971, 1975); Nelson and Winter (1974, 1976).

possibilities are, of course, contrary to the assertion that all firms will exhibit profit-maximizing behaviour because non-maximizers are eliminated by competition. To these problems associated with the natural-selection model we may add the difficulty discussed in chapter I, viz. that natural selection of firms could at most simulate local maximization, unless one assumes that all possible rules of thumb are represented in the market.

The result of these various considerations seems to be that for the analysis of business decisions, and probably for a large number of other decision problems, Simon's theory of satisficing is the most satisfactory yet presented. We have also seen that the satisficing postulates can neither be derived from the assumption of profit-maximizing intentions (as in the third position) nor be used to derive a conclusion of profit-maximizing behaviour (as in the fourth position). It goes without saying that many sub-problems will be optimally resolved by the standard maximizing methods, because we 'see' at once that the calculation will be worthwhile, but I do not believe that the large problems facing the firm or the individual can be solved in this way. I want to stress that this conclusion does not destroy the theses set forward in chapters I and II. The use of indirect strategies does not presuppose full information about the feasible set, only the comparison between two or more options having their rewards distributed differently over time.

Winter's objections to the natural-selection theories of the firm do not, in my opinion, apply to the selection argument about political survival sketched in the preceding section. This is so because politicians are selected not as a result of the consequences of their actions, but as a result of the judgmental qualities that are revealed by their actions. It is difficult to conceptualize this difference, but one important aspect could be summed up by saying that 'In politics you never recover from a single grave mistake in judgment.' That is, the largest amount of political capital can evaporate overnight as the result of one grave mistake, even if the issue at stake is inherently of small importance. When presidential candidates lose their heads in car accidents or are provoked to tears by the impertinence of a journalist, these events are important not for themselves, but for what they reveal about the candidate and his probable behaviour in situations that will be vastly more important. By contrast, firms do not go bankrupt (even though managers may be dismissed) when they commit mistakes of a kind that could have been disastrous in a different situation. This means that the selection of politicians really has nothing to do with *natural* selection. In the terminology of I.5, it is much more like a filter process or *artificial* selection, where a given behaviour is maintained because the beneficiaries both recognize that they are beneficiaries and have the power to maintain that behaviour.

III.6   TRADITIONAL BEHAVIOUR AND RANDOM BEHAVIOUR

In his work on economic theory and irrational behaviour Gary Becker distinguishes usefully between these two categories of non-rational behaviour,[59] i.e. non-rational devices in the second filter referred to above. (Max Weber, incidentally, also discussed traditional behaviour as one alternative to instrumentally rational behaviour, his two other cases being value-oriented behaviour and affectual behaviour. I believe that value-oriented behaviour can be analysed in terms of lexicographic preferences, and that affectual behaviour is akin to weakness of will.) In this section I shall examine, quite independently of Becker's analysis, the status and importance of these two categories.

Where the economist is wont to explain behaviour in terms of rational choice, the sociologist more often invokes tradition, roles or norms, these terms being treated as synonymous for the present purpose. The difference between the two approaches shows up very clearly in the study of crime and the study of education. In both cases the sociologist, or some caricature thereof, argues that the choice of a criminal career or of higher education really is no choice at all, but that the individual is *propelled* into certain channels by subculture-specific norms or values. The economist, by contrast, tends to assume that individuals are *attracted* by differential rewards associated with the available courses of action. The sociologist, that is, looks at the action as a product of its causal antecedents, and the economist regards it as motivated by (the expectation of) future rewards: causality versus intentionality. A testable implication of the sociological view is that changes in the reward system should have

59   Becker (1976), ch. 8.

little efficacy for inducing changes in behaviour, whereas the economist takes it for granted that one can make people behave in virtually any manner, by making suitable changes in the reward system.

More specifically, William Cobb[60] and Gordon Tullock,[61] among others, have distinguished between two hypotheses that purport to explain why some people become criminals: the 'economic hypothesis' that assumes maximization of expected utility, and the 'sociological hypothesis' – Cobb calls it 'the sickness hypothesis' – that links criminal activities to internalized norms and criminal subcultures. According to Tullock there is no doubt which fits the data best; he also states that many of the sociologists who started out to prove that punishment does not deter crime ended up by finding the contrary. Raymond Boudon has argued along similar lines concerning the choice of educational career.[62] Whereas writers like Pierre Bourdieu and Jean-Claude Passeron have seen differential choice of educational career as a cultural mechanism for reproduction of class inequalities,[63] Boudon argues convincingly that to a large extent working-class youths avoid higher education simply because it is too costly.

The sociological hypothesis, in the crude form sketched above, can certainly be invalidated by empirical evidence. In addition we can adduce a simple conceptual argument and a more important theoretical argument. The conceptual argument originates with Becker and states that you cannot abide with tradition if the environment changes so as to make the traditional behaviour lie outside the feasible set.[64] The theoretical argument amounts to a distinction between two ways in which values can influence behaviour. The simplistic sociological theory, which no one, perhaps, has ever held explicitly, says that values *directly* determine behaviour, by singling out one member of the feasible set. A much more plausible theory is that values determine preferences and that preferences and the feasible set jointly determine behaviour. This, I believe, could be used for a more useful statement of the difference between the economic and the sociological approach. The sociologist typically assumes that there are very large socially

[60] Cobb (1973).   [61] Tullock (1974).
[62] Boudon (1973a). The English edition of this work (Boudon 1974) has a less extensive discussion of this particular issue.
[63] Bourdieu and Passeron (1967, 1970).   [64] Becker (1976), ch. 8.

determined differences in preferences between individuals; that, for example, workers and women use higher discount rates when evaluating the present utility of future rewards (the problem of 'deferred gratification').[65] The economist, on the other hand, would tend to think that preferences are basically similar, and that most of the observed differences in behaviour can be explained through differences in the opportunity set. Another formulation, not quite equivalent to the preceding one, is that for the sociologist the most efficient method, dollar for dollar, of bringing about, say, educational equality is to work on the value system, whereas for the economist manipulation of the reward system is likely to bring more results. A third way of stating the distinction, equivalent to none of the others, is that for the sociologist social change typically begins with changes in the value system, whereas for the economist changes in the feasible set are prior to and induce (endogenous) change of preferences.[66]

This reinterpretation tends to close the gap between economists and sociologists, in the sense that the modified – and much more sensible – sociological position recognizes that for any given individual, action is governed by preferences, even if preferences vary over individuals. The gap could – and should – also be closed from the other side, by getting economists to admit that there are genuine cases of traditional, stereotyped and rigid behaviour. I shall return to this question in III.10, and here I only make the polemical point that people sometimes act stupidly out of stupidity and rigidly out of rigidity. Inertia may be a rational way of coping with a too rapidly changing environment, but it may also be just what it is: inertia.

On the (simplistic) theory of traditional behaviour, actions will remain the same following a change in the feasible set, assuming that the traditional behaviour remains feasible. On the rational-choice theory, changes in the feasible set will often induce a change in behaviour. On the third approach, to be discussed now, behaviour could change even with a constant feasible set and no assumption of changing preferences. This is the theory that behaviour is sometimes *random*, in the sense of being realized according to some probability distribution defined over the feasible set. Random behaviour in this sense is assumed in many

[65] See Ainslie (1975) for a survey.   [66] Cp. Elster (1976a) for this mechanism.

models of social mobility,[67] in the Asch–Cohen model for conformity[68] and in Rapoport's model for sequential Prisoner's Dilemmas,[69] to name but a few. In all such models individuals are seen as the bearers of *states* rather than of *intentions*, and their behaviour as governed by causal antecedents rather than by future rewards. Both traditional and random behaviour belong to the causal rather than the intentional image of man, even though they differ fundamentally in other respects.

The interpretation of stochastic models is often ambiguous. Are the stochastic models just useful approximations to some underlying deterministic mechanism (as in coin-tossing), or is it exactly the other way around, so that we assume deterministic causality in spite of our knowledge of random disturbances? Actually both answers may be true simultaneously. At the deepest level coin-tossing presumably is governed by the objectively random quantum processes; at a more aggregate (but still microscopic) level these processes can be given some very complex deterministic representation; and at the molar level this approximation is itself approximated by a stochastic process, which does not, however, bear any relation to the original random process. (The situation is somewhat similar to the cases where a real process in discrete time is mathematically represented in continuous time, which for computational purposes is then represented in a discrete time that bears no significant relation to the original discrete process.)[70] This implies that stochastic models in the social sciences have a rather unsatisfactory character; they describe rather than explain.

There is one exception to this statement, the case where the agent deliberately acts randomly. In this case the transition probabilities (or whatever) would be more than a compact representation of some unknown determinism underlying the process; they would stem directly from the assumption of rationality. A typical example is the use of mixed strategies in game theory. Here, however, we encounter the contention of John Harsanyi, cited above in III.2, that only equiprobabilistic mixed strategies will be chosen by rational actors and that these are

[67] Boudon (1973b).   [68] Snell (1965).
[69] Rapoport and Chammah (1965).
[70] Bellman (1961), pp. 67–8; see also pp. 130ff for brief and perceptive remarks on the relation between deterministic and stochastic models.

generated by some objectively random mechanism inside their heads rather than by deliberate choice. This, if correct, would imply that we fall back upon the causal image of man once again. While recognizing that there are strong arguments in favour of Harsanyi's thesis, I have also given my reasons for believing that it is not adequate for all cases. I certainly believe that the efforts of Raymond Boudon, discussed in I.4, to explain mobility behaviour through models involving mixed strategies are very much worth while, but there clearly is a need for further conceptual analysis in this domain.

In conclusion, we may assert that both of the cases discussed by Becker may be, but are not necessarily, genuine exceptions to rational-choice theory. There are no doubt cases where values, norms and traditions have a direct impact upon behaviour, but in most cases the influence is mediated through the preference structure. And even if there are cases where random behaviour stems from a deliberate choice to act unpredictably, the more common case is certainly that the randomness is the superficial expression of some unknown causal determinism operating behind the back of the agent.

III.7 EXPLAINING ALTRUISM

In the older body of literature rational-choice models were often associated with the assumption that behaviour is motivated merely by egoistic, hedonistic or narrowly self-interested purposes, and the phenomena of altruistic behaviour were either denied or believed to create an insuperable anomaly for these models. At a superficial level this link between rationality and narrowly conceived self-interest can no longer be upheld. Economists of most persuasions agree that the consumption (or even the utility) of other people can enter as an argument in my utility function. My utility may go down as a result of an increase in other people's consumption (as in envy) or it may go up (as in altruism).[71] My welfare may depend in part upon the consumption of some

[71] In fact a stronger definition of altruism would seem needed, viz. that some reduction in my own consumption could be compensated by increases in other people's consumption so as to give the same utility level. The 'lexicographic altruism' where other people's welfare makes a difference for my utility only when my own consumption is held constant would not be altruism as the word is usually employed.

specific person or persons (as in love)[72] or upon the average level of consumption (as in the search for status).[73] In altruistic gift-giving, the very act of giving may be evaluated positively, over and above the positive evaluation of the pleasure taken in the gift by the recipient.[74]

At a deeper level some problems remain. In the first place most authors seem to believe that if an explanation for a given behaviour can be found invoking only (narrowly defined) self-interest, this is always preferable in principle to explanations invoking concern for others, in much the same way as rational-choice explanations in general are preferred to causal models of behaviour. As is spelt out more fully in III.10 below, the economist has a moment of triumph each time he succeeds in showing up the rational logic of some behaviour previously believed to be irrational, and I also think he has the same feeling when an apparently altruistic behaviour is shown to be a par-ticularly subtle form of self-interest. In part this preference for the narrow definition of self-interest is purely methodological, a preference for the simple over the complex. In part it also seems to rest upon a substantive assumption about human nature: altruism does not come natural to man. In the second place – and this is linked to the same substantive assumption about human nature – there seems to be a widespread belief that the concern for others, when invoked to explain behaviour, should itself be explained. In this section, then, I shall look briefly at some proposed mechanisms for explaining apparently altruistic be-haviour as being really egoistic in motivation, and for explaining the emergence of behaviour whose altruistic character is *not* an apparent one only. The logical or the evolutionary reduction of altruism to egoism remains characteristic of rational-choice theory.

The paradigm for such questions is the choice of the cooperative strategy in the Prisoner's Dilemma. Generally speaking this choice may be explained along one of three distinct lines of argument. First, we may assume that the real payoff matrix is a Prisoner's Dilemma, but that the actors are not rational. This approach belongs to the causal rather than the intentional image of man.

---

[72] Becker (1976), pp. 233ff.
[73] Haavelmo (1970); also Hirsch (1976).
[74] I refer here to unpublished work by Serge-Cristophe Kolm (Paris).

It is associated especially with the experimental work of Anatol Rapoport and his associates on sequential Prisoner's Dilemmas, briefly referred to in III.6. It is also invoked in passing by Mancur Olson, in the course of a discussion of the free-rider problems in collective action.[75] Secondly, we may assume that the actors are rational, but that the real – as distinct from, say, the monetary – payoff matrix is not a Prisoner's Dilemma. Below I return briefly to this position. Thirdly, and most ambitiously, one may attempt to show that it can be rational to cooperate even when the game is a genuine Prisoner's Dilemma. In II.4 we saw that Descartes argued that it can pay to be helpful; here I comment briefly upon some recent proposals.

I believe we may dismiss without prolonged discussion the 'meta-game' analysis offered by Nigel Howard.[76] The asymmetry of his 'solution' is, in my opinion, enough to disqualify it for counting as a solution at all. Much more promising is the 'supergame' analysis offered by Martin Shubik and Michael Taylor.[77] Taylor, in particular, has explored in great detail the conditions under which the cooperative strategy will be consistently chosen by two rational players in sequential Prisoner's Dilemmas where future rewards are discounted to present value. I have, nevertheless, some objections to his analysis. By assuming that threats and promises are enforceable, it begs the very question under discussion. Moreover, it only shows that (given certain conditions) there is a cooperative equilibrium point, not that there is a cooperative solution. Finally, and most important, the conditions under which this equilibrium point, assuming it to be the solution, will actually be *realized* are such as to make it likely that the underlying game will have been transformed into something different from the Prisoner's Dilemma. The conditions which ensure a way out of the dilemma also do away with the dilemma itself. I return to this point below.

A third variety of the 'rationality of altruism' approach is the theory proposed by Gary Becker in recent work.[78] His analysis does not, and indeed cannot, deal with Prisoner's Dilemma-type situations, but rather refers to cases where one genuine altruist may lead other (egoistic) persons to act towards him as if they, too,

[75] Olson (1965), p. 108.   [76] Howard (1971).
[77] Shubik (1970), M. Taylor (1976a).   [78] Becker (1976), chs. 12, 13.

were altruists, because they may be able to get more in return than they give. My objection to this ingenious theory is my feeling that the genuine altruist would cease being an altruist if and when he realised that the false altruists really are egoists. Altruism may be pure and disinterested, in the sense that you derive positive utility from the well-being of another, regardless of his character or conduct, but more frequently you act altruistically towards someone as a function of his character, a minimum condition being that he is not trying to cash in on your altruism. (But see IV.3 for some exceptions to this statement.) The egoistic strategy of simulating altruism would be successful only if successfully kept hidden, unless, of course, behaving as if you were an altruist ends up by making you into an altruist. The latter possibility might even be an incentive to start acting altruistically in the first place, on an analogy to the argument expounded in II.3, and subject to the same qualifications.

Turning now from logical to evolutionary reductionism, what are the conditions that could make genuine altruism likely to emerge? Evolutionary biology offers several possible avenues for exploring this issue. For reasons given in I.4, I do not accept Gary Becker's attempt to extend his 'theory of social interaction' from short-term human choices to long-term natural selection. I shall also disregard group selection, not because the conditions required for its operation are inherently impossible, as in the case of Becker's theory, but because it seems widely agreed that they involve an extremely improbable coincidence of circumstances.[79] More promising are the mechanisms of kin selection and reciprocal altruism. Kin selection[80] may produce behaviour that is harmful to the actor if it is sufficiently beneficial to some sufficiently near relative. In an example offered by Richard Dawkins, 'A gene for suicidally saving five cousins would not become more numerous in the population, but a gene for saving five brothers would.'[81] Actually kin selection may produce behaviour that is *indiscriminately* altruistic, i.e. that benefits everyone within helping distance, if the chances are that there are disproportionately many relatives in the near vicinity and if it is either too costly (in terms of genetic

[79] Wilson (1975) offers a good discussion of this subject.
[80] Hamilton (1964) is the originator of this concept.
[81] Dawkins (1976), p. 100.

material that could be better employed elsewhere)[82] or technically impossible to reserve help for relatives only.

No one has yet, as far as I know, proposed a working model for how kin selection could produce altruistic behaviour in humans. Robert Trivers has argued, however, that his theory of *reciprocal altruism* can explain such psychological attitudes as guilt, friendship or gratitude as (ultimately self-interested) means for maintaining altruistic behaviour.[83] Roughly speaking, the mechanism of reciprocal altruism favours the emergence, or – as was explained in I.4 – at least the non-disappearance of the conditional strategy often called 'tit for tat': 'You scratch my back, I'll ride on yours.'[84] If to this conditional strategy we add that the initial strategy against an unknown individual always is to cooperate, it is clear that in a population of reciprocating altruists a mutant egoist would be at a disadvantage. He would receive some favours from the others, but they would cease as soon as they saw that he failed to reciprocate. A 'subtle cheater' who reciprocated to some extent, giving less than he got, might fare better, at least before the others develop the counteradaptations enabling them to detect such 'calculated altruism'. Trivers suggests that guilt will be favoured by natural selection 'in order to motivate the cheater to compensate his misdeed and to behave reciprocally in the future'.[85]

I lack the competence to evaluate the soundness of this analysis. One should observe, however, that the account is reductionist only in the sense that the altruistic behaviour is explained as being ultimately in the evolutionary self-interest of the organism, but not in the sense that the concern for others is simulated, as in Becker's analysis. On the contrary, Trivers argues that natural selection will evolve the capacity to detect attempts to simulate altruism. The altruism is the more efficient because it is *not* derived from calculated self-interest. Another important feature of the explanation is that it does not purport to explain specific instances of altruistic behaviour, such as, say, the tendency to save a drowning person. Rescue attempts are explained by a general tendency to perform acts of altruism, and this tendency is then made the object

---

[82] Williams (1966), p. 206. Trivers (1971) sees this as an 'explanation of last resort', but I am not sure it should be dismissed so quickly. From economic theory we can learn much about the costs of internalizing external economies, and I cannot see why this problem should be less important in natural selection.   [83] Trivers (1971).
[84] Dawkins (1976), ch. 10.   [85] Trivers (1971), p. 50.

of the evolutionary explanation. As was also argued in I.3, this two-step reductionism is more satisfactory than the attempts to reduce behaviour *directly* to natural selection.

The emergence of altruism could also be explained along strictly sociological lines. Given a Prisoner's Dilemma such as trade-union formation,[86] it can be argued that prolonged inter-action between the workers will make the real payoff structure diverge from the purely monetary one, because the welfare of others will enter into the utility function of the individual. This could change the game into an Assurance Game, as defined in I.4, where the worst alternative still is to be Sucker, but the best alternative is *not* to be Free Rider. The Assurance Game does not have a dominant strategy, so that the cooperative solution will only be realized if there is perfect information. Now I submit that the very same conditions that tend to transform the game from a Prisoner's Dilemma into an Assurance Game, viz. that the actors form a small and stable group, also will tend to generate the information required for the solution to the latter game to be realized: affection for others and information about them tend to grow *pari passu*. This explains the third objection offered above to Michael Taylor's theory. He stresses very strongly that the cooperative behaviour in the Prisoner's Dilemma supergame will only be realized in small and stable communities where the strong information requirements are likely to be satisfied,[87] but I have just argued that the sustained interaction in such communities may do away with the problem itself by transforming the nature of the game.

Altruism, then, is an anomaly for the theory of rational choice only in the sense that attempts to explain altruistic behaviour as the result of narrowly defined self-interest do not seem likely to succeed in all cases. Altruism, trust and solidarity are genuine phenomena that cannot be dissolved into ultra-subtle forms of self-interest. This argument, taken together with the comments in III.3, points to the need for a broad notion of rationality. *Economic man* may be defined through continuous preferences and narrow self-interest, but *rational man* can have non-Archimedean preferences and be moved by concern for others.

[86] Olson (1965); also Elster (1978a), ch. 5.   [87] M. Taylor (1976a), p. 93.

III.8   INCONSTANCY

Rational behaviour in the standard definition means acting in accordance with a complete and transitive set of preferences. The behaviour of an individual who is rational in this sense can be predicted by himself and others, provided his preferences do not change. What shall we say, however, about an individual who at every moment of time exhibits complete and transitive preferences, but who never settles down to a stable pattern? A failure of rationality in this connection may stem from two sources. Inconstancy in itself may be a form of irrationality, as may also the inability to adopt a strategic attitude towards the endogenously changing preferences. The perfectly rational individual is free from inconstancy. A second-best rationality is to be inconstant *and* take precautions against this tendency. In II.6 the last problem was extensively discussed; here the notion of first-best rationality will be the focus of the discussion. The problem is *how to sort out the good reasons for changing or not changing one's mind from the bad reasons.* I believe that the question is a very important one, which if resolved could have consequences for many fields of human behaviour. To take but one example, the theory of social choice would have to be totally transformed if one could give reasons for disregarding the preferences of individuals who constantly change their minds so as to conform with (or to differ from) the socially adopted preferences. To state this problem is, of course, to show how far it is from being resolved; indeed, I do not imply that it could ever be solved to everybody's satisfaction. At the level of even greater generality, we are dealing here with the issue of *moral hysteresis.*[88] Even if in principle only present factors are relevant for the purpose of causal explanation and prediction, this need not be so for moral evaluation. Here the genesis of the preferences, or of the distribution of property,[89] could be relevant for an assessment of moral worth.

Among the good reasons for changing one's mind we should include experience and training. *Experience* can be formalized as

---

[88]   Elster (1978b, 1978c) gives a fuller discussion of this notion.
[89]   Nozick (1974) holds that moral hysteresis is important for a theory of just income distribution. He uses the term 'historical theories of justice', as opposed to 'end-result theories', for this notion.

the difference between *ex ante facto* and *ex post facto* preferences.[90] A given consumption bundle may look more (or less) attractive after the actual consumption than it did before. The larger the part of the commodity space already explored, the smaller, presumably, the induced change in preference after each choice. *Training* has been formalized through the distinction between utility and consumption capital.[91] Training, in this conceptualization, does not change the enjoyment that I derive from a given amount of time spent on, say, listening to music, everything else being the same. It does, however, make a difference for the 'everything else', by increasing the consumption capital that enables me to get more enjoyment out of a given time spent listening to music. (This approach, due to George Stigler and Gary Becker, may be a useful restatement of some well-known facts, but it is hard to follow the authors when they also use it to argue that preferences are essentially stable. By transferring the changing element in the preference structure to the category of consumption capital, they are indeed able to say that what remains is essentially stable, but we must be allowed to doubt the substantial content of this statement.)

Among the bad reasons we should include the sheer desire for novelty, and its converse, pure inertia; also the sheer desire to be different, and its converse, pure conformism. If a person always wants to be in New York when in San Francisco and vice versa, this should qualify for the epithet 'irrational'. Also, if someone has a consuming desire for novelty and change, he can be led to 'improve himself to death' by a series of small changes, each of which is an improvement in terms of the current preferences.[92] A pure conformist and a pure non-conformist may unsuccessfully chase each other in their preferences, as most tourists know.[93] In such cases the individual is in the grip of causal forces operating 'behind his back' and governing his preferences in a way that he does not himself understand. I believe that most readers will agree that in many cases the reasons specified are bad reasons indeed. The catch is the number of counterexamples that also come to mind immediately. Leibniz, for one, made the desire for change

[90] See in particular Cyert and De Groot (1975).   [91] Stigler and Becker (1977).
[92] Von Weiszäcker (1971) shows the conditions under which this can occur.
[93] Gibbard (1974) has proposed a formal model of this phenomenon.

into a defining characteristic of man: 'Je trouve que l'inquiétude est essentielle à la félicité des créatures, laquelle ne consiste jamais dans une parfaite possession qui les rendrait insensibles et comme stupides, mais dans un progrès continuel et ininterrompu à des plus grands biens.'[94]

I shall return briefly to this point in IV.3, where it is argued that in love (or some forms of love) the desire for change and growth is essential. In other contexts the extreme form of constancy that I have called inertia may be an admirable trait which we should hesitate to call irrational. (I am here not referring to someone who deliberately manipulates his preferences so as to resist the endogenous forces making for change, but to the character trait of *unplanned* inertia.) Don Quixote was irrational because he refused to adopt to the changing circumstances, but we all know of cases where the stature of a person is enhanced because he has remained unmoved by the ebb and tide of fashion.

Some formal criteria for irrational inconstancy may nevertheless be proposed. In the first place, whenever a person 'improves himself to death', we are definitely dealing with a case of irrationality. This case covers not only the endogenously changing preferences mentioned above, but also intransitive preference structures.[95] In the second place, cyclically changing preferences would seem to be an unambiguous mark of irrationality. Let it be observed, however, that cyclically changing preferences should not be confused with cyclically changing *behaviour*. The latter may stem from the former, but also from inconsistent preferences (discussed in the next section) or from indifference, as in Harsanyi's theory of mixed strategies discussed in III.2 and III.6 above. In the third place, we might want to call irrational the 'inverse dictator' whose preferences always coincide with the social preferences, not because he is able to dictate them, but rather the other way around.[96] (Here I assume of course that the coincidence is not dictated by some meta-preferences adopted by the individual, but comes about by a purely causal mechanism.) I do not believe that

94 Leibniz (1875–90), v, p. 175.
95 Raiffa (1968), p. 78, shows how an individual with intransitive preferences could be bled to death by being made to give up some money for each link in the cyclical chain of preferences.
96 Such a person is also referred to as a 'chameleon'. For the conceptual problems created by such individuals for the theory of power, see Goldman (1972).

these criteria capture all or even most cases of irrational inconstancy (of which irrational constancy may be seen as a particular case), but they should at any rate suffice to give the reader an idea of the set of problems which I have in mind under this heading.

III.9   PARADOX

Inconstancy and inconsistency are related but different notions, as already explained in II.5 and II.6. In chapter IV I deal with some forms of inconsistent attitudes that are particularly important in human affairs: hate, love, self-deception. Elsewhere[97] I have tried to spell out the formal structure of these contradictions, and I shall not here repeat these analyses. I limit myself, therefore, to some brief remarks that link the problem of inconsistency to the general theory of rational behaviour.

Paradox, contradiction and inconsistency have traditionally been explored by poets and novelists, recently also by psychiatrists, but rarely by the social scientist. A charitable interpretation of this fact is that the social scientists have been so aware of their limitations that they have preferred to start with the more accessible, even if less important, facets of human behaviour. I fear that in many cases a less charitable interpretation, that they have mistaken the accessible for the important, is to be preferred. In particular I cannot help feeling that the enthusiasm with which economists have applied the tools of consumption analysis to love, marriage, worship or suicide is somewhat misplaced. I am not objecting to the use of formal methods *per se*, rather to the jejune assumptions that love is an externality in the utility function[98] or that the value of eternal life must be discounted to present value.[99]

'Contradictions of the mind' come in many varieties, and the ones most amenable to formal techniques are not always the most interesting. By this I mean the following. In some cases an individual holds a set of preferences or of beliefs from which a contradiction can be formally and immediately deduced, a simple case being that the individual believes or desires p and not-p

[97]   Elster (1978a), ch. 4.   [98]   Becker (1976), p. 234.
[99]   Azzi and Ehrenberg (1975). To my mind this article is a *reductio ad absurdum* proof against 'the economic approach to human behaviour'.

simultaneously. Here the contradictory attitudes coexist passively, and it is possible for the individual to abandon one of them when the inconsistency is pointed out to him. It is well known, for example, that most persons correct their preferences if made aware of intransitivities.[100] Vastly more interesting are the cases where the contradiction stems from a *single* desire (or a single belief), from which a contradiction can somehow be deduced. The word 'somehow' covers the murky notions of conceptual implication,[101] pragmatic implication[102] and the like, which I do not here intend to discuss. The reader will see for himself, through the examples given here and in the next chapter, the kind of situation I have in mind. The crucial point in the present context is the following. When confronted with the contradictory project of, say, 'trying to forget', we are not dealing with a meaningless attitude. We can understand it, even though it cannot be realized. By contrast, if someone asserts '*p* and not-*p*', we cannot even grasp what he has in mind. When the contradiction or inconsistency follows from a single unitary project, it may be constitutive of the personality as a whole and far from easily given up.

Leslie Farber has coined the phrase 'willing what cannot be willed' for one subset of these contradictory projects:

I can will knowledge, but not wisdom; going to bed, but not sleeping; eating, but not hunger; meekness, but not humility; scrupulosity, but not virtue; self-assertion or bravado, but not courage; lust, but not love; commiseration, but not sympathy; congratulations, but not admiration; religion, but not faith; reading, but not understanding.[103]

Paul Watzlawick and his associates have given many examples of the same general kind: You ought to love me; I want you to dominate me; Don't be so obedient; I thought I could train you to become a real man; Be spontaneous; and so on.[104] In my own family there is a story of a remote ancestor who instructed his children 'Do it quickly and with pleasure.' In II.3 I referred to Bernard Williams's analysis of the impossibility of carrying out a decision to believe, and to Emily Dickinson's observation about the

---

[100] Raiffa (1968), p. 75, reports, however, that some subjects in an experiment preferred to retain their preferences even after the intransitivities were pointed out to them.
[101] Elster (1978a), chs. 4 and 5, offers some remarks upon this elusive notion.
[102] For a possible-world model of 'assertion logic', see Gullvåg (1977).
[103] Farber (1976), p. 7.
[104] Watzlawick *et al.* (1967), ch. 6; Watzlawick *et al.* (1974), ch. 6. See also ch. IV below.

equally impossible decision to forget. The general thesis of chapter II also shows up a sense in which such decisions and injunctions need *not* be paradoxical or impossible to carry out, viz. through the use of indirect strategies, by making action generate conviction rather than the other way around. It is doubtful whether the strategy of 'going through the motions' would work for all the cases cited here. It may work for belief, but not for forgetfulness; for altruism, not for love; for virtue, not for a sense of humour. In any case there is a trace of paradox even in successful applications of the strategy, for the intending altruist may find to his dismay that he is not accepted as a genuine altruist and the intending believer might end up in the wrong place.

Another set of paradoxes occurs when status X gives you the right to status Z, on the condition that you also perform action Y, which automatically disqualifies you from being X. The paradigm is *Catch 22*, succinctly described thus by Paul Watzlawick:

Anybody willing to fly combat missions would have to be crazy, and being crazy, could be grounded for psychiatric reasons. He has only to ask to be. But the very process of asking, of not wanting to fly more combat missions, is evidence of normalcy and rules out being grounded for psychiatric reasons.[105]

It is easy to think up variations on this example, such as the use of special forms to be filled in by the individuals who are so needy that they cannot even fill in a form, etc. In II.9 I quoted the Russian nobleman case constructed by Derek Parfit – a person setting up for himself a situation where he cannot make a certain request without ceasing to be himself and thus losing all grounds for being obeyed. Leslie Farber's analysis of suicide goes along similar lines, as when he argues that 'the despairer takes his own life in order to prove that he is not responsible for taking his own life',[106] forgetting that after the event he will no longer be around to cash in on the demonstration. A similar wish lies behind the desire to be present at one's own funeral and to hear the funeral oration spelling out one's essence 'tel qu'en lui-même enfin l'éternité le change'.[107]

A further category of paradoxes is paradigmatically given by

---

[105] Watzlawick (1977), p. 25.   [106] Farber (1976), p. 80.
[107] When Sartre (1943, *passim*) asserts that the basic contradiction of man is the desire to be simultaneously *en-soi* and *pour-soi*, he quotes this verse of Mallarmé as an illustration, but the funeral episode from *Tom Sawyer* would do equally well. For the history of the notion of 'becoming who one is', see Peyre (1963), p. 294.

Groucho Marx's saying 'I would not dream of belonging to a club that is willing to have me as a member.' (In a sense this is a reversal of the master–slave paradox, of which more in IV.2.) Someone willing to recognize *me* must obviously be unworthy of recognition, and his recognition of me equally worthless. (In the master–slave paradox the worthlessness of the recognizer, i.e. the slave, is the starting point, while the lack of worth of the recognition, and thus of the recognized, is the conclusion. It can truly be said, therefore, that Marx stood Hegel on his head.) Anyone observing small children at play will have seen this paradox, when one refuses to accept an object that he has solicited because he reckons that it must be pretty worthless if the other is willing to part with it. I also believe that writers sometimes fall victim to this fallacy; if anyone praises their work this automatically disqualifies him from being a serious critic. This, of course, is a form of hubris rather than of excessive modesty, for if anyone fails to praise their work this is seen as equally disqualifying.

I submit that it is a shallow kind of social science that denies or disregards such phenomena. I also believe that there is an important conceptual lesson to be drawn from such cases, viz. that *intentional analysis does not presuppose rational actors.* Hitherto I have tacitly used 'rationality' and 'intentionality' as if they were synonyms, a practice that was justified in the cases discussed above. The examples given here show that this is not always so. Contradictory and paradoxical intentions may be intelligible in terms of a project even if that project is not rational. In one sense, therefore, such paradoxes limit the scope of rational-choice models, but in another sense they open up the possibility of making sense of behaviour that would otherwise be thought of as pathological and as subject to causal analysis only. To be sure, the analysis of contradictory attitudes must also draw upon causal models in order to predict what the actor is going to *do* in a given situation, for here the intentional model, predicting *too much*, is useless.

III.10   AND SO WHAT?

As is strongly argued by Donald Davidson, there is a general *presumption of rationality* in human affairs. In a recent article

Davidson explains what made him switch from the causal to the intentional (or rational) image of man. He was engaged at the time in testing Frank Ramsey's theory of utility and subjective probability, an early and, according to Davidson, superior version of the von Neumann–Morgenstern theory of cardinal utility. Although the subjects often exhibited intransitive preferences in single experiments, a succession of trials showed some more rational patterns:

It was found that as time went on, people became steadily more consistent; intransitivities were gradually eliminated; after six sessions, all subjects were close to being perfectly consistent. This was enough to show that a static theory like Ramsey's could not, even under the most carefully controlled conditions, yield accurate predictions: merely making choices (with no reward or feedback) alters future choices. There was also an entirely unexpected result. If the choices of an individual over all trials were combined, on the assumption that his 'real' preference was for the alternative of a pair he chose most often, then there were almost no inconsistencies at all. Apparently, from the start there were underlying and consistent values which were better and better realized in choice. I found it impossible to construct a theory that could explain this, and gave up my career as an experimental psychologist.[108]

From this experiment, and from more general considerations, Davidson concludes not only 'that data are open to more than one interpretation', but 'that if we are intelligibly to attribute attitudes and beliefs...we are committed to finding, in the pattern of behaviour, belief and desire, a large degree of rationality and consistency'.[109] The point may, perhaps, be made in the following paradoxical terms: in order to gather the very evidence on which rationality could be denied in the case of a given individual, we must assume him to be rational if the outwardly observable behaviour is to be translatable into evidence. Irrational behaviour only makes sense against a background of rationality; and the pattern may always be reinterpreted so as to make the irrationality appear in a different part of the system of behaviour.

This argument corresponds very well to what has for a long time been the standard practice among economists. They have worked according to what has been called a *principle of charity*, stating that one should always assume, as a working hypothesis, the rationality of any given action, however strange and unadapted it might appear to be at first glance. The social scientist should be prepared to spend time and imagination in thinking up rational

[108] Davison (1976), p. 107.   [109] *Ibid.* p. 108.

explanations for the action he observes, and only after repeated failure should he tentatively label the action as irrational.

The successes of the principle of charity are numerous. In II.4 and II.8 we discussed at some length the reasons why it may be rational to act inflexibly and rigidly, deliberately refusing to adapt to the current environment. In III.6 we observed that what looks like random behaviour may stem from the deliberate adoption of a mixed strategy. Also people may have different goals from what the observer initially assumes. The mercantilist policy of protectionism was irrational if we assume that absolute wealth was the goal, but not if we replace that goal by power (and relative wealth).[110] Planters' behaviour in the ante-bellum South may have been irrational if judged by the standards of profit-maximizing, but not if judged by the standards of utility-maximizing.[111] (But see IV.2 below for a more nuanced statement.) Also people may act in terms of probability distributions rather than of average values. The resistance to technical change in underdeveloped countries may be a rational response to methods which combine higher average yields with larger dispersions around the mean, rather than irrational traditionalism.[112] Also the time perspective of the actors may be longer or shorter than initially believed. The lack of responsiveness of peasants to price changes appears rational once we take account of the price fluctuations in the past that make it rational to form cautious expectations about future prices, even if these expectations turn out to be wrong *ex post facto*. A landlord refusing to adopt new and superior techniques may do so because he fears that the increased yields will enable the sharecroppers to repay their debts and to liberate themselves from the state of semi-serfdom, which in the long run would more than offset the short-term gains that would accrue to him.[113] Also people may have changing preferences rather than inconsistent preferences. Consumption choices inconsistent with the axiom of revealed preferences may be explained on the assumption of a change in tastes. Finally, people may deliberately refuse to adapt themselves because of the 'psychic costs' involved. 'The greatest of all monopoly profits is a quiet life.'[114]

[110] Gerschenkron (1970), p. 65.   [111] Elster (1976b); also (1978a), ch. 6.
[112] Wharton (1971); but see Roumasset (1976).   [113] Bhaduri (1973).
[114] This dictum by John Hicks is quoted after Hirschman (1971), p. 55.

Some of these gambits stretch charity to the limit. In II.4 I referred to Douglass North's contention that *ideologies* are a rational response to the 'cost of information' problem. This, I submit, is to carry the presumption of rationality too far. Douglass North again, in another context, explains peasant conservatism as a 'cost–benefit decision: the psychological and transaction costs of instituting the three-field system counterbalanced the significant benefits it promised'.[115] I simply refuse to believe that peasants living at subsistence level would sacrifice an improvement in their standard of living for the sake of a 'quiet life'. Also there comes a point when cautious expectations cease to be rational. More generally, as was also observed in I.5, the manipulation of the time perspective in order to lend rationality to apparently unmotivated behaviour is often an *ad hoc* solution to be used with circumspection. This, indeed, is the general problem with the principle of charity, that so many of its gambits involve *ad hoc* reasoning perilously close to tautologies. To postulate costs of information, costs of transaction, psychic costs or different time perspectives just to make the behaviour fit the theory is an unacceptable way out. Some independent evidence for these additional variables should always be given; the *ad hoc* hypotheses should have some independent predictive power.

As will be clear from III.2 and III.5 above, I also believe that there are more radical objections to the principle of charity. The infinite regresses involved in games without solution and in the problem of the optimal amount of information prevent the rational-choice model from even getting off the ground. This does not mean that people in such cases cannot make rational choices, only that there is no choice which is *the* rational one. The situation is not a 'single-exit' one,[116] but this does not mean that all exits are equally good. More precisely, to make the situation into a single-exit one we must add some causal assumptions to the purely intentional ones, in order to be able to predict which of the non-discarded options will actually be realized.

---

[115] North and Thomas (1973), p. 42.
[116] For this notion, see Latsis (1976), pp. 19ff.

IV

IRRATIONALITY: CONTRADICTIONS OF THE MIND

IV.1 INTRODUCTION

Thwarted intentions, frustrated wants, unsatisfied desires, failed projects: this is the stuff of everyday life, of world literature, of the social sciences. Some failures are due to external obstacles, to excusable false beliefs, to unforeseeable accidents, to calculated risks, to malevolent behaviour of others. These cases range from the trivial to the tragic, from Wodehouse to *Oedipus Rex*; their common feature is that failure does not imply lack of rationality. Other failures arise when people act rationally on irrational assumptions about the behaviour of others, i.e on inexcusable false beliefs. Such assumptions may arise in many ways. In some cases, discussed in III.2, the actors falsely assume themselves to be the only active agents and treat their environment as if it were a constant one, or at least made up of agents less sophisticated than themselves. In other cases wishful thinking is at work, as may happen when people act on the subjective probabilities discussed in III.4. In a third category of cases self-deception is behind the irrational assumptions. This is a more radical source of irrationality, as the agent somehow manages both to believe and not to believe the same ideas. Exactly *how* this feat is performed is the subject of IV.4.

Finally intentions may remain unrealized because they are inherently unrealizable. Some varieties of these were briefly surveyed in III.9, such as 'willing what cannot be willed', double binds, the *Catch 22* paradox and the Groucho Marx paradox. In IV.2 and IV.3 I explore the sense in which hate and love are emotions exhibiting such built-in contradictions which prevent them from finding a durable satisfaction. In the analysis of these

157

structures I draw upon three distinct traditions, which I shall
briefly discuss before coming to the point.

Within the philosophical tradition, the insistence upon contradictions as a feature of reality goes back to Heraclitus, and in recent
times is associated with the name of Hegel. I have discussed
elsewhere Hegel's theory of contradictions, concluding that we
should distinguish between the *Logic*, where the principle of
contradiction is squarely denied, and the *Phenomenology of Mind*,
where a much more acceptable position is worked out.[1] In the
former work Hegel actually says that two contradictory beliefs may
both be true, but in the latter the main assumption is that the
human mind often entertains contradictory beliefs, or single
beliefs from which a contradiction may be deduced. Similarly the
Phenomenology of Mind explores the stances characterized by
contradictory desires, the paradigm being the desire to eat one's
cake and have it. After Hegel Jean-Paul Sartre has shown an acute
insight into these paradoxical intentions. Indeed, *L'être et le néant*
argues that man's fundamental project is the desire to be
simultaneously an object and a consciousness, *en-soi* and *pour-soi*,
an argument which is spelled out in a number of masterful
analyses of specific attitudes. As was briefly observed in III.9,
Sartre's philosophy could be summed up by saying that man is
haunted by the desire to listen to his own funeral oration, so that
finally he can *know* what he *is*, two verbs that are mutually
incompatible.

Sartre is as much a novelist and playwright as a philosopher; and
the *Phenomenology of Mind* has been called a philosophical novel.
The second tradition, indeed, is found in the literary expressions
of the contradictions of the mind, especially in what we think of
as the modern period. To see the difference between the classical
and the modern attitudes, take Hermione's question in *Andromaque*: 'Je t'aimais inconstant, qu'aurais-je fait fidèle?' The implicit
answer, of course, is that if the object of her love had been more
constant, her love would have been even greater. The modern
answer, by contrast, is exactly the opposite, that inconstancy in the
love object is a condition of love. Stendhal and Proust are the
names that come to mind here, and through them the attitude has
spread so as to become virtually omnipresent. 'Modern' should not

[1]   Elster (1978a), ch. 4.

here be interpreted too strictly in a chronological sense. John Donne, writing before Racine, has an attitude perfectly congenial to the twentieth century. I believe, indeed, that Donne is the writer with the ear most fine-tuned to the contradictions involved in most human projects. Take, for example, his conceptual analysis of why it is contradictory to use the verb 'love' in the past tense:

> He is stark mad, who ever says,
>   That he hath been in love an hour,
> Yet not that love so soon decays,
>   But that it can ten in less space devour;
> Who will believe me, if I swear
> That I have had the plague a year?
> Who would not laugh at me, should I say,
> I saw a flask of powder burn a day?[2]

The argument is that there is a pragmatic inconsistency[3] in saying 'I loved', for love so transforms a person as to make him into a different individual. (The reader will perceive the link to the *Catch 22* paradox of III.9.) The extensive use made below of Donne's poetry warrants a brief discussion of his specificity. The paradoxical and twisted ways of Donne have not always been a source of admiration, and there is some truth in Samuel Johnson's observation: 'The most heterogeneous ideas are yoked by violence together; nature and art are ransacked for illustrations, comparisons, and allusions; their learning instructs, and their subtlety surprises; but the reader commonly thinks his improvement dearly bought, and, though he sometimes admires, is seldom pleased.'[4] As a characterization of Donne's best poems, this is definitely untrue, but some of his more explicit paradoxes may justifiably evoke this reaction. As the explicit paradoxes are often the most useful for the present purposes, I do not claim that the poems cited here are uniformly good poetry, though some of them certainly are. For Donne at his worst, we should go to the early *Paradoxes and Problems* or to the elegies, where implausible positions are defended with a strained wit that is only sometimes redeemed by the sheer exuberance of the performance.[5] Donne at his best is

---

[2] 'The Broken Heart'; cp. also 'The Paradox': 'I cannot say I loved, for who can say/He was killed yesterday?'
[3] Hintikka (1967) and Gullvåg (1977) deal with some aspects of this notion.
[4] Quoted from Clements (ed.) (1966), p. 107.
[5] An exception is Paradox 10, on wit and wisdom, biting itself in the tail in the most disarming manner; cp. also Sanders (1971), p. 28.

too movingly complex to permit encapsulation in a simple formula, albeit a paradox. Between the two extremes there are, however, many poems of very high quality which do hinge upon simple conceptual paradoxes of the kind discussed here.

Among my other authorities is Stendhal, both for his insight into the paradoxes of love and for the way he tried to overcome the paradoxes of sincerity. Julien Sorel and Lucien Leuwen act out the paradoxes of *De l'amour*; *Souvenirs d'égotisme* and *Vie de Henri Brulard* try valiantly to refute the thesis that sincerity is but the continuation of self-deception by other means. There is mathematics in Stendhal, as well as passion; an eighteenth-century mind allied to a nineteenth-century sensibility. Strange as the *rapprochement* may appear to be, these are the very same qualities which to me distinguish Emily Dickinson, who is also often cited in these pages. Her early training in science comes through very strongly not only in her metaphors from botany or geology, but in the formal precision of her verse; formal in the sense of being about objects in general.[6] The authors mentioned here – Donne, Stendhal, Dickinson – are all strange voices, if compared, for example, to the robustness of Shakespeare, Balzac or Whitman. They are, moreover, strange in a uniquely defined manner that makes them appropriate for the present purpose. William Blake, to cite another strange writer, would not provide the same material. His paradoxes, e.g. his *Proverbs of Hell*, are often deep, but they are paradoxes only in the weaker sense of being surprising truths. 'The road of excess leads to the palace of wisdom', spelled out as 'You never know what is enough unless you know what is more than enough', expresses a genuine and lasting insight, and not an inconsistent attitude. (It can, of course, be transformed into a stronger paradox, by observing that it would be impossible to find out by experience where the border is without ever crossing it, and inconsistent to form the project to do so.)

The third tradition, finally, is made up of some strands from the history of psychology and psychiatry. Freud, of course, has hate, love and self-deception at the very centre of his work, but the uneasy coexistence in his writings of causal and intentional models of man makes it hard to reconstruct a coherent theory of

6   Hagenbüchle (1974).

contradictions from them. Some recent attempts to restate psy-
choanalytic theory in 'action language', to get rid of the reified
terminology of causal structures behaving strangely like intentional actors, do not appear wholly successful, though I believe
them to point in the right direction. At a more superficial level
the student of self-deception can learn much from cognitive
psychology, from Festinger to Janis and Mann; 'superficial'
because these studies mostly eschew the crucial philosophical
problem of how self-deception is at all possible, and sometimes are
demonstrably in error because of this negligence. Finally it will not
come as a surprise to the reader that the work of Bateson,
Watzlawick and other members of the Palo Alto school is
highlighted here. Their topic is not so much one of persons
setting up contradictory goals for themselves, as one of persons
issuing contradictory orders to other people, who are then caught
in a 'double bind' when trying to realize them. In their work, as
in most of the other examples cited in this chapter, the contradictions are of a pragmatic kind rather than of a straightforward
logical character: the implicit presuppositions of the instructions
are incompatible with their overt content.

IV.2   HATE

> Take heed of hating me,
> Or too much triumph in the victory.
>   Not that I shall be mine own officer,
> And hate with hate again retaliate;
>   But thou wilt lose the style of conqueror,
> If I, thy conquest, perish by thy hate.
>   Then, lest my being nothing lessen thee,
>   If thou hate me, take heed of hating me.[7]

This verse captures so perfectly the paradox of hate that nothing
more is really required by way of conceptual analysis. Some
variations on the theme, nevertheless, may be useful for bringing
out how and when this attitude is likely to arise. First, we may
observe how the notion fits into Hegel's analysis of self-
consciousness in ch. IV of the *Phenomenology of Mind*. The main
theme of that chapter is the mind's attempt to come to grips,
practically, with the external world, having in the preceding

---

[7]   Donne, 'The Prohibition'.

chapters failed to arrive at a theoretical understanding. The defining project of self-consciousness in its initial stage of *desire* (*Begierde*) is described in the following terms:

Das Bewusstsein hat als Selbstbewusstsein nunmehr einen gedobbelten Gegenstand, den einen, den unmittelbaren, den Gegenstand der sinnlichen Gewissheit und des Wahrnehmens, der aber *für es* mit dem *Charakter des Negativen* bezeichnet ist, und den zweiten, nämlich *sich selbst*, welcher das wahre *Wesen* und zunächst nur erst im Gegensatze des ersten vorhanden ist. Das Selbstbewusstsein stellt sich hierin als die Bewegung dar, worin dieser Gegensatz aufgehoben und ihm die Gleichheit seiner selbst mit sich wird.[8]

To dominate the external world through desire means to assimilate it physically, by eating and drinking. (Sexual gratification appears at a later stage in the *Phenomenology*, with essentially the same paradoxical features.)[9] Self-consciousness finds, however, that this means dependence upon the world rather than liberation from it:

In dieser Befriedigung aber macht es die Erfahrung von der Selbständigkeit seines Gegenstandes. Die Begierde und die in ihrer Befriedigung erreichte Gewissheit seiner selbst ist bedingt durch ihn, denn sie ist durch Aufheben dieses Andern; *dass dies Aufheben sei, muss dies Andere sein.* Das Selbstbewusstsein vermag also durch seine negative Beziehung ihn nicht aufzuheben; es erzeugt ihn darum vielmehr wieder, so wie die Begierde.[10]

The phrase that I have italicized again gives the paradox in a nutshell. If a mode of consciousness is defined through the negation of another object, then consciousness depends upon that object in its very being. The phrase 'inner negation' is sometimes used for this attitude, which is also exemplified in the *decision to forget* discussed in II.3. By 'trying to forget' something, I negate it *and* affirm it. The injunction 'Forget it' may set up a double bind of a rather vicious variety, as when a child is told by a parent 'Remember that you must not even think about this forbidden thing.' Without Communism the anti-Communist of the God-that-failed category would lose the very meaning of life; for the militant atheist the death of God, or of all believers, would be equally disastrous.

---

[8]   Hegel (1807), p. 135.   [9]   *Ibid.* pp. 262–6.

[10] *Ibid.* p. 139. I believe that Marx's views on the relation between capitalism and feudalism can be interpreted in a similar manner. Capitalism is viable only so long as it can expand into the precapitalist sectors of the economy. With the complete penetration of capitalism in all sectors comes also a fall in the rate of profit and the rise of the working class. The capitalists, therefore, 'strive to avoid every forcible collision with the aristocracy; but historical necessity and the Tories press them onwards' (*New York Daily Tribune*, 25 Aug. 1852).

Having discovered, with the self-consciousness whose Odyssey he is following, that desire can give no durable satisfaction, Hegel goes on to a more complex attitude where self-consciousness relates itself to another self-consciousness. The transition to this stage is made in a passage immediately following the last text quoted above:

Es ist in der Tat ein Anderes als das Selbstbewusstsein, das Wesen der Begierde; und durch diese Erfahrung ist ihm selbst diese Wahrheit geworden. Zugleich aber ist es ebenso absolut für sich, und ist dies nur durch Aufheben des Gegenstandes, und es muss ihm seine Befriedigung werden, denn es ist die Wahrheit. Um der Selbständigkeit des Gegenstandes willen kann es daher zur Befriedigung nur gelangen, indem dieser selbst die Negation an ihm vollzieht; und er muss diese Negation seiner selbst an sich vollziehen, denn er ist *an sich* das Negative, und muss für das Andre sein, was er ist. Indem er die Negation an sich selbst ist und darin zugleich selbständig ist, ist er Bewusstsein.[11]

If the self-consciousness can make the object *negate itself*, then it can be freed from the perpetual need to find new objects to negate; or so it believes. This self-negating object can only be another consciousness, which as a *slave* is the property of the original self-consciousness, the *master*. The details of the master–slave dialectic are so well known that I shall not repeat them here, but refer to the expositions given elsewhere.[12] The idea to be retained is simply that the master sets himself the contradictory goal of achieving a *unilateral recognition*. The goal is contradictory, because for this recognition to have any worth and give the 'satisfaction' desired by the master, it must come from a being which he himself recognizes, and this cannot be a slave or an *instrumentum vocale*. The master cannot simultaneously achieve the satisfaction which he gets from dominating the slave and, through him, the external world laboured by the slave, *and* the satisfaction derived from recognition. Or, more simply, you cannot force another being to respect you. To the 'Be spontaneous' paradoxes explored by Watzlawick and his associates, we can add the 'Be respectful' paradox of slavery.

Eugene Genovese has shown that in American slavery this paradox was important indeed. The dual status of the slave as a human being and an object showed up, for example, in the law: if the slave has the capacity to commit crime, is it not also a crime

[11]   Hegel (1807), p. 139.
[12]   Elster (1976b), pp. 260ff; Elster (1978a), pp. 70ff, 208ff.

to mistreat him? How can you be a human being as an offender and a thing as a victim?[13] Also, the masters became dependent upon their slaves, by the very mechanism described by Hegel: 'The masters desperately needed the gratitude of their slaves in order to define themselves as moral human beings. The slaves, by withholding it, drove a dagger into their masters.'[14] As in Donne's phrase, there really was no need for the slave to be 'mine own officer, / And hate with hate again retaliate', for the masters in their own interest were led to avoid excessive brutality 'lest my being nothing lessen thee'.

The Hegelian progression is repeated, with some variations, in Sartre's work. The attitude which we have described as hate appears in Sartre as sadism:

Toutefois le sadisme lui-même...renferme le principe de son échec...C'est en effet la liberté transcendentale de la victime qu'il cherche à s'approprier. Mais précisément cette liberté demeure par principe hors d'atteinte. Et *plus le sadique s'acharne à traiter l'Autre en instrument, plus cette liberté lui échappe.*[15]

For Sartre, the attempt to *possess the liberty* of the other is characteristic of many human relations, an ideal which is equally contradictory in the form of love as in the form of hate or sadism. In sadism, however, as is indicated by the phrase that I have italicized, there is the added contradiction that by treating the victim as a thing, the sadist destroys the very thing he is trying to appropriate. We do not find, however, the twist whereby the master is turned into the slave of his slave. Nor is this insight to be found in Freud's writings on the subject. To be sure, Freud recognizes that sadism can turn into its opposite, masochism; indeed, and in contradistinction to Sartre, he sees all masochism as converted sadism.[16] In other cases sadism is turned into self-torture without an external agent; the active verb is converted to the reflexive rather than the passive voice. These 'transformations', however, are causal and not intentional; they occur, but we cannot understand them. By contrast, the Hegelian dialectic

[13] Genovese (1974), pp. 25ff.
[14] *Ibid.* p. 146.   [15] Sartre (1943), pp. 475–6.
[16] Freud (1969), x, pp. 219ff, in particular p. 220: 'Ein ursprünglicher Masochismus, der nicht auf die beschriebene Art aus dem Sadismus entstanden wäre, scheint nicht vorzukommen.' Sartre, by contrast, discusses masochism before sadism, though it is not certain whether this order is a causal–chronological one, or a logical–phenomenological one (as in the development of the *Phenomenology of the Mind*).

is moved by consciousness attempting to work out the implications of its successive projects, so that we can *understand* how strength is turned into weakness or dominance into dependence. Freud's language of desires changing their object, while somehow remaining the same desires, is exceedingly hard to accept, and the intentional language seems much more appropriate to these phenomena. I also believe that intentional language is better suited than the 'action language' proposed by Roy Schafer;[17] you can form contradictory intentions but not perform contradictory actions. Schafer's notion of paradoxical action is inadequate because it does not capture the idea that the opposed modes of behaviour stem from a *single unitary project*.

I V.3   LOVE

> Love, oh love, oh loveless love,
> We set our hearts on goalless goals,
> With dreamless dreams and schemeless schemes,
> We wreck our love-boat on the shoals.

This ditty by W. C. Handy may not be great poetry, but it tells us more about the paradoxes of love than the first verse of the poem by Donne of which the second verse was cited as epigraph to IV.2:

> Take heed of loving me,
> At least remember, I forbade it thee:
> Not that I shall repair my unthrifty waste
> Of breath and blood, upon thy sighs, and tears,
> By being to thee then what thou to me wast;
> But, so great joy, our life at once outwears,
> Then, lest thy love, by my death, frustrate be,
> If thou love me, take heed of loving me.

This, I submit, is distinctly weak, both as poetry and as paradox. The contradictions of love are made of less sentimental stuff. I begin by excluding the notion of irrational love as being somehow founded on false beliefs[18] about the loved person. As was stated in IV.1, I am concerned here with love as an inherently unrealizable project. I should also state that I do not imply that

---

[17] Schafer (1976) is very close to Gilbert Ryle (1949) in his conceptualization, whereas I believe that the tradition stemming from Husserl and revitalized by recent Anglo-American thought will ultimately prove more fruitful. It should be added, however, that Schafer's demolition of the traditional Freudian language is performed with unprecedented clarity and force.

[18] G. Taylor (1975–6), pp. 157ff, has a discussion of this notion.

love is necessarily paradoxical and contradictory. Indeed, I will not attempt to define the emotion, which is best recognized through its clinical symptoms. These symptoms may correspond to a stable project, or to an unstable and inconsistent one. I am here concerned with the latter only, but let me briefly state how a satisfactory and stable love relationship could be conceptualized. To this end two features of love will be stressed: the transformation of the lover and the need for reciprocity. Taken together, these imply that in love both persons are mutually and conditionally transformed, the metamorphosis of each being contingent upon that of the other. Here we can draw upon Charles Taylor's theory of the responsibility for self, as exposed and discussed in II.9 above. If another person changes the boundary conditions for my life so as to permit me to redefine myself in a way that would otherwise have been unattainable, and my redefined self likewise changes the boundary conditions for that person, then we are bound to each other in a state of love that is certainly precarious, like the solution to a game without dominant strategies, but not necessarily evanescent or inconsistent. The 'inter-assured of the mind' are like 'twin compasses'; in an extraordinary line Donne also exhorts us 'True and false fears let us refrain',[19] as if saying could make it so, which indeed it can.

It is correct that reciprocation in this sense is the object of love,[20] but it may also mean the death of love. I have already touched upon this in IV.1, commenting upon a line from *Andromaque*. The point is strongly driven home by Stendhal in his description of the seesaw relation between Julien Sorel and Mathilde de la Mole. The simplest, and perhaps the best, conceptualization of this pheno- menon is by way of the Groucho Marx paradox of III.9: I would not dream of loving someone who would stoop so low as to love *me*. Henri Peyre attributes to Rousseau 'that strangely pre- Proustian notion that to possess a woman . . . is also to debase her',[21]

---

[19] 'The Anniversary'; the preceding phrases are from 'A Valediction: Forbidding Mourning'.

[20] Newton-Smith (1973), p. 126, writes that 'It does seem to be a g-necessary truth that if A loves B, A wishes to be loved by B', the concept of g-necessity being one of a necessary connection in the general case, some exceptions being permitted. I do not believe that the seesaw relations discussed in the text constitute exceptions to this statement; rather that the wish could not survive its fulfilment.

[21] Peyre (1963), p. 99. On p. 93 Peyre also quotes (in his own translation) the following letter from Rousseau to Madame d'Houdetot: 'If you are mine, I lose, though possessing you, her whom I honor.'

a notion that also finds its natural explanation through this paradox. The lover in this case is not possessed by the hubris implicit in some forms of the paradox, for he does see non-reciprocation as a sign of superiority and loveworthiness. As in all varieties of the paradox, however, reciprocation is seen as a sign of inferiority. The lover strives to be recognized by a person whose recognition has worth only when withheld, in contradistinction to the Hegelian master who strives to be recognized by a person whom he has already refused to recognize, denying him thereby the very condition that could give worth to the recognition. (This contrast is also noted by Sartre, in much the same terms.)[22]

Reciprocated love can be explained, as was suggested above, on an analogy, not to be taken too literally, with the realization of the solution in a game without a dominant strategy. The paradoxical form of love discussed in the previous paragraph is more like a game without a solution, discussed in III.2. An intermediate case could be conceived on an analogy with games where the solution exists but is not realized, precisely because it does not consist of dominant strategies. In this category of cases, in other words, there is a failure of information that prevents the relationship from emerging. This information breakdown may be due to external causes, in which case it is not particularly interesting, but it may also stem from the nature of the relation itself. Thus Lucien Leuwen and Madame de Chasteller are unable to declare their love for each other, because the very qualities which make them lovable also prevent them from speaking out. When Madame de Chasteller for the first time answers a letter from Lucien, Stendhal observes that

'Ah! Madame de Chasteller répond', aurait dit le jeune homme de Paris, un peu plus vulgairement élevé que Leuwen. 'Sa grandeur d'âme s'y est enfin décidée. Voilà le premier pas. Le reste est une affaire de forme; ce sera un mois ou deux, suivant que j'aurai plus ou moins de savoir-faire, et elle des idées plus ou moins exagérées sur ce que doit être la défense d'une femme de la première vertu.'[23]

Lucien, by contrast, perceives only the severe tone of the answer, and lacks the wit to disregard the content and to see that the very fact of having been answered is the real message. On the other hand Stendhal tells us over and over again that it is only this very

---

[22] Sartre (1943), p. 438: 'Ce que le maître hégélien est pour l'esclave, l'amant veut l'être pour l'aimé. Mais l'analogie s'arrête ici, car le maître n'exige, chez Hegel, que latéralement et, pour ainsi dire, implicitement, la liberté de l'esclave, au lieu que l'amant exige *d'abord* la liberté de l'aimé.'   [23] Stendhal (1952), I, p. 960.

lack of *savoir-faire* which makes Lucien acceptable to Madame de Chasteller; he cannot simultaneously inspire love and be able to exploit it.

Sartre sees love as an essentially futile attempt to 'possess a liberty'.[24] (An illustration is found in *The Collector* by John Fowles.) The lover wants the subjection of his object, freely given. This paradox is reflected, for example, in an everyday phrase like the following: 'If you promise me to do it without my asking you to, I will promise not to ask you.' We are clearly dealing with a variety of the 'Be spontaneous' paradox, but with an added twist that can be stated as follows. In the standard order 'Be spontaneous', the contradiction is between the form and the content of the injunction. The same content in another syntactical form might be quite consistent, e.g. 'I wish that he were spontaneous.' The paradox of love, on the other hand, goes deeper, for here part of the wish is that it shall be fulfilled *as* obedience to an order. This, at any rate, is Sartre's contention:

Ainsi l'amant ne désire-t-il pas posséder l'aimé comme on possède une chose; il réclame un type spécial d'appropriation. Il veut posséder une liberté comme liberté. Mais, d'autre part, il ne saurait se satisfaire de cette forme éminente de la liberté qu'est l'engagement libre et volontaire. Qui se contenterait d'un amour qui se donnerait comme pure fidélité à la foi jurée? Qui donc accepterait de s'entendre dire: 'Je vous aime parce que je me suis librement engagé à vous aimer et que je ne veux pas me médire; je vous aime par fidélité à moi-même?' Ainsi l'amant demande le serment et s'irrite du serment. Il veut être aimé par une liberté et réclame que cette liberté comme liberté ne soit plus libre.[25]

Further paradoxes relate to the function of *time* in love. Donne, in several poems, explores the importance of *growth* for love. We can certainly impute to him one thesis about this element, and possibly also a slightly stronger one. The weak thesis is this:

> Except our loves at this noon stay,
> We shall new shadows make the other way,
>   As the first were made to blind
>   Others; these which come behind
> Will work upon ourselves, and blind our eyes.
> If our loves faint, and westwardly decline;
>   To me thou, falsely, thine,
>   And I to thee mine actions shall disguise.
> The morning shadows wear away,
> But these grow longer all the day,
> But oh, love's day is short, if love decay.

[24] Sartre (1943), p. 434.   [25] *Ibid.*

> Love is a growing or full constant light;
> And his first minute, after noon, is night.[26]

If the satisfaction (*Befriedigung*) derived from love is a function both of the intensity of the emotion and of its rate of change, this text says that if the second variable takes on negative values, then the value of the function is zero. Compare Emily Dickinson on a similar topic:

> Crumbling is not an instant's Act
> A fundamental pause
> Dilapidation's processes
> Are organized Decays
>
> 'Tis first a Cobweb on the Soul
> A Cuticle of Dust
> A Borer in the Axis
> An Elemental Rust –
>
> Ruin is formal – Devil's work
> Consecutive and slow –
> Fail in an instant, no man did
> Slipping – is Crash's law.[27]

Both may be right, because they are not necessarily concerned with the same processes. The *anticipation* of decay can make the decay come about instantaneously, the dark future working backwards on the present, as in a sequential Prisoner's Dilemma.[28]

The stronger thesis says that love must grow if it is to exist at all; that the function defined above takes on the value zero if either of the variables is zero. In III.8 a similar assertion was quoted from Leibniz;[29] imagine also a downhill race on bicycle or ski, where the pleasure depends both upon speed and acceleration. The psychological foundation for this thesis is very different from that of the former one; the lack of an actual experience of growth rather than an anticipation of decay. It is not certain whether it can be

---

[26] 'A Lecture upon the Shadow'.   [27] Dickinson (1970), no. 997.

[28] When the future is known precisely, e.g. the number of games to be played finite and known in advance, then the compelling rationality of the non-cooperative strategy in the last game has a contagious effect on the next but last, which for all practical purposes appears as the last; and so on to the first game in the sequence. A similar problem arises in the 'examination paradox', where a number of students are told that they will have an unexpected examination some time during the next week; it is easy to show that no such examination can take place. It has often been remarked that human life would be completely transformed if men were immortal; I believe that no less profound transformations would occur if the span of life was known in advance.

[29] Cp. Elster (1978a), p. 64, for some remarks on the mathematical structure of this view.

imputed to Donne, who only states that an indefinitely growing love is possible:

> And though each spring do add to love new heat,
> As princes do in action get
> New taxes, and remit them not in peace,
> No winter shall abate the spring's increase.[30]

These are paradoxical phenomena not in the strict sense of inherently unrealizable projects, but in the looser sense of inherently unstable and evanescent emotions, present only when emerging or already gone when disappearing.

Time also makes for paradox by a different mechanism, related to the structure of inner time. As explained by Husserl,[31] the consciousness of inner time is a network of temporal intentions: retentions, impressions and protentions, directed towards the past, present and future respectively. The object of any such intention is an integral experience, complete with its own retentions, impressions and protentions. This means that when I grasp the past, I also grasp the present as the future of that past; similarly the present is embodied in the future as what will then have been. These correspondences may be only latently or implicitly known to consciousness, but they always contribute something to the tonality of the present, making it both the fulfilment of an expectation and the birth of a memory. In love these overtones may take on a pathological dominance, so that the present meeting with the beloved is experienced *only* as the meeting place of past expectations and future regrets. The experience may be richly comic in its outward manifestations, but inwardly the paradox is lived with the mute frenzy well described by Stendhal in ch. XXIV of *De L'Amour*:

Lorsqu'on doit voir le soir la femme qu'on aime, l'attente d'un si grand bonheur rend insupportable tous les moments qui en séparent.

Une fièvre dévorante fait prendre et quitter vingt occupations. L'on regarde sa montre à chaque instant, et l'on est ravi quand on voit qu'on a pu faire passer dix minutes sans la regarder; l'heure tant désirée sonne enfin, et quand on est à sa porte, prêt à frapper, l'on serait aise de ne pas la trouver; ce n'est que par réflexion qu'on s'en affligerait: en un mot, l'attente de la voir produit un effet désagréable.

Voilà de ces choses qui font dire aux bonnes gens que l'amour déraisonne.

[30] 'Love's Growth'; cp. also 'Lovers' Infiniteness'.
[31] Husserl (1966), in particular §§24, 25.

C'est que l'imagination, retirée violemment de réveries délicieuses où chaque pas produit le bonheur, est ramenée à la sévère réalité.

L'âme tendre sait bien que dans le combat qui va commencer aussitôt que vous la verrez, la moindre négligence, le moindre manque d'attention ou de courage sera puni par une défaite empoisonnant pour longtemps les rêveries de l'imagination.

This collapse of inner time is distantly related to another time-bound paradox of love, which also turns upon the anticipation of future regret. In the situations described by Stendhal, the lover often has the certainty that he will regret whatever he does. The obvious strategy for coping with this problem is to simulate a decision, and then do exactly the opposite, in the hope of catching oneself unawares. 'Being the kind of person I am, this is the kind of irredeemable error I am liable to commit, so I should be on safe ground if I yield to the opposite impulse.' But then, inescapably, comes the second thought: what if *this* strategy is the kind of error by which all will be destroyed? The general structure of this reasoning is related to Newcomb's Problem, a paradox first discussed by Robert Nozick.[32] Here a person is given instructions summarized as follows:

On the table before you are two boxes A and B. Box B contains 100 dollars. Box A contains either 0 dollars or 1000 dollars. You have the choice between either opening A and taking as your reward what is inside, or opening both A and B and taking as your reward what is inside both. The money is placed inside box A *before* you make your choice, by a Being who in the past has had an uninterrupted run of one million correct guesses as to which choice would be made by other subjects (given these very same instructions) subsequent to the placing of the money, and he has consistently placed the money so that everyone who opened A has got 1000 dollars and everyone who has opened both boxes has got 100 dollars only. In other words, when the Being foresees that someone is going to open both boxes, he places nothing inside box A. Otherwise he places 1000 dollars in it, and he has always been successful in his anticipations so far. Now make your choice.

The dilemma of the person given these instructions is obvious. His best option would seem to be to outguess the Being; to scrutinize himself to see whether he is the kind of person who is liable to open box A only, and, if so, to open both boxes. The catch, of course, is that he cannot be sure whether he is not rather the kind of person liable to calculate in this way, in which case the Being

---

[32]   Nozick (1969b); also Elster (1978a), pp. 85ff.

is not going to place any money in box A. We see that this is really a variety of the paradoxical attempt to be simultaneously *en-soi* and *pour-soi*. The lover or the recipient of the instructions tries to contemplate himself from the outside, as if he were a fixed essence with an immutable nature, and then adds a grain of consciousness to exploit the knowledge thus acquired. This is like an attempt to catch your own shadow by turning around swiftly and unexpectedly. The lover feels that there *is* one action that can save him, viz. the action he is not going to choose: from this he is necessarily led to the attempt to be a *pour-soi* contemplating his *en-soi*. Sartre believes this project to be constitutive of human reality, but this is an extreme and unwarranted conclusion. The desire to catch oneself when one is not looking arises from the compulsion of specific situations, be they set up by an omniscient Being or by an impossible love.

IV.4 SELF-DECEPTION

Il y a donc deux manières de falsifier: l'une par le travail d'*embellir*, l'autre par l'application à *faire vrai*.[33]

Here Valéry, foreshadowing Sartre,[34] says that self-deception may lodge in sincerity as well as in insincerity. Man simply cannot help being false to himself, and the injunction 'To thine own self be true' is an impossible one. The omnipresence and the necessity of self-deception is an extreme thesis. At the other extreme is the contention that self-deception is impossible, as it would entail the same person both knowing and not knowing the same thing in the same respect. Between the two stands common sense, which tells us that men sometimes but not always deceive themselves. I shall try to show that this position is well in line with the theory of imperfect rationality sketched in chapter II, though I do not claim that this approach can deal with all varieties of self-deception. Some of the remaining cases can be handled with additional conceptual machinery, and still other cases will remain unresolved. This partial success is no great achievement, as the cases left in suspense may be said to be the hard ones. On the other hand no competing theory can be said to have completely solved this

---

[33] Valéry (1957), p. 571. Cp. p. 570: 'C'est une loi de la nature que l'on ne se défende d'une affectation que par une autre.'   [34] Sartre (1943), pp. 102ff.

problem, which to my mind is the crucial test that any theory of human nature has to pass. Freud's theory of the mind is notoriously unable to make sense of the notion of self-deception in resistance and defence,[35] recent refinements notwithstanding.[36] Sartre, here as elsewhere, solves the problem by the method of overkill, making self-deception so omnipresent as to disappear as a distinctive phenomenon. Fingarette, in the most recent full-length analysis,[37] stumbles at the crucial point where the emergence of a unitary self is to be explained. The recent developments in cognitive psychology[38] do not even seem to have grasped the nature of the difficulty. Self-deception may indeed be a form of 'hot cognition',[39] but it also has specific features that require a different approach.

Let me begin with a number of classificatory observations, in order to place self-deception on the map of contradictions of the mind. To begin with, as has been observed by many writers,[40] self-deception is related to weakness of will, either as a cognitive analogy to that phenomenon or as its condition of possibility. By deceiving yourself as to the nature of the good, you may do the bad while knowing 'in your heart' what is good. It is clear that this cannot be a solution to the problem of *akrasia*. In the first place there are standard cases of weakness of will where I do the bad

[35] Ibid. pp. 88ff, Gardiner (1969–70), Schafer (1976), pp. 235ff; also Fingarette (1969), ch. VI, and Pears (1974).

[36] Schafer (1976), while criticizing the traditional Freudian framework, tries to restate and solve the problem of self-deception in his 'action language'. I do not feel, however, that his basic concepts are sufficiently clarified for this reinterpretation to be convincing. For a typical – and to me incomprehensible – statement, consider the following: '...people do frequently resolve consciously, preconsciously or unconsciously to think only certain thoughts, feel only certain emotions, and perform only certain deeds' (p. 197). How this feat of unconscious resolution is performed is to me a total mystery; a restatement of the problem, not a solution.

[37] Fingarette (1969), pp. 107ff. On p. 109 he states that 'the world is such as to bring it about that individuals do become persons', i.e. that the community of selves acquires a dominant and integrating member, the others being subordinated to and transformed by this central self. He then adds that how this comes about 'is an issue we need not debate here'. I believe, on the contrary, that his model of the self and of consciousness requires an explanation of this process if it is to be taken seriously. Some of the ideas from chapter II above might be relevant here, if the emergence of *a* self among the selves is seen as the result of strategic planning (and possibly counterplanning). In this case, however, the problem of self-deception can be treated in a quite different manner, as argued below.

[38] See in particular the recent synthesis by Janis and Mann (1977).

[39] Abelson (1963) is at the origin of this notion.

[40] Rorty (1972), p. 405; Fingarette (1969), pp. 76ff.

in full awareness of the good; and in the second place the explanation, where apt, is only a case of *obscurium per obscurius*. The formal analogy between the two phenomena is more interesting than the purported causal links. At the most general level, there have been intensive discussions as to whether self-deception and weakness of will are at all possible; whether they represent contradictory notions about mental phenomena rather than notions about contradictory mental phenomena.[41] At a more specific level, both notions involve a conflict where there are reasons on both sides, the stronger side losing out to the weaker. This is obviously the case in weakness of will. To see that it also holds for self-deception, consider the case of a person who deliberately refuses to gather all available evidence because he strongly fears that it will tell against some of his cherished beliefs. The lack of this evidence does count as evidence of a sort for his belief, though it is weak evidence indeed. I return to this point below. Here I shall only point to some differences between *akrasia* and self-deception. In addition to the obvious difference between the practical and the theoretical spheres where these paradoxes occur, there is the fundamental dissimilarity that self-deception, unlike weakness of will, is an intentional *project*. We can, at least roughly, conceptualize weakness of will as some kind of mental *surdity*[42] where the intentional projects of the mind are thwarted by causal mechanisms. Self-deception, on the other hand, essentially *is* a project, the project to deceive oneself; paradox arises because 'je dois savoir très précisément cette vérité *pour* me la cacher soigneusement'.[43]

As is implicit in this last remark, and as is stressed correctly by Fingarette,[44] self-deception should be clearly distinguished from the simultaneous entertainment of incompatible beliefs. It implies this, but also something more, viz. the intentional element just referred to. Self-deception should also be distinguished from wishful thinking, where there is neither contradiction nor intentionality.[45] Wishful thinking arises because one is causally

---

[41] For this distinction, see Elster (1978a), pp. 67ff. Also Rorty (1972), p. 395: 'Attributions of self-deception are attributions of incoherence, not incoherent attributions.'

[42] Davidson (1969), p. 113.

[43] Sartre (1943), p. 87; his italics.

[44] Fingarette (1969), ch. II.

[45] For discussions of the relation between self-deception and wishful thinking, see Fingarette (1969), pp. 19–20, and Pears (1974).

influenced by one's desires and preferences when assessing evidence; it is, in a sense, closer to weakness of will than to self-deception. The psychic processes going on behind my back may induce me to follow the weaker reasons over reasons known to be stronger (weakness of will) or make the weaker reasons appear the stronger (wishful thinking); both cases are different from the deliberate attempt to overlook the stronger reasons. The decision-making studies of cognitive psychology focus intensively on wishful thinking, under the term 'defensive avoidance'. In the recent and exhaustive study by Janis and Mann many of the sub-strategies of defensive avoidance seem very close to self-deception, as when subjects persuade themselves to disregard remote consequences of their actions.[46] (Here, of course, the cases may shade over into weakness of will as well.) There is, surprisingly, no discussion of self-deception in their work, nor any reference to the large body of philosophical literature in this field. In this respect they perpetuate the philosophical naïveté of earlier work in cognitive psychology, in particular of the Festinger school. The consequences of this neglect are discussed below.

Some hurdles related to sincerity should also be cleared. As is shown by Henri Peyre in his extensive study of sincerity in literature,[47] many authors have assimilated sincerity with inconsistency. To present oneself as made of one block is necessarily deception, of oneself or of others; real sincerity implies that all the contradictory facets of the self are given free expression. This strongly contrasts with Fingarette's approach, where a main theme is that self-deception arises because the self has not achieved an integrated structure but keeps some of its officially disavowed projects alive in the wings.[48] At one level it is easy to side with Fingarette and with Peyre, when the latter remarks that

Morally as well as psychologically, the passive acceptance of our contradictions and the laying bare of them in self-analyzing fictional characters who watch for every symptom of disunity in themselves and record all that is ignoble in their desires or in their dreams may not be distinctly superior to establishing a hierarchy, an order of priority among all the promptings which solicit our attention.[49]

The hubris of confession, 'professing guilt to claim credit for the sin', as John von Neumann is reported to have said of Robert

---

[46] Janis and Mann (1977), p. 92.
[48] Fingarette (1969), ch. IV.
[47] Peyre (1963), pp. 38ff, 88ff, 319ff.
[49] Peyre (1963), p. 322.

Oppenheimer,[50] is indeed a constant theme of the literature on sincerity. Both Valéry and Sartre find this fault in Stendhal,[51] though I cannot help suspecting this to be a case of one-upmanship. Be this as it may, we should add that it is also possible to be more or less honest towards one's self-deception. The recidivist self-deceiver who refuses to become aware of his habit doubly deceives himself, whereas the self-deceiver who knows his propensity in this respect can deal strategically with his problem, as was explained in chapter II above. The unity of the mind does not imply an absence of contradictions, only an awareness of them and the ability to reduce their impact on behaviour.

The key to my own approach to self-deception is the notion of *responsibility for self*, with the Aristotelian and Sartrian varieties distinguished in II.9 above. Many apparent cases of self-deception can be reinterpreted as (successful or unsuccessful) attempts at self-modification. To each of the two sub-varieties corresponds a particular form of self-deception, as I shall now explain.

The self-deception associated with character formation, in the Aristotelian sense, has already been discussed at some length in II.3. Paradigmatic cases are the decision to believe and the decision to forget. These, if carried out successfully, would certainly qualify as examples of self-deception. Such decisions can occur in three modalities. At one extreme is the attempt to carry out, say, the decision to believe in a direct and fully conscious manner; this, as is argued by B. A. O. Williams, is conceptually impossible. At the other extreme is the use of indirect strategies, with the double effect of bringing about the desired state of belief and of inducing forgetfulness. (A related strategy is discussed by Fingarette, in an example involving a man drinking himself into a stupor so as to make himself liable to self-deception.)[52] In this case the person is indeed deceiving 'himself', but the deception can be successful only if the earlier and deceiving incarnation of the self can stage the scene so that it will be killed off by the later and deceived self. A lack of continuity in the self is the condition for successful self-deception in this case, just as lack of integrity may be a condition in other cases. Among these 'other cases' – the 'hard

[50]   Ulam (1976), p. 224.
[51]   Valéry (1957), p. 570; Sartre (1943), p. 105. Against this I prefer the interpretation of Wood (1971), p. 100.   [52]   Fingarette (1969), pp. 31, 80.

cases' referred to above – is the third modality of deciding to believe, intermediate between the two varieties defined above. In this mode the self-deceiver intentionally and instantaneously adopts a new belief, but somehow manages to hide this very intention from himself.[53] How this feat is performed has become *the* problem of self-deception. I am not going to propose a solution, except to express the hope that the residual class of cases that cannot be given a more straightforward analysis will ultimately be reduced to an empty set.

I have already cited the line from Donne 'True and false fears let us refrain'. The exhortation to avoid false fears is fairly conventional, but the reference to true fears sounds strangely like an invitation to self-deception. As was suggested above, however, it should rather be understood as an invitation to self-modification in the Sartrian sense of the term. This approach has indeed been chosen by several recent writers on self-deception.[54] Even if they do not follow Sartre in his emphasis on the self's unrestricted freedom to define itself ('il n'y a aucune inertie dans la conscience'),[55] they agree that 'within limits, saying makes it so', to repeat a phrase used in II.9. One can in this sense intentionally adopt new beliefs and attitudes, trying them on, as it were, to see whether they are compatible with the boundary conditions of one's life. In some cases, of course, they may turn out not to be so compatible; no amount of bootstrap-pulling could change Garcin in Sartre's *Huis clos* from a coward into a different kind of person. Garcin appeals to the idea implicit in a phrase cited elsewhere by Sartre,[56] 'Je suis trop grand pour moi', a manifest piece of self-deception. In other cases, however, these manoeuvres may be successful. It *is* possible to overcome fear by repeating to oneself 'I am not afraid', even though initially the statement was false. The failure of the enterprise is not a sufficient condition for us to talk about self-deception in such cases, for this would imply that one can always know beforehand whether it will be successful. There is a 'zone of indeterminacy' within which saying makes it so, and

---

[53] 'Thus the adoption of the *policy* of not spelling-out an engagement is a "self-covering" policy. To adopt it is, perforce, never to make it explicit, to "hide" it' (Fingarette 1969, p. 49).

[54] Rorty (1972), p. 392; de Sousa (1971), p. 312. For the general notion involved, see C. Taylor (1971, 1976).

[55] Sartre (1943), p. 101.   [56] *Ibid.* p. 96.

the borders of this zone are themselves indeterminate, i.e. incompletely known. Once we become accustomed to this way of looking at the world, I suspect that much of our experience can fit into this conceptual frame, so that many cases harshly dismissed as self-deception should be redescribed as unforeseeable failures of self-modification.

Some other cases of self-deception can be understood by a variant of Fingarette's theory that self-deception is the refusal to *spell out* one's engagement in the world. The variety of spelling-out that I have in mind is the gathering of all available evidence, self-deception arising when one deliberately refuses to collect threatening evidence. (We may observe in passing that the theory of rationality stressing the cost of information is tailor-made as a rationalization of this attitude.) The paradigmatic case is the dictator telling his underlings 'I do not want to know the details': even though he does know that there are unsavoury details to be known, the lack of specific knowledge permits him to say to himself and to others that he has no knowledge of such things occurring. The ability of millions of Germans to overlook the extermination of Jews can be explained on this model: they must have observed that their Jewish acquaintances disappeared, and they must have known that this had some gruesome explanation, but as long as they managed to remain ignorant of the details they could say to themselves that they were genuinely unaware of what went on. This is not a hard or paradoxical case of self-deception, because we do not have to impute to the self-deceiver a knowledge of the facts that he does not want to know, only a knowledge that there are such facts. The 'Preface paradox' of stating in the preface to a book that one believes that some of the statements made in the book are false,[57] and the 'Slander paradox' of saying that one would be liable to the laws of slander if one spoke one's true opinion of a person and that therefore one will not do so, also express this distinction between specific and general statements.

In cognitive psychology this variety of self-deception is often referred to as 'selective exposure to information'.[58] I believe that Leon Festinger's theory of cognitive dissonance acquired a rather

[57] Cp. Elster (1978a), p. 88.
[58] The following draws upon *ibid.* pp. 88ff.

fatal flaw because of his neglect of the paradoxical implications of this notion. The general thesis of the Festinger school being that people seek to reduce cognitive dissonance, Festinger in his first work singled out as a particularly important strategy the selective exposure to information, i.e. the tendency to expose oneself to information sources which will produce consonance and to avoid information sources that will increase dissonance. The glaring paradox latent in this formulation cropped up in several of the experimental studies used to buttress the argument. One study referred to the tendency of buyers of a product, such as a car of a certain make, to seek out and read advertisements for that brand even *after* the purchase, and to avoid ads for other brands. Here the problem is that we hesitate to talk about *information* in such cases. Information, like recognition, must come from an independent source in order to be worth while; to seek confirmation by reading ads for the product you have just bought is like seeking recognition from a slave. In another study the results predicted by the theory did not materialize, and this led Festinger, in his later work, to recognize the paradox: 'Once the person has been told that the information exists that does not support his decision, additional evidence has already been introduced – in a sense it is impossible for him to avoid it since he knows it exists.'[59] If this elementary observation had been made at the outset, the design of the entire sequence of experiments presumably would have been different. The neglect of the paradox in both the studies cited above amounts to an implicit assumption that the subjects were self-deceivers: that they could persuade themselves to take sham information for the real thing and to refrain from spelling out the details. This is certainly an interesting assumption to test, but it is not the hypothesis which the tests were devised for.

In brief conclusion, I believe that the interpretations of self-deception as self-modification and as a refusal to collect available evidence can account non-paradoxically for many important cases of bad faith. To repeat, I do not believe they can handle all 'hard cases', but at any rate they contribute to a reduction of the number of such cases. Further progress can only be made by further reductions.

[59] Festinger (1964), p. 82.

REFERENCES

Abelson, R. P. 1963. Computer simulation of hot cognition. In S. Tomkins and S. Messick (eds.), *Computer simulation of personality*, pp. 277–98. New York: Wiley.

Adserballe, H. 1977. *Frihedsberøvelse og trang i psykiatrien*. Copenhagen: FADL's Forlag.

Ainslie, G. 1975. Specious reward. *Psychological Bulletin* 82, 463–96.
1977. A behavioral understanding of the defense mechanism. Mimeographed.

Alchian, A. 1950. Uncertainty, evolution and economic theory. *Journal of Political Economy* 58, 211–22.

Arrow, K. 1963. *Social choice and individual values*, 2nd ed. New York: Wiley.

Arrow, K. and Hurwicz, L. 1972. An optimality criterion for decision-making under uncertainty. In C. F. Carter and J. L. Ford (eds.), *Uncertainty and expectation in economics*, pp. 1–11. Clifton, N.J.: Kelley.

Azzi, C. and Ehrenberg, R. 1975. Household allocation of time and church attendance. *Journal of Political Economy* 83, 27–56.

Bagehot, W. 1966. *The English constitution*. Ithaca, N.Y.: Cornell University Press.

Banton, M. (ed.) 1961. *Darwinism and the study of society*. London: Tavistock.

Barash, D. P. 1976. *Sociobiology and behavior*. New York: Elsevier.

Barth, F. 1967. Economic spheres in Darfur. In R. Firth (ed.), *Themes in economic anthropology*, pp. 149–74. London: Tavistock.

Baumol, W. 1952. *Welfare economics and the theory of the state*. London: Bell.

Becker, G. 1976. *The economic approach to human behavior*. Chicago: Chicago University Press.

Bellman, R. 1961. *Adaptive control processes*. Princeton, N.J.: Princeton University Press.

Bhaduri, A. 1973. A study in agricultural backwardness under semi-feudalism. *Economic Journal* 83, 120–37.

Bohannan, P. 1955. Some principles of exchange and investment among the Tiv. *American Anthropologist* n.s. 57, 60–70.

Borch, K. 1968. *The economics of uncertainty*. Princeton, N.J.: Princeton University Press.

Boudon, R. 1973a. *L'inégalité des chances*. Paris: Armand Colin.
1973b. *Mathematical structures of social mobility*. Amsterdam: Elsevier.
1974. *Education, opportunity and social inequality*. New York: Wiley.
1977. *Effets pervers et ordre social*. Paris: Presses Universitaires de France.

Bourdieu, P. and Passeron, J.-C. 1967. *Les héritiers*. Paris: Editions de Minuit.
1970. *La reproduction*. Paris: Editions de Minuit.

Bourdieu, P., Passeron, J.-C. and Chamboredon, J.-C. 1968. *Le métier de sociologue.* The Hague: Mouton.

Bowles, S. and Gintis, H. 1976. *Schooling in capitalist America.* London: Routledge and Kegan Paul.

Brams, S. 1976. *Paradoxes in politics.* New York: Free Press.

Brooke, M. 1972. Problems in the decision-making process. In M. Brooke and H. Remmers (eds.), *The multinational company in Europe*, pp. 93–109. London: Longman.

Cargile, J. 1966. Pascal's wager. *Philosophy* 35, 250–7.

Clements, A. L. (ed.) 1966. *John Donne's poetry.* New York: Norton.

Cobb, W. 1973. Theft and the two hypotheses. In S. Rottenberg (ed.), *The economics of crime and punishment*, pp. 19–30. Washington, D.C.: American Enterprise Institute for Public Policy Research.

Coddington, A. 1968. *Theories of the bargaining process.* London: Allen and Unwin.

Cody, M. L. 1974. Optimization in ecology. *Science* 183, 1156–64.

Cohen, S. N. 1977. Recombinant DNA: fact and fiction. Science 195, 654–7.

Coser, L. 1971. Social conflict and the theory of social change. In C. G. Smith (ed.), *Conflict resolution: contributions of the behavioral sciences*, pp. 58–65. Notre Dame, Ind.: University of Notre Dame Press.

Cotgrove, S. and Box, S. 1970. *Science, industry and society.* London: Allen and Unwin.

Curio, E. 1973. Towards a methodology of teleonomy. *Experientia* 29, 1045–58.
  1976. *The ethology of predation.* Berlin: Springer.

Cyert, R. M. and De Groot, M. H. 1975. Adaptive utility. In R. H. Day and T. Groves (eds.), *Adaptive economic models*, pp. 223–46. New York: Academic Press.

Darlington, C. D. 1969. *The evolution of man and society.* New York: Simon and Schuster.

David, P. 1975. *Technical choice, innovation and economic growth.* Cambridge: Cambridge University Press.

Davidson, D. 1969. How is weakness of the will possible? In J. Feinberg (ed.), *Moral concepts*, pp. 93–113. Oxford: Oxford University Press.
  1970. Mental events. In L. Foster and J. W. Swanson (eds.), *Experience and theory*, pp. 79–101. Amherst, Mass.: University of Massachusetts Press.
  1973. The material mind. In P. Suppes *et al.* (eds.), *Logic, methodology and philosophy of science IV*, pp. 709–24. Amsterdam: North Holland.
  1976. Psychology as philosophy. In J.Glover (ed.), *The philosopohy of mind*, pp. 101–10. Oxford: Oxford University Press.

Dawkins, R. 1976. *The selfish gene.* New York: Oxford University Press.

Dennett, D. 1971. Intentional systems. *Journal of Philosophy* 68, 87–106.
  1976. Conditions of personhood. In A. Rorty (ed.), *The identities of persons*, pp. 175–96. Berkeley: University of California Press.

Descartes, R. 1897–1910. *Oeuvres complètes*, ed. C. Adam and P. Tannery. 11 vols. Paris: Vrin.

Dickinson, Emily. 1970. *Complete poems*, ed. Thomas H. Johnson. London: Faber and Faber.

Dorfman, R., Samuelson, P. and Solow, R. 1958. *Linear programming and economic analysis.* New York: McGraw-Hill.

Dworkin, G. 1972. Paternalism. *The Monist* 56, 64–84.

Edmunds, M. 1974. *Defence in animals.* Harlow, Essex: Longman.

Ellsberg, D. 1971. The quagmire myth and the stalemate machine. *Public Policy* 19, 217–74.

Elster, J. 1975a. *Leibniz et la formation de l'esprit capitaliste.* Paris: Aubier.

1975b. Review of Francis Sejersted, *Ideal, teori og virkelighet. Economic History Review* 2nd ser. 28, 160.

1976a. A note on hysteresis in the social sciences. *Synthese* 33, 371–91.

1976b. Some conceptual problems in political theory. In B. Barry (ed.), *Power and political theory*, pp. 245–70. London: Wiley.

1978a. *Logic and society.* London: Wiley.

1978b. Exploring exploitation. *Journal of Peace Research* 15, 3–17.

1978c. The labor theory of value. *Marxist Perspectives* 1, 70–101.

Evans-Pritchard, E. 1940. *The Nuer.* Oxford: Oxford University Press.

Fararo, T. S. 1973. *Mathematical sociology.* New York: Wiley.

Farber, L. 1976. *Lying, despair, jealousy, envy, sex, suicide, drugs and the good life.* New York: Basic Books.

Feller, W. 1968. *An introduction to probability theory and its applications*, vol. 1, 3rd edn. New York: Wiley.

Fellner, W. 1961. Two propositions in the theory of induced innovations. *Economic Journal* 71, 305–8.

1965. *Probability and profits.* Homewood, Ill.: Irwin.

Festinger, L. 1964. Conflict, decision and dissonance. Stanford, Calif.: Stanford University Press.

Fingarette, H. 1969. *Self-deception.* London: Routledge and Kegan Paul.

Finley, M. I. 1973. *Democracy: ancient and modern.* London: Chatto and Windus.

Fishburn, P. 1973. On the foundations of game theory: the case of non-Archimedean Utilities. *International Journal of Game Theory* 2, 65–71.

Foreyt, J. P. (ed.) 1977. *Behavioral treatment of obesity.* Oxford: Pergamon Press.

Frankfurt, H. M. 1971. Freedom of will and the concept of a person. *Journal of Philosophy* 68, 5–20.

Frazzetta, T. H. 1975. *Complex adaptations in evolving populations.* Sunderland, Mass.: Sinauer.

Freud, S. 1969. *Gesammelte Werke.* Frankfurt a. M.: Fischer.

Friedman, M. 1953. The methodology of positive economics. In M. Friedman, *Essays in positive economics*, pp. 3–43. Chicago: University of Chicago Press.

Gardiner, P. 1969–70. Error, faith and self-deception. *Proceedings of the Aristotelian Society* n.s. 70, 197–220.

Genovese, E. 1965. *The political economy of slavery.* New York: Pantheon.

1974. *Roll, Jordan, Roll.* New York: Pantheon.

Georgescu-Roegen, N. 1950. The theory of choice and the constancy of economic laws. *Quarterly Journal of Economics* 64, 125–38.

1954. Choice, expectations and measurability. *Quarterly Journal of Economics* 68, 503–34.

Gerschenkron, A. 1970. *Europe in the Russian mirror.* Cambridge: Cambridge University Press.

Gibbard, A. 1974. A Pareto-consistent libertarian claim. *Journal of Economic Theory* 7, 388–410.

Glantz, S. A. and Albers, N. V. 1974. Department of Defense R & D in the university. *Science* 186, 706–11.

Goldman, A. 1972. Toward a theory of social power. *Philosophical Studies* 23, 221–68.

Gorman, W. M. 1967. Tastes, habits and choices. *International Economic Review* 8, 218–22.

Gould, S. J. 1976. D'Arcy Thompson and the science of form. In M. Greene and E. Mendelsohn (eds.), *Topics in the philosophy of biology*, pp. 66–97. Dordrecht: Reidel.

Griffin, D. R. 1976. *The question of animal awareness.* New York: Rockefeller University Press.

Grindheim, S. 1975. Hvorfor fikk aristokratiet regjere når borgerskapet hersket? Master's thesis in history, University of Oslo. Mimeographed.

Gullvåg, I. 1977. The logic of assertion. University of Trondheim. Mimeographed.

Haavelmo, T. 1944. The probability approach in econometrics. *Econometrica* (supplement) 12, 1–118.

   1970. Some observations on welfare and economic growth. In W. A. Eltis, M. Scott and N. Wolfe (eds.), *Induction, growth and trade: essays in honour of Sir Roy Harrod*, pp. 65–75. Oxford: Oxford University Press.

Hacking. I. 1975. *The emergence of probability* Cambridge: Cambridge University Press.

Hagenbüchle, R. 1974. Precision and indeterminacy. in the poetry of Emily Dickinson. *Emerson Society Quarterly* 20, 33–56.

Hájek, O. 1975. *Pursuit games.* New York: Academic Press.

Hamilton, W. 1964. The genetical theory of social behaviour. *Journal of Theoretical Biology* 7, 1–52.

   1967. Extraordinary sex ratios. *Science* 156, 477–88.

Hammond, P. 1976. Changing tastes and coherent dynamic choice. *Review of Economic Studies* 43, 159–73.

Harsanyi, J. 1955. Cardinal welfare, individualistic ethics and interpersonal comparisons of utility. *Journal of Political Economy* 63, 309–21.

   1976. Can the maximin principle serve as a basis for morality? *American Political Science Review* 69, 594–606.

   1977. *Rational behavior and bargaining equilibrium in games and social situations.* Cambridge: Cambridge University Press.

Heal, G. 1973. *The theory of economic planning.* Amsterdam: North Holland.

Hegel, G. W. F. !807. *Die Phänomenologie des Geistes.* Hamburg: Felix Meiner, 1953.

Henry, C. 1974. Investment decisions under uncertainty: the 'irreversibility effect'. *American Economic Review* 64, 1006–12.

Hicks, J. 1932. *The theory of wages.* London: Macmillan.

Himes, J. H. 1971. The functions of racial conflict. In C. G. Smith (ed.), *Conflict resolution*, pp. 170–9. Notre Dame, Ind.: University of Notre Dame Press.

Hintikka, J. 1967. *Cogito ergo sum*: inference or performance? In W. Doney (ed.), *Descartes*, pp. 108–39. London: Macmillan.

Hirsch, F. 1976. *Social limits to growth.* Cambridge, Mass.: Harvard University Press.

Hirschman, A. O. 1971. *Exit, voice and loyalty.* Cambridge, Mass.: Harvard University Press.

   1977. *The passions and the interests.* Princeton, N.J.: Princeton University Press.

Hobsbawm, E. 1959. *Primitive rebels.* Manchester: Manchester University Press.

Howard, N. 1971. *Paradoxes of rationality.* Cambridge, Mass.: MIT Press.

Husserl, E. 1966. *Zur Phänomenologie des inneren Zeitbewusstseins* (= Husserliana, vol. x). The Hague: Martinus Nijhoff.

184   *References*

Isaacs, R. 1965. *Differential games.* New York: Wiley.
Jacob, F. 1970. *La logique du vivant.* Paris: Gallimard.
James, W. 1896. The will to believe. In *The will to believe and other essays in popular philosophy.* New York: Dover, 1897.
Janis, I. 1972. *Victims of group-think.* Boston: Houghton Mifflin.
Janis, I. and Mann, L. 1977. *Decision making.* New York: Free Press.
Jarvie, I. C. 1968. Limits to functionalism and alternatives to it in anthropology. In R. A. Manners and D. Kaplan (eds.), *Theory in anthropology,* pp. 196–203. London: Routledge and Kegan Paul.
Jeffrey, D. B. 1975. Self-control: methodological issues and research trends. In M. J. Mahoney and C. E. Thoresen (eds.) (1975), pp. 166–99.
  1977. Introduction to part VI of Foreyt (ed.) (1977).
Jewell, D. 1977. *Duke: a portrait of Duke Ellington.* New York: Norton.
Johansen, L. 1973. On the optimal use of forecasts in public policy. *Journal of Public Economics* 1, 1–24.
  1977. *Lectures on macro-economic planning,* vol. I. Amsterdam: North Holland.
Kalecki, M. 1971. Political aspects of full employment. In M. Kalecki, *Selected essays on the dynamics of the capitalist economy,* pp. 138–45. Cambridge: Cambridge University Press.
Keeney, R. L. and Raiffa, H. 1976. *Decisions with multiple objectives.* New York: Wiley.
Kennedy, C. 1964. Induced innovation and the theory of distribution. *Economic Journal* 74, 541–7.
Kydland, F. and Prescott, E. 1977. Rules rather than discretion: the inconsistency of optimal plans. *Journal of Political Economy* 85, 473–92.
Lancaster, K. 1973. The dynamic inefficiency of capitalism. *Journal of Political Economy* 81, 1092–1109.
Latsis, S. 1976. A research programme in economics. In S. Latsis (ed.), *Methods and appraisal in economics,* pp. 1–41. Cambridge: Cambridge University Press.
Laudan, L. 1977. *Progress and its problems.* Berkeley: University of California Press.
LeClair, E. and Schneider, H. (eds.) 1968. *Economic anthropology.* New York: Holt, Rinehart and Winston.
Leibniz, G. W. 1875–90. *Die philosophische Schriften,* ed C. J. Gerhardt. 7 vols. Berlin: Weidmannsche Buchhandlung.
Leigh, E. G. 1971. *Adaptation and diversity.* San Francisco: Freeman and Cooper.
Lindbeck, A. 1976. Stabilization policy in open economies with endogenous politicians. *American Economic Review: Papers and Proceedings* 66, 1–19.
Luce, R. D. and Raiffa, H. 1957. *Games and decisions.* New York: Wiley.
Luce, R. D. and Suppes, P. 1965. Preference, utility and subjective probability. In R. D. Luce, R. R. Bush and E. Galanter (eds.), *Handbook of mathematical psychology,* vol. III, pp. 249–410. New York: Wiley.
McFarland, A. S. 1969. *Power and leadership in pluralist systems.* Stanford, Calif.: Stanford University Press.
Mahoney, M. J. 1972. Research issues in self-management. *Behavior Therapy* 3, 45–63.
Mahoney, M. J. and Thoresen, C. E. (eds.) 1975. *Self-control: power to the person.* Monterey, Calif.: Brooks/Cole.
Mangset, D. 1974. Industri, stat og karteller. Master's thesis in history, University of Oslo. Mimeographed.
March, J. 1977. Bounded rationality, ambiguity and the engineering of choice. Stanford University, Calif. Mimeographed.

de Marsily, G. *et al.* 1977. Nuclear waste disposal. *Science* 197, 519–27.

Marx, K. 1845–6. *Die deutsche Ideologie.* In Marx–Engels Werke, vol. III. Berlin: Dietz, 1962.

  1852. *Louis Napoleon's 18 Brumaire.*

  1857–8. *Grundrisse der Kritik der politischen Ökonomie.* Berlin: Dietz, 1953.

  1867. *Capital*, vol. I, tr. S. Moore and E. Aveling. New York: International Publishers, 1967.

  1971. *The unknown Karl Marx*, ed. R. Payne. New York: New York University Press.

Marx, K. and Engels, F. 1848. *The Communist Manifesto.*

  1971. *Articles on Britain.* Moscow: Progress Publishers.

Masters, R. D. 1975. Politics as a biological phenomenon. *Social Science Information* 14, 7–63.

  1976. Functional approaches to analogical comparisons between species. In M. von Cranach (ed.), *Methods of inference from animal to human behaviour*, pp. 73–102. The Hague: Mouton.

Maynard Smith, J. 1973. The logic of animal conflict. *Nature, London* 246, 15–18.

  1974. The theory of games and the evolution of animal conflict. *Journal of Theoretical Biology* 47, 209–21.

Mayr, E. 1970. *Populations, species and evolution.* Cambridge, Mass.: Harvard University Press.

Meisner, M. 1967. *Li Tao-chao and the origins of Chinese communism.* Cambridge, Mass.: Harvard University Press.

Merton, R. K. 1957. *Social theory and social structure.* Glencoe, Ill.: Free Press.

  1973. *The sociology of science.* Chicago: University of Chicago Press.

Millay, Edna St Vincent 1975. *Collected poems*, ed. N. Millay. New York: Harper and Row.

Miller, D. 1976. *Social justice.* Oxford: Oxford University Press.

Monod, J. 1970. *Le hasard et la nécessité.* Paris: Le Seuil.

de Montmort, R. 1713. *Essai d'analyse sur les jeux de hazard.* 2nd ed. Paris.

Morgenstern, O. 1964. Pareto-optimum and economic organization. In *Systeme und Methoden in den Wirtschafts- und Sozialwissenschaften: Festschrift für Erwin von Beckerath*, pp. 573–86. Tübingen: Mohr.

  1972. Thirteen critical points in contemporary economic theory. *Journal of Economic Literature* 10, 1163–89.

  1976. Some reflections on utility. In A. Schotter (ed.), *Selected economic writings of Oskar Morgenstern*, pp. 65–70. New York: New York University Press.

Morishima, M. and Seton, F. 1961. Aggregation in Leontief matrices and the labour theory of value. *Econometrica* 29, 203–20.

Mortimore, G. W. (ed.) 1971. *Weakness of will.* London: Macmillan.

Nagel, T. 1970. *The possibility of altruism.* Oxford: Oxford University Press.

Needham, J. 1956. *Science and civilisation in China*, vol. II. Cambridge: Cambridge University Press.

Nelson, R. and Winter, S. G. 1974. Neoclassical vs. evolutionary theories of economic growth. *Economic Journal* 84, 886–905.

  1976. Technical change in an evolutionary model. *Quarterly Journal of Economics* 90, 90–118.

Newton-Smith, W. 1973. A conceptual investigation of love. In A. Montefiore (ed.), *Philosophy and personal relations*, pp. 113–35. London: Routledge and Kegan Paul.

Nivison, D. 1976. Motivation and moral action in Mencius. Stanford University, Calif. Mimeographed.

Nordhaus, W. 1975. The political business cycle. *Review of Economic Studies* 42, 169–90.

North, D. 1971. Institutional change and economic growth. *Journal of Economic History* 31, 118–25.

North, D. and Thomas, R. 1973. *The rise of the western world.* Cambridge: Cambridge University Press.

Nozick, R. 1969a. Coercion. In S. Morgenbesser *et al.* (eds.), *Philosophy, science and method: essays in honor of Ernest Nagel,* pp. 440–72. New York: St Martin's Press.

  1969b. Newcomb's Problem and two principles of choice. In N. Rescher (ed.), *Essays in honor of Carl G. Hempel,* pp. 114–46. Dordrecht: Reidel.

  1974. *Anarchy, state and utopia.* Oxford: Blackwell.

Olson, M. 1965. *The logic of collective action.* Cambridge, Mass.: Harvard University Press.

Owen, G. 1968. *Game theory.* Philadelphia: Saunders.

Padulo, L. and Arbib, M. 1974. *System theory.* Philadelphia: Saunders.

Parfit, D. 1973. Later selves and moral principles. In A. Montefiore (ed.), *Philosophy and personal relations,* pp. 137–69. London: Routledge and Kegan Paul.

Pears, D. 1974. Freud, Sartre and self-deception. In R. Wollheim (ed.), *Freud,* pp. 97–112. New York: Anchor Books.

Peston, M. H. 1967. Changing utility functions. In M. Shubik (ed.), *Essays in mathematical economics in honor of Oskar Morgenstern,* pp. 233–6. Princeton, N.J.: Princeton University Press.

Peyre, H. 1963. *Literature and sincerity.* New Haven, Conn.: Yale University Press.

  1967. *The failures of criticism.* Ithaca, N.Y.: Cornell University Press.

Phelps, E. S. and Pollak, R. A. 1968. On second-best national saving and game-theoretic equilibrium growth. *Review of Economic Studies* 35, 185–99.

Pollak, R. A. 1968. Consistent planning. *Review of Economic Studies* 35, 201–8.

  1970. Habit formation and dynamic demand functions. *Journal of Political Economy* 78, 745–63.

  1976. Habit formation and long-run preferences. *Journal of Economic Theory* 13, 272–97.

Popper, K. 1957. *The poverty of historicism.* London: Routledge and Kegan Paul.

  1972. *Objective knowledge.* Oxford: Oxford University Press.

Quirk, J. and Saposnik, R. 1968. *Introduction to general equilibrium theory and welfare economics.* New York: McGraw-Hill.

Raiffa, H. 1968. *Decision analysis.* Reading, Mass.: Addison-Wesley.

Rapoport, A. 1966. *Two-person game theory.* Ann Arbor: University of Michigan Press.

Rapoport, A. and Chammah, A. 1965. *Prisoner's Dilemma.* Ann Arbor: University of Michigan Press.

Rapoport, A., Guyer, M. J. and Gordon, D. G. 1976. *The 2×2 game.* Ann Arbor: University of Michigan Press.

Rapport, D. J. and Turner, J. E. 1977. Economic models in ecology. *Science* 195, 367–73.

Rawls, J. 1971. *A theory of justice.* Cambridge, Mass.: Harvard University Press.

Reid, C. 1970. *Hilbert: the life and story of David Hilbert.* Berlin: Springer.

Reisner, R. 1974. *Bird: the legend of Charlie Parker.* London: Quartet Books.
Richerson, P. J. and Boyd, R. (forthcoming). A dual inheritance model of the human evolutionary process I. *Journal of Human and Social Biology.*
Rigby, P. W. J., Burleigh, B. D. and Hartley, B. S. 1974. Gene duplication in experimental enzyme evolution. *Nature, London* 251, 200–4.
Riker, W. and Ordeshook, P. C. 1973. *An introduction to positive political theory.* Englewood Cliffs, N.J.: Prentice-Hall.
Robbins, S. M. and Stobaugh, R. B. 1974. *Money in the multinational enterprise.* Harlow, Essex: Longman.
Robinson, J. 1956. *The accumulation of capital.* London: Macmillan.
Rorty, A. 1972. Belief and self-deception. *Inquiry* 15, 387–410.
Rosen, R. 1972. Morphogenesis. In R. Rosen (ed.), *Foundations of mathematical biology,* vol. II, pp. 1–77. New York: Academic Press.
Rosenberg, N. 1976. *Perspectives on technology.* Cambridge: Cambridge University Press.
Roumasset, J. A. 1976. *Rice and risk: decision-making among low-income farmers.* Amsterdam: North Holland.
Ruse, M. 1974. Cultural evolution. *Theory and Decision* 5, 413–40.
Russell, R. 1973. *Bird lives: the high life and hard times of Charlie Parker.* New York: Charterhouse.
Ryle, G. 1949. *The concept of mind.* London: Hutchinson.
Salter, W. E. G. 1960. *Productivity and technical change.* Cambridge: Cambridge University Press.
Salthe, S. 1972. *Evolutionary biology.* New York: Holt, Rinehart and Winston.
Sanders, W. 1971. *John Donne's poetry.* Cambridge: Cambridge University Press.
Sartre, J.-P. 1943. *L'être et le néant.* Paris: Gallimard.
Schafer, R. 1976. *A new language for psychoanalysis.* New Haven, Conn.: Yale University Press.
Schelling, T. S. 1963. *The strategy of conflict.* Cambridge, Mass.: Harvard University Press.
Schlanger, J. 1971. *Les métaphores de l'organisme.* Paris: Vrin.
Schoffeniels, E. 1973. *L'anti-hasard.* Paris: Gauthier-Villars.
Schumpeter, J. 1934. *The theory of economic development.* Cambridge, Mass.: Harvard University Press.
  1954. *A history of economic analysis.* London: Allen and Unwin.
Sejersted, F. 1973. *Ideal, teori og virkelighet.* Oslo: Cappelen.
  1978. Rettsstaten og den selvdestruerende makt. In R. Slagstad (ed.), *Om staten,* pp. 46–84. Oslo: Pax.
Sen, A. K. 1967. Isolation, assurance and the social rate of discount. *Quarterly Journal of Economics* 80, 112–24.
  1970. *Collective choice and social welfare.* San Francisco: Holden Day.
  1973. *On economic inequality.* Oxford: Oxford University Press.
  1974. Choice, orderings and morality. In S. Körner (ed.), *Practical reason,* pp. 54–67. Oxford: Blackwell.
  1975. *Employment, technology and development.* Oxford: Oxford University Press.
Shapley, L. and Shubik, M. 1967. Ownership and the production function. *Quarterly Journal of Economics* 80, 88–111.
Shefrin, H. and Thaler, R. 1977. An economic theory of self-control. University of Rochester, N.Y. Mimeographed.

Shubik, M. 1970. Game theory, behavior and the paradox of the Prisoner's Dilemma. *Journal of Conflict Resolution* 14, 181–202.

Simon, H. 1954. A behavioral theory of rational choice. *Quarterly Journal of Economics* 69, 99–118.

1976. From substantive to procedural rationality. In S. Latsis (ed.), *Method and appraisal in economics*, pp. 129–48. Cambridge: Cambridge University Press.

Simon, M. 1971. *The matter of life.* New Haven, Conn.: Yale University Press.

Snell, J. L. 1965. Stochastic processes. In R. D. Luce, R. Bush and E. Galanter (eds.), *Handbook of mathematical psychology*, vol. III, pp. 411–86. New York: Wiley.

de Sousa, R. 1971. Review of Fingarette (1969). *Inquiry* 14, 308–21.

Stanford Research Institute 1976. The economic and social costs of coal and nuclear electric generation. Report prepared for the National Science Foundation. Stanford, Calif.

Stark, W. 1962. *The fundamental forms of social thought.* London: Routlege and Kegan Paul.

Stebbins, G. L. and Lewontin, R. C. 1972. Comparative evolution at the levels of molecules, organisms and populations. In L. M. Le Cam, J. Neyman and E. L. Scott (eds.), *Proceedings of the sixth Berkeley symposium on mathematical statistics and probability*, vol. v, pp. 23–42. Berkeley: University of California Press.

Stendhal (1952). *Romans et nouvelles*, ed. H. Martineau. 2 vols. Paris: Gallimard (Editions de la Pléiade).

Stigler, G. and Becker, G. 1977. De gustibus non est disputandum. *American Economic Review* 67, 76–90.

Stinchcombe, A. 1968. *Constructing social theories.* New York: Harcourt, Brace and World.

Strotz, R. H. 1955–6. Myopia and inconsistency in dynamic utility maximisation. *Review of Economic Studies* 23, 165–80.

Stuart, R. B. 1971. A three-dimensional program for the treatment of obesity. *Behaviour Research and Theory* 9, 177–86.

Suttmeier, R. 1974. *Research and revolution.* Lexington, Mass.: Lexington Books.

Taylor, A. J. 1960. Progress and poverty in Britain 1750–1850. *History* 45, 16–31.

Taylor, C. 1971. Interpretation and the sciences of man. *Review of Metaphysics* 25, 3–51.

1976. Responsibility for self. In A. Rorty (ed.), *The identities of persons*, pp. 281–300. Berkeley: University of California Press.

Taylor, G. 1975–6. Love. *Proceedings of the Aristotelian Society* n.s. 76, 147–64.

Taylor, M. 1973. The problem of salience in the theory of collective decision-making. In H. R. Alker, K. W. Deutsch and A. H. Stoetzel (eds.), *Mathematical approaches to politics*, pp. 231–56. Amsterdam: Elsevier.

1976a. *Anarchy and cooperation.* London: Wiley.

1976b. Altruism and cooperation: their evolution by natural selection and their role in primitive societies. University of Essex. Mimeographed.

Tisdell, C. 1971. Economic policy, forecasting and flexibility. *Weltwirtschaftliches Archiv* 106, 34–51.

Trivers, R. 1971. The evolution of reciprocal altruism. *Quarterly Review of Biology* 46, 35–57.

1972. Parental investment and sexual selection. In B. Campbell (ed.), *Sexual selection and the descent of man*, pp. 136–79. Chicago: Aldine.

Tullock, G. 1974. Does punishment deter crime? *The Public Interest* 36, 103–11.

Tversky, A. and Kahneman, D. 1974. Judgement under uncertainty. *Science* 185, 1124–30.

Ulam, S. 1976. *Adventures of a mathematician.* New York: Scribner.

Valéry, P. 1957. Stendhal. In *Oeuvres*, vol. I, pp. 553–82. Paris: Gallimard (Editions de la Pléiade).

Watzlawick, P. 1977. *How real is real?* New York: Vintage Books.

Watzlawick, P., Beavin, J. H. and Jackson, D. D. 1967. *Pragmatics of human communication.* New York: Norton.

Watzlawick, P., Weakland, C. E. and Fisch, R. 1974. *Change.* New York: Norton.

Weiszäcker, C. C. von 1971. Notes on endogenous change of tastes. *Journal of Economic Theory* 3, 345–72.

    1973. Notes on endogenous growth of productivity. In J. A. Mirrlees and N. H. Stern (eds.), *Models of economic growth*, pp. 101–14. London: Macmillan.

Wharton, C. 1971. Risk, uncertainty and the subsistence farmer. In G. Dalton (ed.), *Economic development and social change*, pp. 566–74. New York: Natural History Press.

Williams, B. A. O. 1973. Deciding to believe. In *Problems of the self*, pp. 136–51. Cambridge: Cambridge University Press.

    1976. Persons, character and morality. In A. Rorty (ed.), *The identities of persons*, pp. 197–216. Berkeley: University of California Press.

Williams, G. C. 1966. *Adaptation and natural selection.* Princeton, N.J.: Princeton University Press.

Williams, J. D. 1954. *The compleat strategyst.* New York: McGraw-Hill.

Wilson, E. O. 1975. *Sociobiology.* Cambridge, Mass.: Harvard University Press.

Winter, S. G. 1964. Economic 'natural selection' and the theory of the firm. *Yale Economic Essays* 4, 225–72.

    1971. Satisficing, selection and the innovating remnant. *Quarterly Journal of Economics* 85, 237–61.

    1975. Optimization and evolution. In R. H. Day and T. Groves (eds.), *Adaptive economic models*, pp. 73–118. New York: Academic Press.

Wittgenstein, L. 1953. *Philosophische Untersuchungen.* Oxford: Blackwell.

Wood, M. 1971. *Stendhal.* Ithaca, N.Y.: Cornell University Press.

Wright, S. 1970. Random drift and the shifting balance theory of evolution. In K. Kojima (ed.), *Mathematical topics in population genetics* (= *Biomathematics*, vol. I), pp. 1–31. Berlin: Springer.

INDEX

191